up

dn

88 Spins with Bill Pechet

Leslie Van Duzer

with
Greg Girard
Pablo Mandel
Bill Pechet
Michael Perlmutter
Bill Richardson
Thena Jean-hee Tak
Lőrinc Vass

ORO EDITIONS

ABC

36 Views of Sulphur Mounds

BURRARD INLET, NORTH VANCOUVER, BC • 2003–

"One of the greatest joys of living in Vancouver is taking a seaplane." [BP]

As fleets of seaplanes come and go from Coal Harbour, passengers are treated to spectacular views of downtown Vancouver, the North Shore mountains, and for as long as anyone can remember, the shocking canary of the sulphur piles. Originating in the Alberta tar sands, the sulphur rails into Vancouver and ships out to Asia, coming to rest in transit on the Vancouver Wharves. Some find the yellow mounds beautiful, popping out against the blue-green landscape of the Burrard Inlet like Wolfgang Laib's pollen piles on a gallery floor, others consider them a blight. For Bill, they offer an unlikely bridge to Japan.

Inspired by Hokusai's series, *Thirty-six Views of Mount Fuji,* and enabled by frequent seaplane flights to Victoria, *36 Views of Sulphur Mounds* references Hokusai's depictions of Mt. Fuji from multiple perspectives. For this project, and many others, Bill borrows a device, *mitate,* often associated with such *ukiyo-e* prints. *Mitate* is a way of "reseeing" something. In *ukiyo-e*, allusions to older forms of art, landscapes, and material culture are in-jokes, puns, *shukô* or double meanings. "This project not only resees an embarrassment (raping nature) as potentially beautiful, but also adopts the 36 views as a referent. The visually acrid colour of the sulphur piles challenges the notion that Vancouver sits in a pure and harmonious relationship to its natural surroundings." [BP]

Indeed, the uninitiated may be disturbed by the proximity of the loose substance to the water, wondering about the fate of powder exposed to rain and worrying about the runoff. But those in the know know that these piles of sulphur, like pollen, do not dissolve in water. Sulphur does not harm fish, but it does kill fungi on contact and insects when digested, making it a key ingredient in fertilizers and pesticides. As a highly flammable substance, sulphur (a.k.a. brimstone) is also the Biblical source of Hell's fire and fury. In *36 Views of Sulphur Mounds*, smokin' hot Mt. Fuji meets Vancouver's industrial firepower.

WOODBLOCK PRINTS: Hokusai, Library of Congress, public domain, composite by Lőrinc Vass • **PHOTOS:** Bill Pechet • **STATUS:** Ongoing

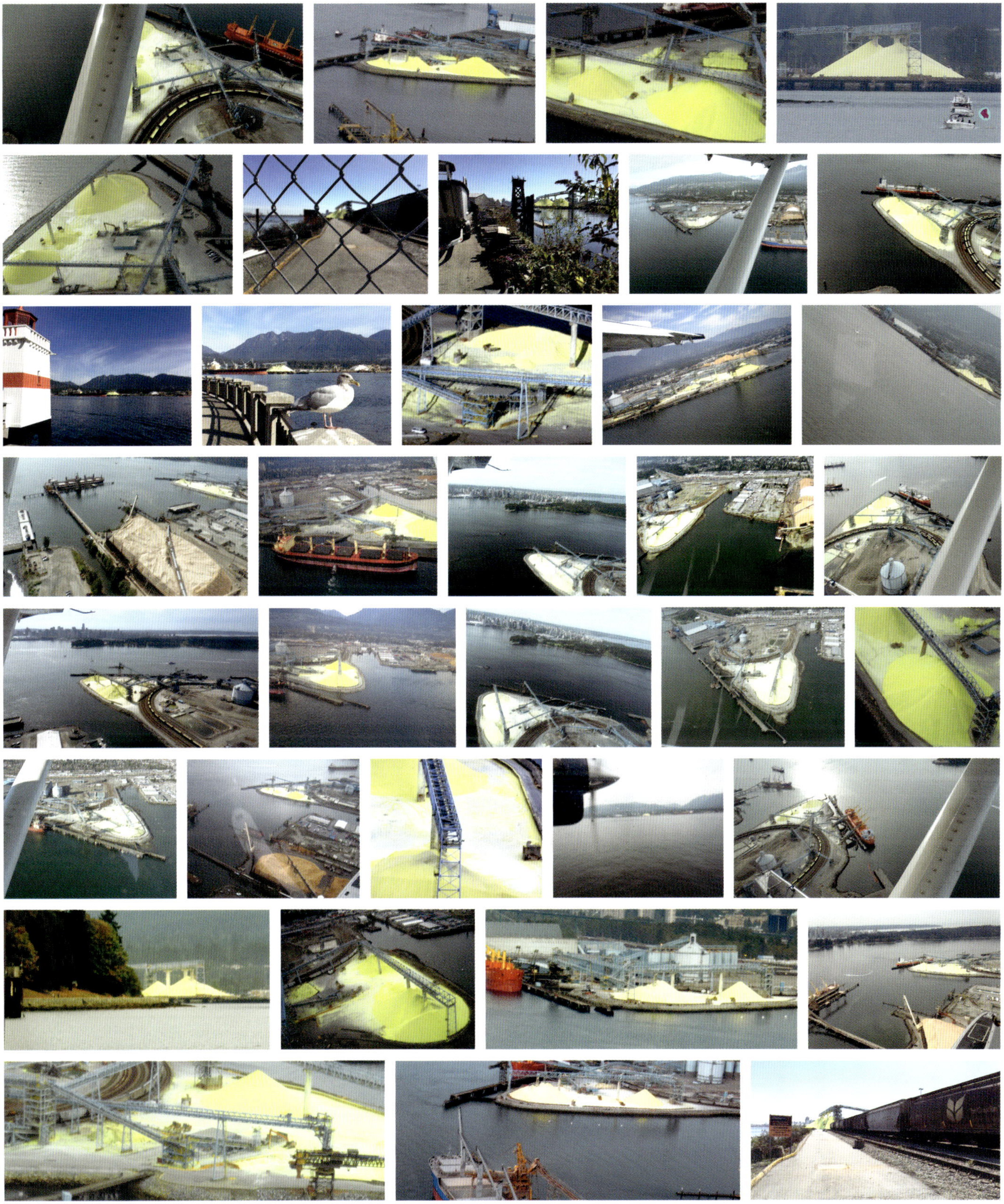

A Walking Table

PAPERNY FAMILY JEWISH COMMUNITY CENTRE, CALGARY, AB • 2018

Simultaneously a recognition of a diaspora and a gathering, an embodiment of the centripetal and centrifugal forces acting on the Jewish community, *A Walking Table* honours contributors to the Community Centre expansion project. The table top, an open-ended display of generosity cast in bronze, will expand as the list of donors grows, and the table's legs, so human with their knobbed knees and skinny calves, feet pointing this way and that, will multiply in support.

The current siting of the table, tucked away in the backyard of the existing centre, on land earmarked for the expansion, feels suitably temporary, as if the table merely sought out shade while on a longer journey.

PECHETStudio

CLIENT: Calgary Jewish Federation Campus Committee • **TEAM:** Bill Pechet with Nikolay Kuchin • **CONSTRUCTION:** Elliott Steinberg (manager) • **FABRICATION:** Dura Stainless and Sheet Metal MFG / Ductal Lafarge / Behrends Group • **PHOTOS:** Michael Perlmutter (top left, bottom), Bill Pechet (top right, middle)• **DRAWING:** Lőrinc Vass • **STATUS:** Built

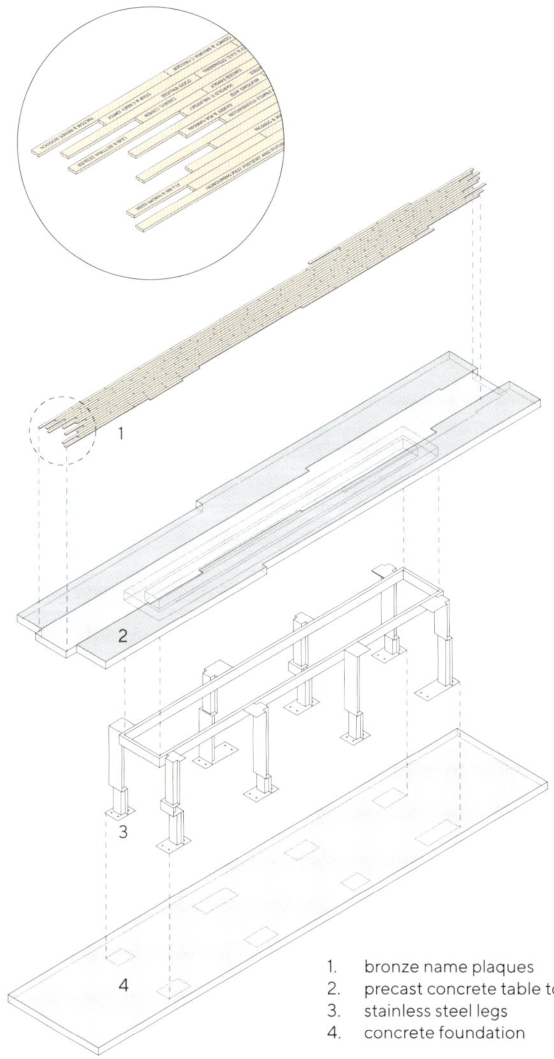

1. bronze name plaques
2. precast concrete table top
3. stainless steel legs
4. concrete foundation

Acer Gigantis

WEST 10TH & MAPLE, VANCOUVER, BC • 2013

As this story goes, to the great delight of botanists everywhere, gigantic petrified acer seed pods from an ancient tree were discovered during the construction of a new development at West 10th and Maple. Speculation has it that the source of the seed pods was a mythical *Acer Gigantis*, a tree growing over 150′ tall with a humongous, 26′ girth.

The "helicopter seeds," or "samaras" as the scientists like to call them, fly great distances to avoid the shade of their host tree's canopy. It must have been quite a sight: these giant whirligigs propelling across the Kitsilano sky. It is a miracle, a miracle indeed, that there were no reports of downed herons, or swans for that matter. In Bill's vision, the Brobdingnagian seedlings scattered about the site and petrified hard as concrete where they landed, making perfect bum-conforming perches.

PECHETStudio

CLIENT: Pinnacle International • **TEAM:** Bill Pechet with Gabe Daly, Jose Gonzalez • **DRAWING/RENDERINGS:** Gabe Daly, Jose Gonzalez • **STATUS:** Competition finalist

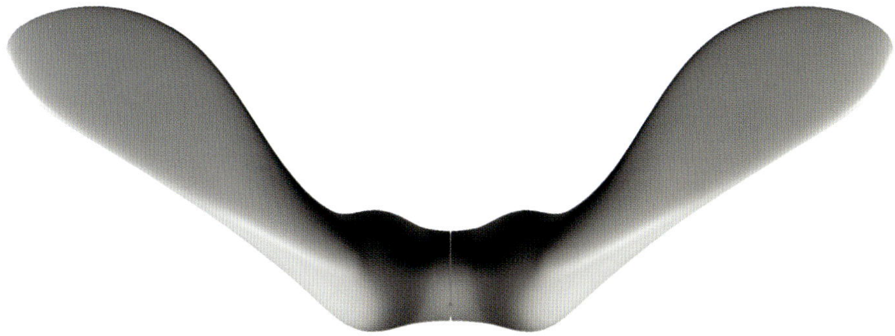

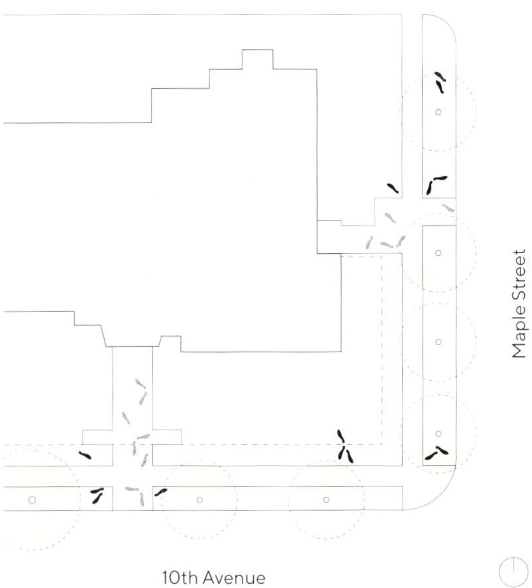

Air Borne

ATMOSPHERE DEVELOPMENT, RICHMOND, BC • 2018

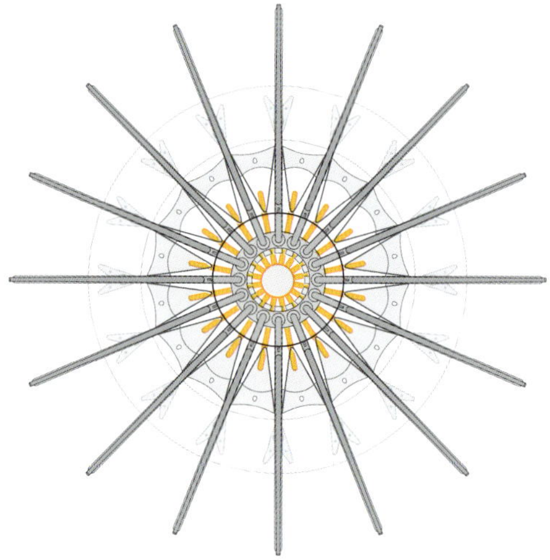

Artfully dodging the giant whirligigs, the largest overwintering population of birds in Canada migrates through the Fraser River Estuary biannually. One billion feathered creatures—shorebirds, waterfowl, raptors—pass this way twice a year. As all snowbirds need rest stops, folks and fowl alike, *Air Borne* proposed a "symbolic roosting space" on the plaza of a new development under the flight path. Like the best of rest stops, no major detour required!

Weighty bodies balancing on skinny bird legs—think ostriches or flamingos or herons—are one of nature's incongruities. Here, the profile of a Great Blue Heron balanced delicately on one leg is multiplied and rotated sixteen times, steadying the big bird and creating a plump container. With the heron well grounded, a golden egg is suspended within its belly, offering a "sign of optimism and completeness." BP The tension in *Air Borne* between flight and stasis brings to mind Constantin Brâncuși's sculptures: his birds defying gravity with their thin profiles balanced just so on weighty bases, his fragile eggs ready to roll off their pedestals with the first breeze, or sneeze.

Had *Air Borne* been realized, it is easy to imagine that the "symbolic" roosting space might have become a favorite rest stop for the migrants. What a sight to behold: hundreds of birds of different species coming to rest on a giant heron! It would be the most magnificent of all their rest stops, to be sure, but maybe it was precisely this popularity that gave the competition judges pause.

PECHETStudio

CLIENT: City of Richmond and South Street Development Group • **TEAM:** Bill Pechet with Lőrinc Vass • **DRAWINGS:** Lőrinc Vass • **STATUS:** Competition finalist

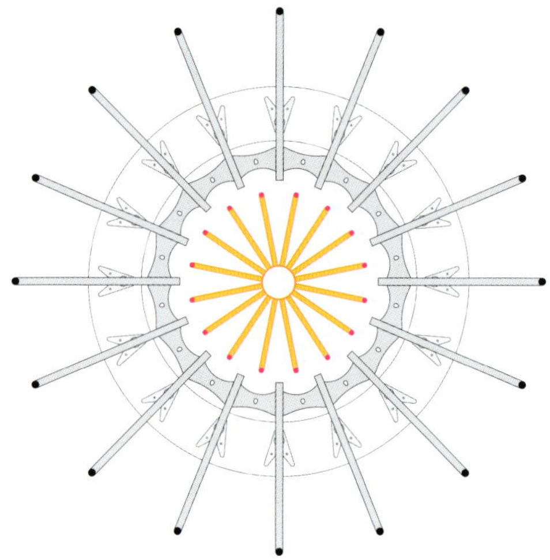

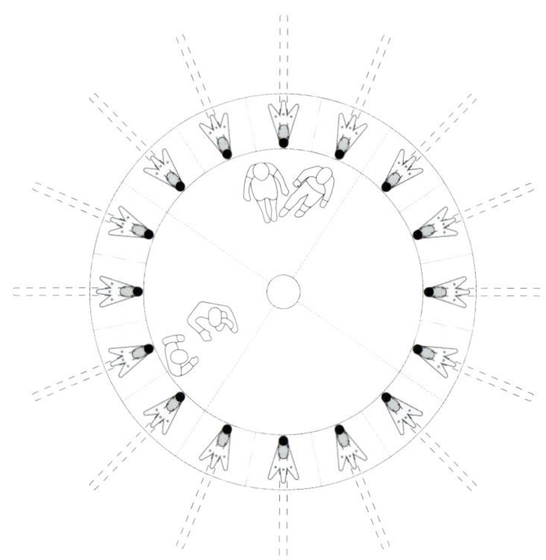

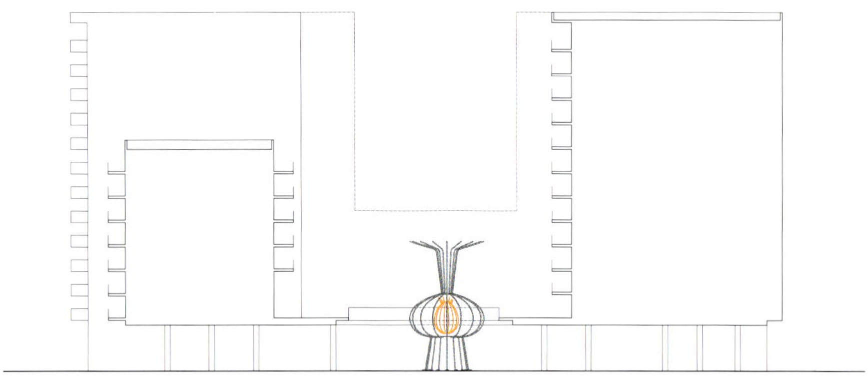

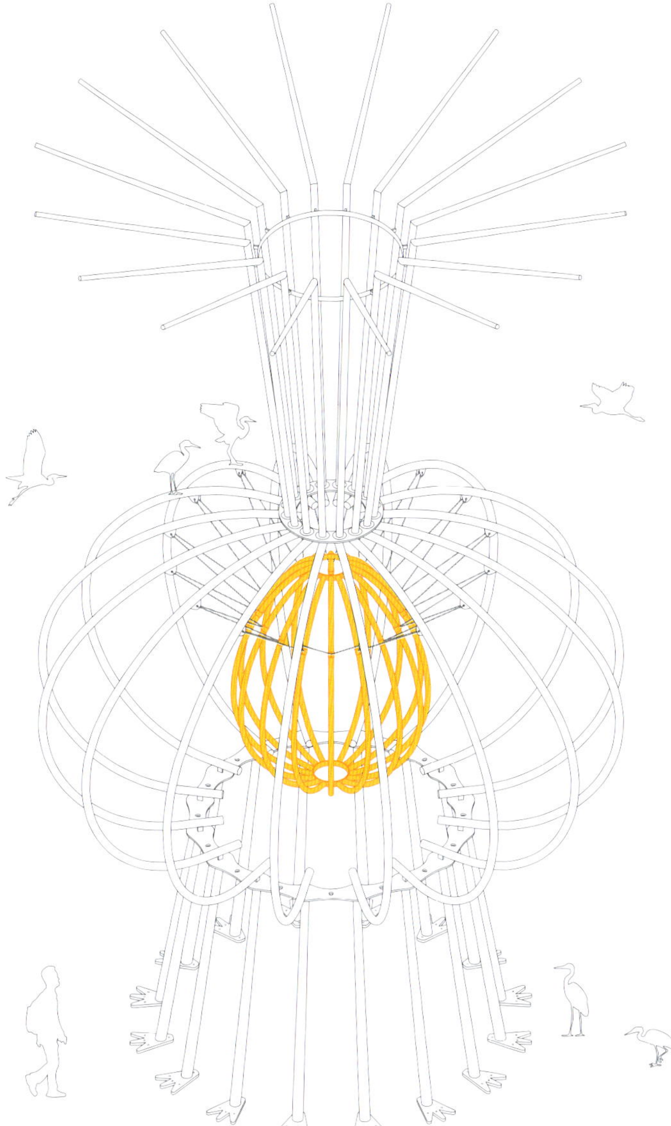

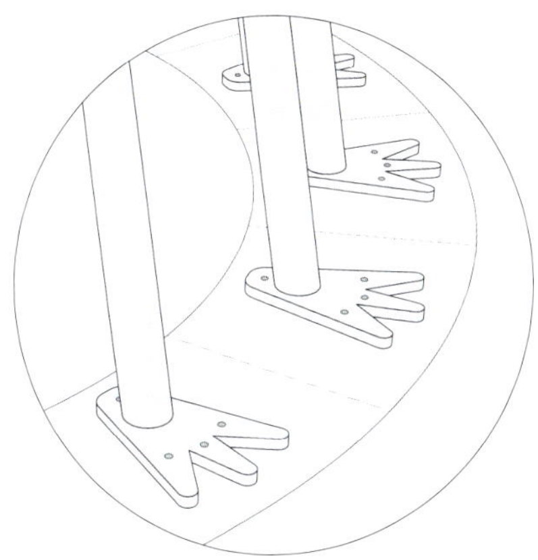

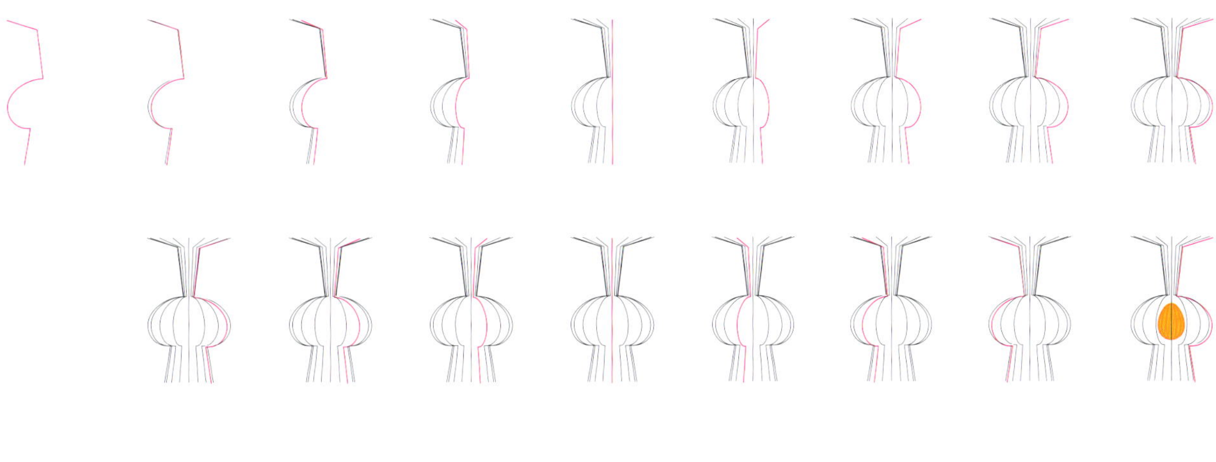

Alton Millpond Art and Infrastructure

ALTON, TOWN OF CALEDON, ON • 2016–

In 1857, provincial surveyor Charles Wheelock identified nine mill privileges on Shaw Creek, a tributary of the Credit River, and by the end of the century, the sleepy little town of Alton had become a thriving industrial village. William Wallace Algie, a free-thinking entrepreneur, built the Beaver Knitting Mill in 1881, and after changing hands twice, it finally closed after 101 years of near continuous operation. In 2009, the old mill reopened as the Alton Mill Arts Centre.

The millpond was an important feature of the site from its earliest days. Over the years, however, the damming of Shaw Creek had unanticipated, adverse consequences. In 2009, the Alton Millpond Rehabilitation Committee was established and a masterplan was completed six years later. The initial plan aimed to modernize the dam by reintroducing natural stream functions for sediment transport and fish passage, generating waterpower/hydroelectricity, and reducing the pollution entering the pond. This plan also showed early concepts for a path around the pond.

PECHETStudio was asked to continue developing the design with the aim of creating flexible and dynamic programming. *Alton Millpond Art + Infrastructure* proposed a suite of spaces strung along a path, encircling the pond, each with a different relationship to the water. The "Nest," surrounded by trees and set back from the pond, provided a small covered gathering and performance space for sixteen. A half dozen "art clearings" framed a variety of views for the pleasure of *en plein air* painters, a strategically located "bird bench" offered prime birdwatching opportunities. Floating on the pond: a picnic table, an "art site" with a viewing platform, and a pavilion.

In addition, the proposal included ideas for the rehabilitation of the dam that went beyond the technical issues addressed earlier. The exposed dam walls would have "swimming" lines of copper, bronze, or maybe concrete to represent the flow of water and fish contained within. A water chute would carry runoff from the pond to the site of the original dam wall, dropping water to mark the historic spot. Giant letters, A and M, cast into the concrete, would be seen from the street. With the old mill now restored and the arts centre thriving, it seems fitting that the rehabilitation of its life blood, the dam and pond, should have its day.

PECHETStudio
CLIENT: Alton Millpond Association • TEAM: Bill Pechet with Lőrinc Vass / DTAH • SKETCHES: Bill Pechet • DRAWINGS: Lőrinc Vass • STATUS: In progress

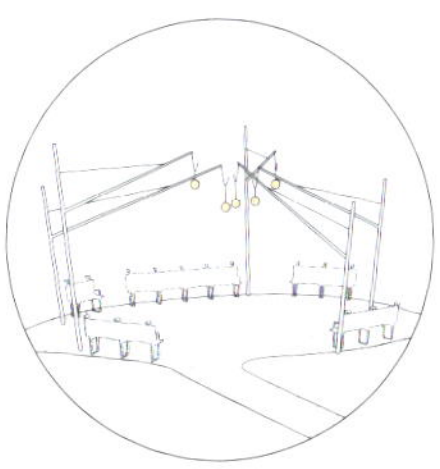

1.
The Nest: Gathering & Performance Space

2.
Art Site Clearing

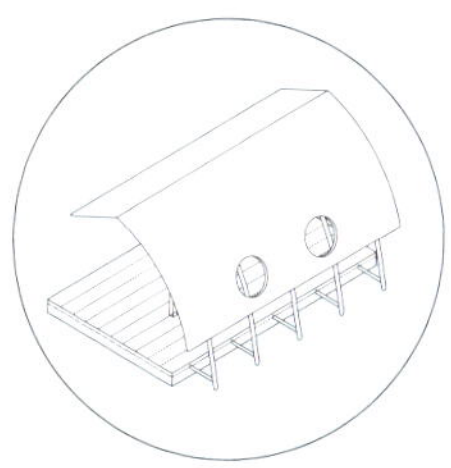

3.
Floating Picnic Table

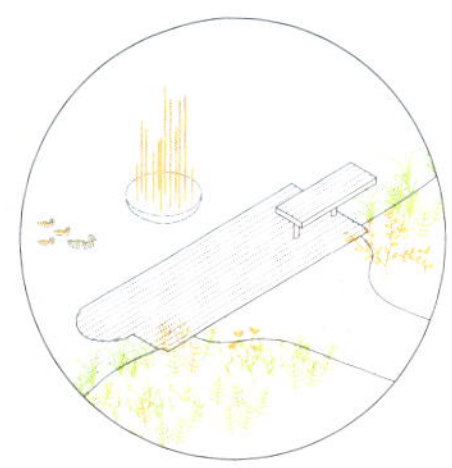

4.
Floating Art Site with Viewing Platform

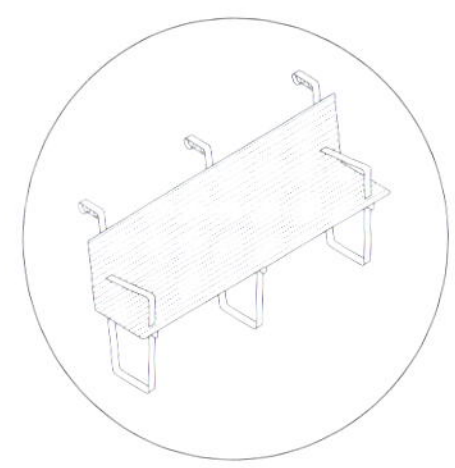

5.
Clearing with Bird Bench

6.
Future Floating Pavilion

Bearing

BEAR CREEK PARK, SURREY, BC • 1999

On the perimeter of Bear Creek Park, an oasis of pristine wilderness in the heart of the sprawling city of Surrey, stands a cluster of ornamental cherry trees. Layering a new order over this cultivated grove, *Bearing* proposed an arrangement of Cobra street lamps that mirrors the constellation Ursa Major, or The Great Bear. Varying the height of each lamp according to its distance from the paired star further strengthens the dialogue between earthly illumination and the heavenly bodies.

Pechet + Robb Studio

CLIENT: City of Surrey • **TEAM:** Bill Pechet and Stephanie Robb with Nicolas Osenton • **PHOTO:** Alamy • **DRAWING:** Lőrinc Vass • **STATUS:** Competition winner, unbuilt

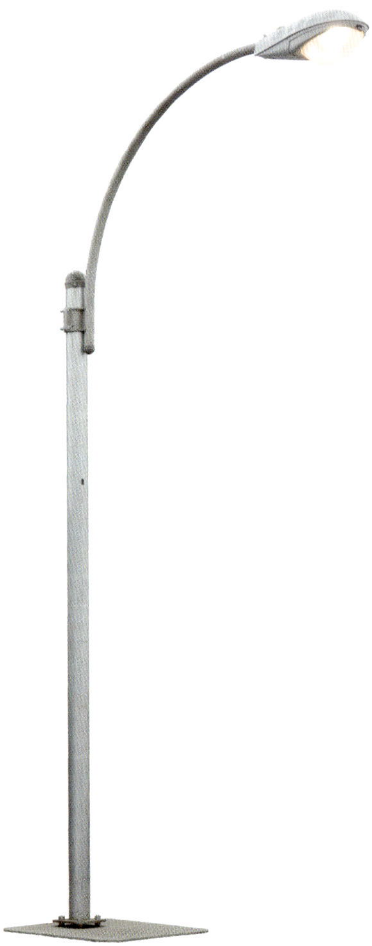

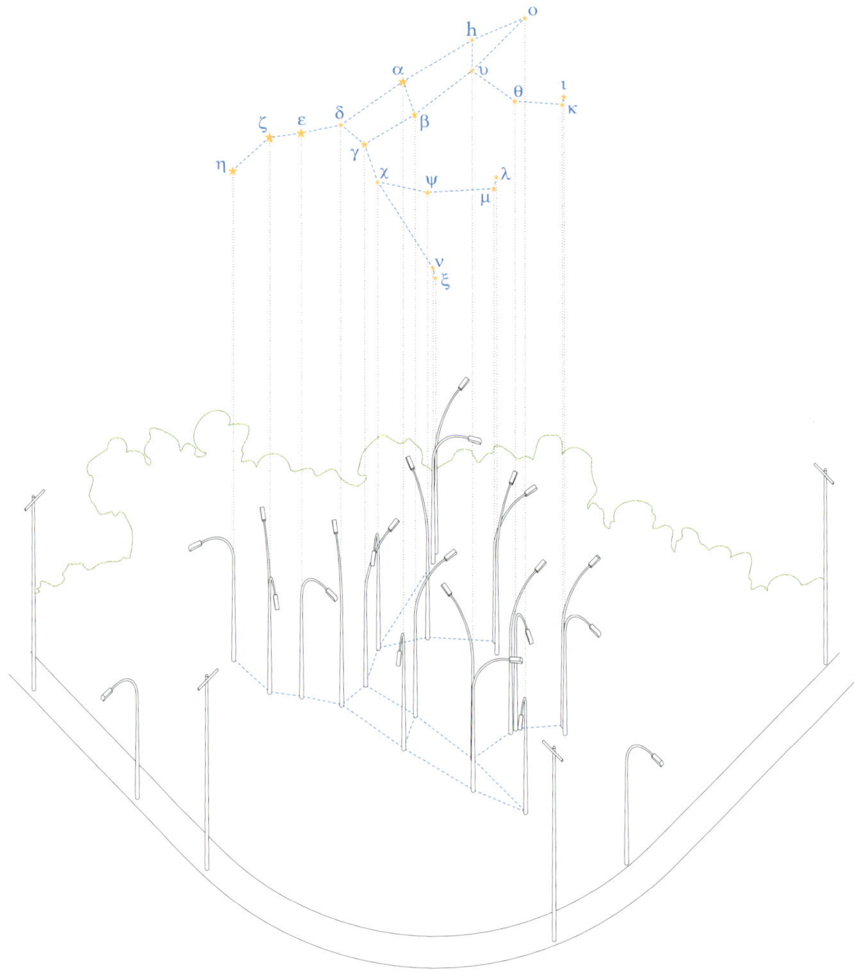

Greek letter	Name	Distance *light years*	Brightness *apparent magnitude **	Pole height *feet*	Light bulb *watts*
η	Alkaid	101 ly	1.86	25′	120 W
ζ	Alcor / Mizar	82 / 83 ly	3.99 / 2.23	23′ (double pole)	75 W x2
ε	Alioth	81 ly	1.77	23′	150 W
δ	Megrez	81 ly	3.31	23′	75 W
γ	Phecda	84 ly	2.44	23′	100 W
β	Merak	79 ly	2.37	23′	100 W
α	Dubhe	124 ly	1.79	25′	150 W
h	(23 UMa)	75 ly	1.83	23′	120 W
o	(Omicron UMa)	184 ly	3.35	27′	75 W
υ	(Upsilon UMa)	115 ly	3.78	25′	75 W
θ	(Theta UMa)	44 ly	2.52	21′	100 W
κ	(Kappa UMa)	423 ly	3.56	35′	75 W
ι	(Iota UMa)	48 ly	3.14	21′	75 W
χ	(Chi UMa)	196 ly	3.72	27′	75 W
ψ	(Psi UMa)	147 ly	3.01	25′	75 W
μ	(Mu UMa)	249 ly	3.06	30′	75 W
λ	(Lambda UMa)	134 ly	3.45	25′	75 W
ν	(Nu UMa)	399 ly	3.49	35′	75 W
ξ	(Xi UMa)	28 ly	4.73	21′	60 W

* the smaller the value, the brighter the star

Beit Olam Cemetery

VICTORIA, BC • 2024–

In 1858, following the end of the California Gold Rush, prospectors turned their attention north to gold deposits discovered at the confluence of the Thompson and Nicomen Rivers in the then Colony of British Columbia. Tens of thousands of people—merchants, prospectors, farmers—eager to make their fortunes, passed through Victoria on their way to the goldfields on the mainland.

In response to the growing Jewish population, the Hebrew Benevolent Society was established in 1859 and a parcel of land was purchased for the first Jewish cemetery in Western Canada. Founded a year later, Beit Olam Cemetery (also called The Jewish Cemetery) is the oldest non-Indigenous cemetery in the province still in use today. The cemetery has a rich and storied history of both neglect and heroic efforts to preserve its integrity and dignity.

Unfortunately, when the hilltop site was first purchased, the challenge of establishing burial grounds on bedrock was overlooked by its founders. For over 150 years, burials had to navigate around a large spine of rock, until finally, much of the rock was blasted and removed to create additional space for interments.

In 2022, a triangular piece of land along Cedar Hill Road was acquired from the city and incorporated into the cemetery to accommodate the growing number of interfaith couples who are now part of the community. A fence, combined with a few subtle landscape features, deliniates this area for this special purpose, while preserving the Garry oaks and outcrops of mossy bedrock.

This is a particularly meaningful project for Bill, as it is in this historic cemetery that his family is buried, and where he too, one day in the distant future, will come to rest.

PECHETStudio

CLIENT: Congregation Emanu-El • TEAM: Bill Pechet with Lőrinc Vass • PHOTOS: City of Victoria Open Data Portal (left), Bill Pechet (right) • DRAWING: Lőrinc Vass • STATUS: In progress

Big Chairs

AMBLESIDE, WEST VANCOUVER, BC • 1994

The chair first appeared as a miniature in the gift shop of *The Museum of Sand*, Bill's graduation project, lending a human scale to a small sandbox. Subsequently, hundreds of the 6″ concrete chairs were roughly cast and many sold before the design was enlarged, first in plywood, then in concrete for a show of young furniture designers at the Charles H. Scott Gallery in Vancouver in the early 1990s.

After the exhibition, a member of the Department of Parks and Recreation requested *Big Chairs* be donated to the municipality and sited at the end of a jetty at Ambleside Beach. The two concrete chairs, warmed by the sun, became a magnet for weddings and funerals and intimate conversations far from busybodies. There they sat "like two people in conversation" for seventeen years, until 2001, when they were moved to make way for the *Squamish Nation Welcome Figure.*

Big Chairs was relocated to a spot further west along the seawall, rather close to the busy waterfront path. While the move changed the intimate nature of the work, it was nonetheless fortuitous. On January 7, 2022, a king tide and windstorm wreaked havoc in Ambleside, damaging much of the waterfront, but *Big Chairs* continued their conversation without missing a beat.

For decades, this interest in the chair has played out at different scales, in various materials and contexts. The chair has been drawn, cast and assembled, made of concrete and plywood, with and without laminates. The chair has been miniaturized and oversized, balanced precariously and fully grounded. Multiples have found their way onto stages and into offices, shops, public spaces, and a private yard.

It is truly remarkable that the design of the chair, with its slightly sloping backrest for comfort, has remained unchanged despite shifting scales and contexts and materials, despite the passing of decades. According to the late great architect Adolf Loos, to be comfortable with repetition, to reject invention for its own sake, was the sign of an enlightened designer. "We have enough original genius. Let us repeat ourselves ad infinitum." [AL]

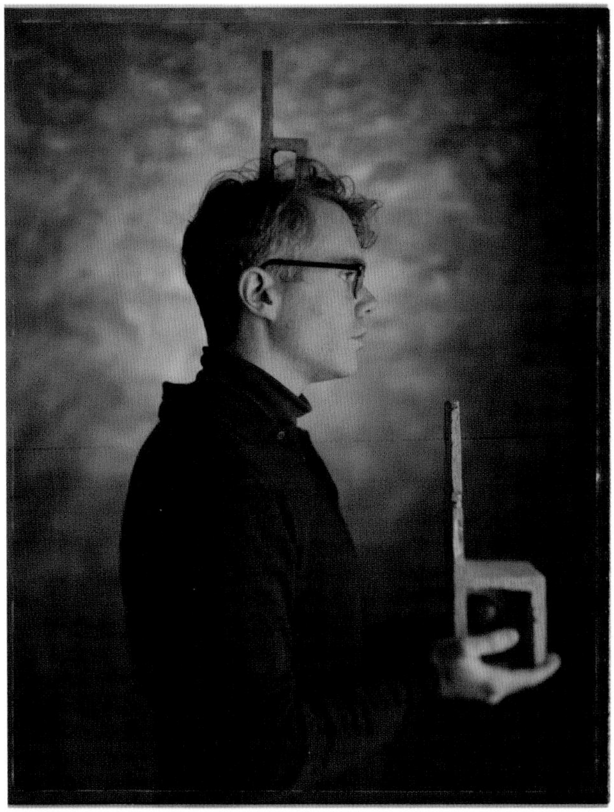

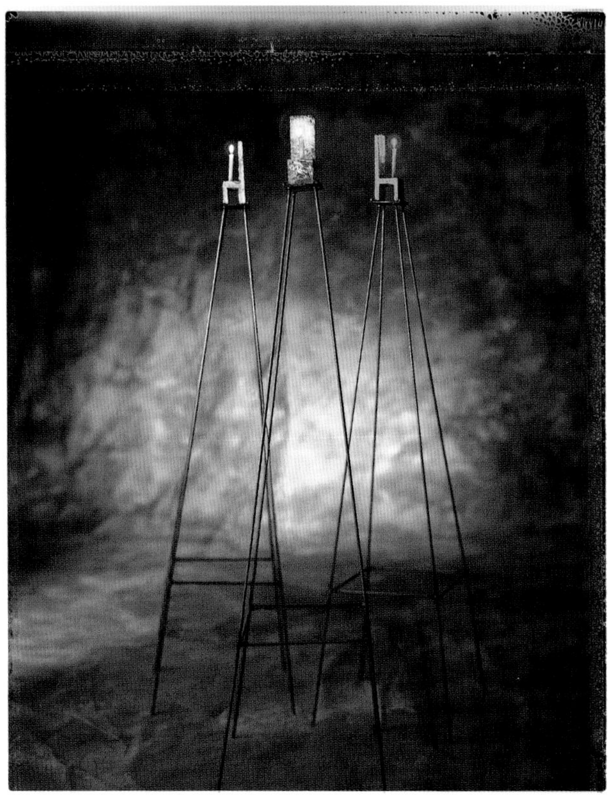

FABRICATORS: molds by Granville Island Woodworks, castings by Bill Pechet with GIWW • **PHOTOS:** Kiku Hawkes (p. 16), Michael Perlmutter (p. 17 top and bottom left), Leslie Van Duzer (p. 17 bottom right)

Brancuzzi's Hope

2007

In the early 2000s, Bill was fascinated by a trend he witnessed in Japan. Young women, mainly found in Shibuya and Ikebukuro, were going to tanning salons, wearing extravagant platform shoes and kooky clothes, dyeing their hair blonde, and applying clown-like makeup, often with white eyeshadow. These "Ganguro Girls" appeared almost alien-like in appearance, taller than everyone else in the crowd and wearing synthetic, otherworldly faces. Bill wondered about the women behind the costumes, about what thoughts and intelligences were masked as their personal identities were erased in favour of a strangely collective uniformity.

Mariko, the protagonist of *Brancuzzi's Hope*, was created to examine a fictional, geeky-brilliant young woman—a genius of sorts—who invents this nonsensical, yet marketable, chemical to be sold in leading department stores. Her friend Tojo is her accomplice. He has a sad story which gives Mariko another dimension, to further remove the mask, as a real friend to someone who needs her.

TEXT: Bill Pechet • **ILLUSTRATIONS:** Bill Pechet • **BOOK DESIGN:** Lisa Marshall • **PUBLISHER:** Helen Pitt Gallery • **STATUS:** Distributed

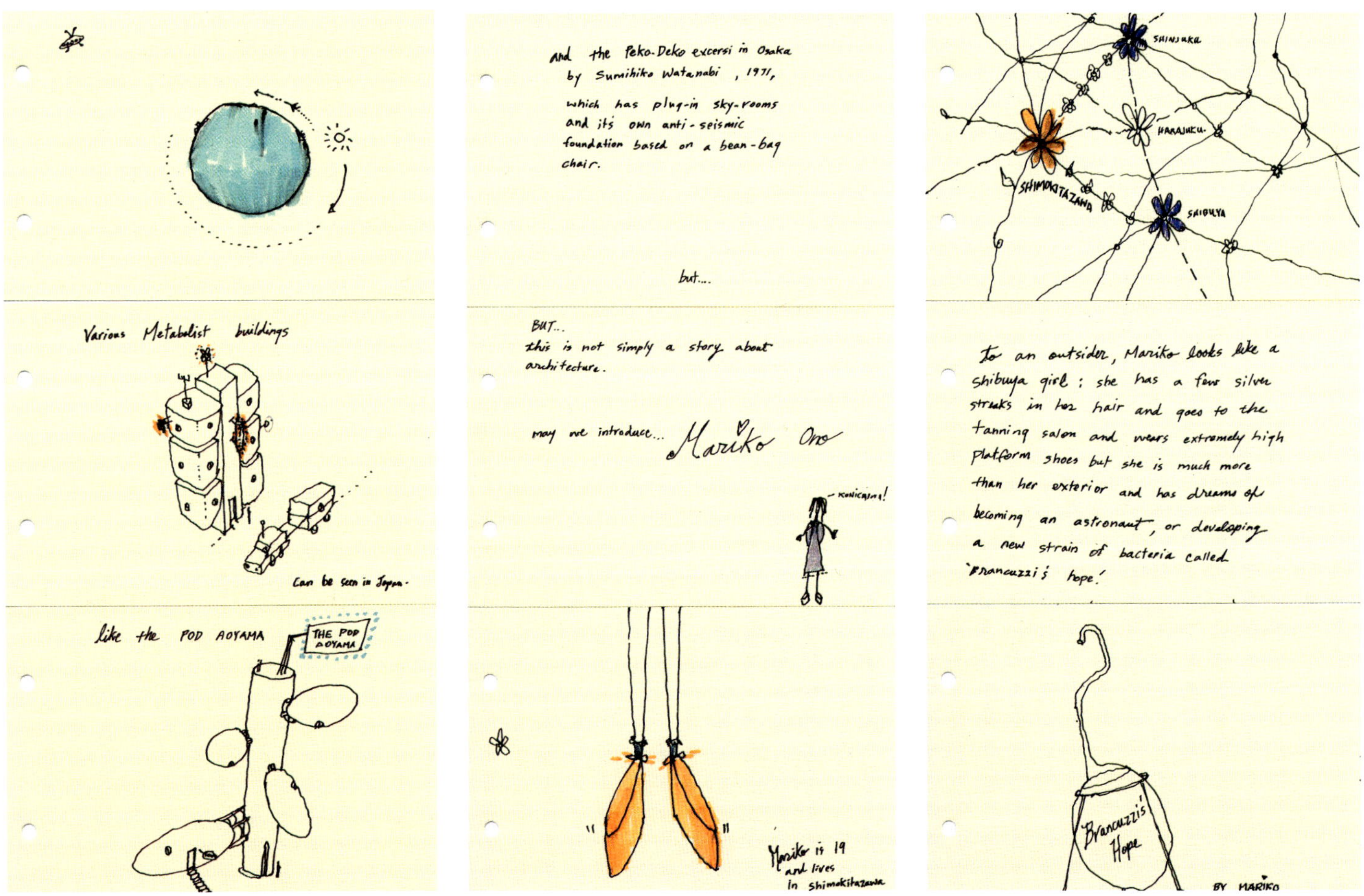

an amalgam of neo-plazmatic receptors regenerated into an inverted monocyte which, when bonded to a T-cell, produces what I call a poki neuron
Tojo and Mariko sometimes go for walks around Shibuya and just talk
young boys
stay tuned
young boys
Especially they talk about Tojo's mom because she died 2 years ago and he really misses her alot.
Mariko always listens and usually brings a sony cd walkman with 2 earphones so that they can also have music while they walk and talk about their pasts and futures
Brancuzzi's Hope will be manufactured in a space station not too far from Earth and will be sold across the world in leading Department Stores and marketed by Mariko's best friend, Tojo who works in a little bar near Mariko's house, by the railway line.
...life is a journey be my friend, my friend along the way...
Brancuzzi's Hope

Burial Estates

HOME OF ETERNITY CEMETERY IN MOUNTAIN VIEW CEMETERY, OAKLAND, CA • 2022–

It was the 1860s and Oakland was booming! The westward expansion of railways created the need for a new rail terminal and port in the West Coast city. With its population exploding, city leaders recognized the need for a large, new cemetery and identified a hillside site with sweeping views of the Bay Area.

As it happened, landscape architect, journalist, and public administrator Frederick Law Olmsted, of Central Park fame, moved to California in 1863 to manage the Mariposa Gold Mine in the Sierra Mountains. While in California for two years, before the gold mine went bust and he headed back to New York, Olmsted designed several significant landscapes, including Mountain View Cemetery, his first solo commission and only cemetery.

The Hebrew Benevolent Society purchased a two-acre site on the northwestern edge of the cemetery, establishing Home of Eternity, a small Jewish cemetery, within its gates. A modern mausoleum, with crypts and niches and gardens, was added later in 1938, and then expanded in the 1940s and 1960s. By 2022, as the Jewish cemetery was running out of space for new interments, a site for expansion was identified to the east of the mausoleum.

The irregular site was defined on three sides by the mausoleum's rectilinear forms, and on the fourth, by a graceful, picturesque arc marking the boundary of the small cemetery.

To navigate between the geometries and to define the cemetery's border, *Burial Estates* proposes two rows of concentric, contiguous "estates:" intimate open-air rooms with grave sites surrounded by 6′ walls and hedges. At the centre of the arc, a path provides access to twenty-one estates and offers a place to stroll and meditate among the magnolias. Backing onto one row, three additional estates open towards the mausoleum. In the large, geometric courtyard defined by wings of the building, a prominent square estate, framed by a circular wall, provides interment space for another eight people.

Burial Estates provides seventy-eight new grave sites in the estates, and, on the eastern wall of the mausoleum, a columbaria wall with 162 double niches. A gracious new entry court, accessed from the main street, provides a ceremonial handwashing basin and space for gathering before and after a ceremony.

Should you find your way to the Home of Eternity Cemetery, look for the tombstone of legendary Simon Argevitch (1915–1986) with the inscription: "He is in Ripley's Believe It or Not Museum and the Guinness Museum of World Records. While smoking 17 cigars he could simultaneously talk, imitate birds, hum, sing and whistle a tune." (Videos can be found on YouTube.)

PECHETStudio

CLIENT: Sinai Memorial • **TEAM:** Bill Pechet with Lőrinc Vass • **DRAWING/RENDERINGS:** Lőrinc Vass • **STATUS:** In development

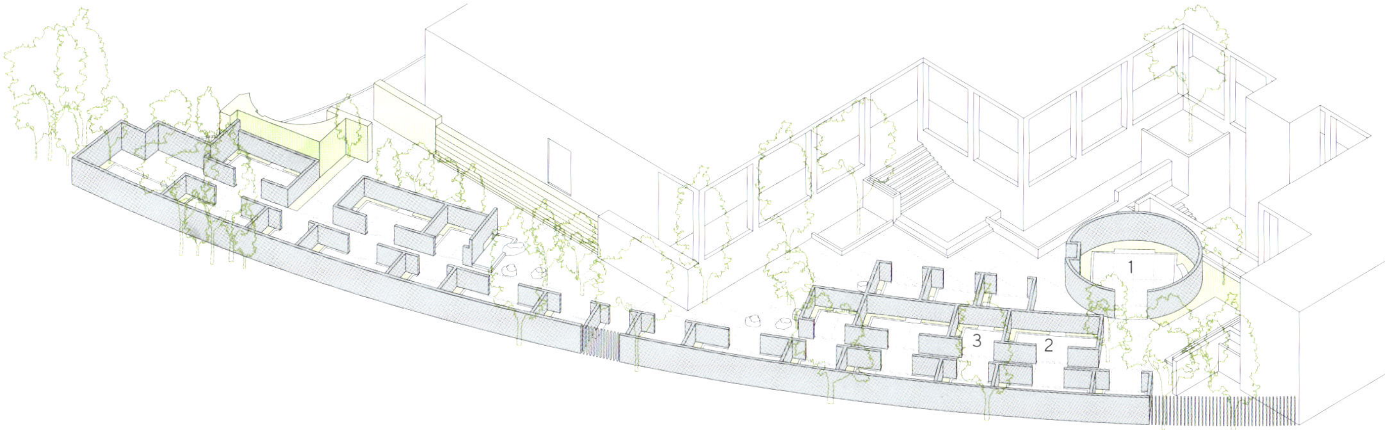

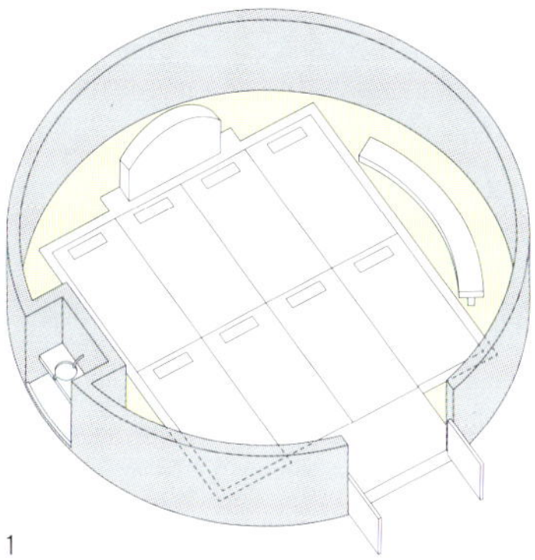

1

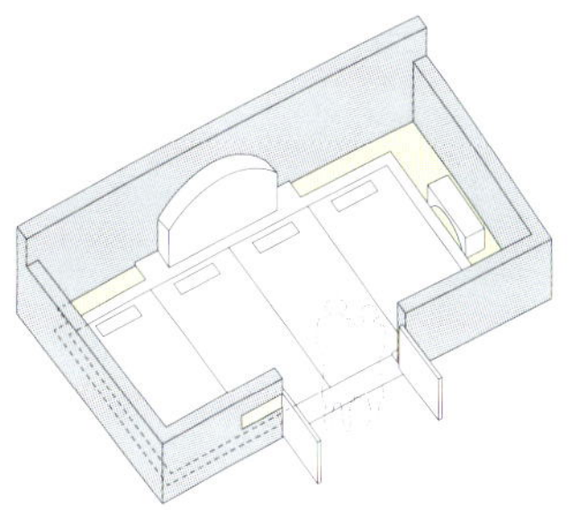

2

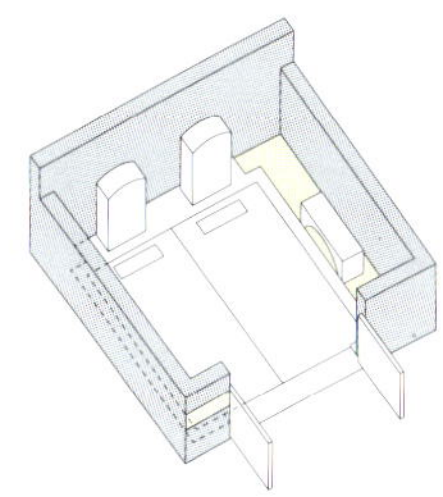

3

Capilano View Memorial Forest

CAPILANO VIEW CEMETERY, WEST VANCOUVER, BC • 2008

The setting for the Capilano View Cemetery could not be more beautiful, surrounded by forest and backgrounded by the North Shore Mountains. As the existing cemetery, nestled into this grand setting, is primarily a flat lawn with little differentiation, Bill was invited to design an alternative environment with interment options and contemplation spaces.

Capilano View Memorial Forest proposes a commemorative space in the forest on the west edge of the cemetery, on the site of an earlier vehicular entry. The *Memorial Forest* would include an open-air pavilion for gathering, eight freestanding memorial walls, a waterway, scattering areas for ashes, and a charming invention: birdhouses designed to hold ashes, "columbary meets columbarium." [BP] A columbarium was originally an oversized birdhouse that contained small alcoves for pigeon nests. Only later did the little alcoves contain cremation urns. The words columbary and columbarium have the same root, so "these birdhouses were a direct 'homecoming' of the word itself." [BP]

The second phase of the project included the addition of a large, labyrinthine bamboo forest and a meditation garden with interment space for ashes. One can imagine the pleasure of tracing the path slowly, and dwelling, even hiding, in its central cul-de-sac.

This project was designed between the completion of *Woods I,* which provided intimate spaces for contemplation, and the adjacent *Woods II*, which defined a generous entry court that could be used for ceremonial gatherings. While *Woods I and II* greatly enhanced the cemetery, *Capilano View Memorial Forest* would not only provide new interment possibilities, but also a space to shelter from the rain, to grieve privately out of the public's gaze, and to enjoy the bittersweet moment when a birdie comes to visit an auntie.

Pechet and Robb Art and Architecture
CLIENT: District of West Vancouver • TEAM: Bill Pechet with Andrew Maclean • SKETCH: Bill Peceht • DRAWING/RENDERINGS: Andrew Maclean, Lőrinc Vass • STATUS: Unbuilt

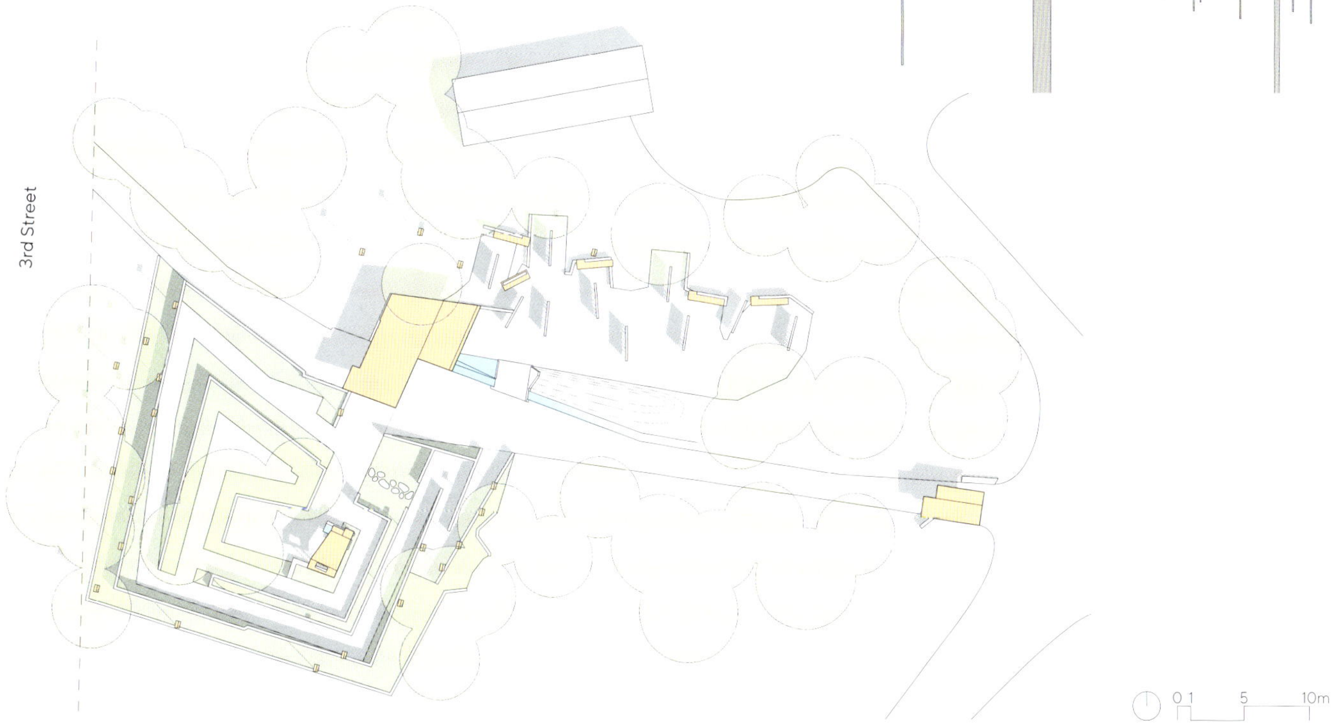
3rd Street
0 1 5 10m

Chumway

TYNEHEAD REGIONAL PARK, SURREY, BC • 2009

Imagine driving along Highway 1, past Tynehead Park, on your way home from IKEA, pleased as punch with your purchases. You're bopping along when suddenly you see, in the distance, what appears to be a giant salmon spanning the road overhead. Your mind is racing trying to make sense of this. Given that the headwaters of the Serpentine River, an excellent habitat for salmon, are in Tynehead Park, for a brief moment, you wonder if you are experiencing a once-in-a-lifetime event. A gargantuan Chinook escapee? Or perhaps a Coho? It is hard to tell. You cannot make out heads or tails, or even fins, but of one thing you are sure: the body has the unmistakable texture and shimmer of salmon skin.

Upon closer inspection—of course you had to pull over to investigate—the giant salmon transforms before your eyes into a pedestrian overpass, connecting Tynehead Regional Park and the Fraser Heights neighbourhood, covered with roadside reflective markers in various colours. It was movement, our movement as we approached by car, that created the illusion of iridescent salmon skin.

To see in a highway reflector a salmon scale (*Chumway*), or in a road construction light the sun (*roger that*), or in a standard Cobra lamp a dialogue with the stars (*Bearing*) or the form of a watchful mother bird (*MAMA*); to see in a security mirror vast new horizons (*Closer Than*): that is what it means to enter a universe of oscillating realities.

Pechet and Robb Art and Architecture
CLIENT: City of Surrey • TEAM: Bill Pechet and Stephanie Robb with Gabe Daly • PAINTING: Stock • PHOTOS: Birigroup Company (left), Bill Pechet (right) • DRAWING: Lőrinc Vass • RENDERING: Gabe Daly • STATUS: Competition finalist

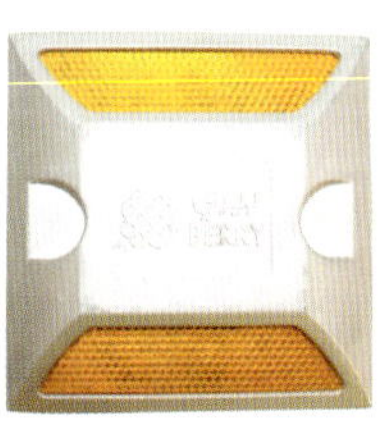

Closer Than

WEST WALL OF MANDARIN RESIDENCE FACING BRIGHOUSE STATION, RICHMOND, BC • 2015–16

"Objects in mirror are closer than they appear."

A sliver of a setback between a residential development and a light rail station hardly seems like an ideal place for expanding one's horizons. But from within this tiny 3′ gap, *Closer Than* offers us nothing less than superhuman (in)sight. By multiplying our horizon line and widening our cone of vision, we are liberated from our natural limitations. *Closer Than* enables the impossible. Like magic, one can approach the LRT station on the street and see the train pulling in directly overhead, or conversely, stand on the elevated platform and watch tardy commuters running into the station.

Closer Than takes as its starting point the humble security mirror, that ubiquitous concave disc found in the corner of convenience stores and at the end of blind driveways. The $135 CAD readymade, commonly found hanging out alone, is here multiplied by 388 and arranged in eight staggered rows, transforming a singular object into a field condition and extending our range of vision supernaturally.

For art lovers, *Closer Than* might bring to mind some of the many artists who depict mirrors or employ them directly: Velázquez, Picasso, Kapoor. But for others, and no doubt some art lovers too, the installation evokes childhood memories of fun house mirrors that turned us into chubby monsters or trifold mirrors in dressing rooms that multiply our chubby bodies into infinite, deep space. In *Closer Than*, our expanded perspective places our multiple selves among other multiple selves, a community of commuters occupying a multitude of spaces simultaneously, "a self-portrait of we and me." BP

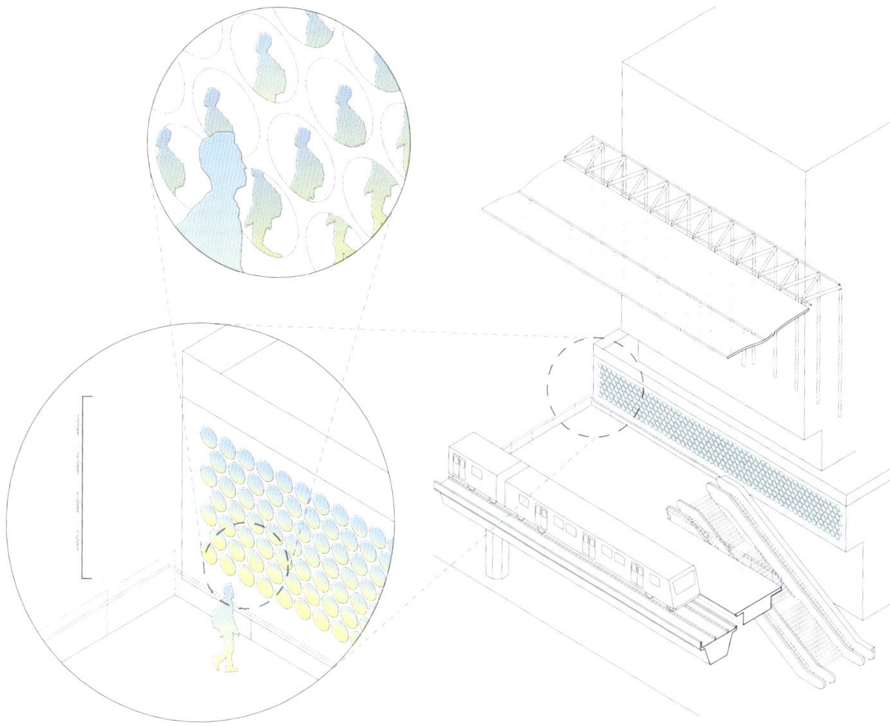

PECHETStudio

CLIENTS: Richmond Public Art Commission and Fairborne • TEAM: Bill Pechet with Gabe Daly, Scotty Keck / C.Y. Loh Associates • FABRICATION: Vision Metalizers, ITC Construction Group • PHOTOS: Michael Perlmutter (p. 25, 26-27) • DRAWING: Lőrinc Vass • STATUS: Competition winner, built

NPC

Cloudy, Mambo Wazo and Wazo Heights

VANCOUVER, BC • 1992

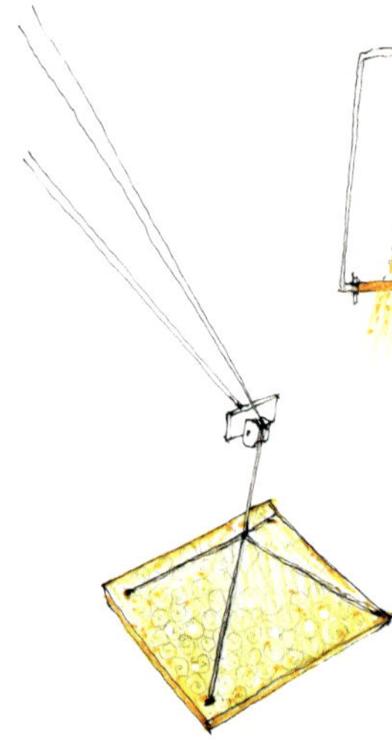

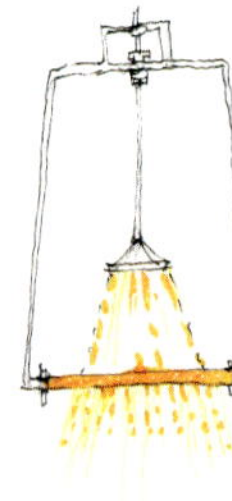

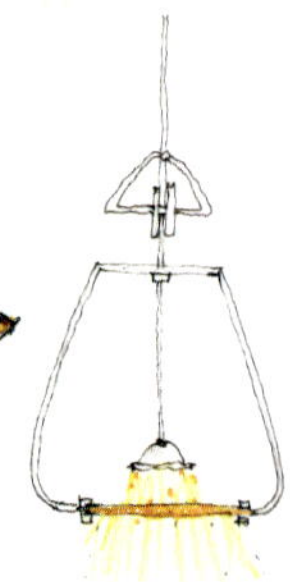

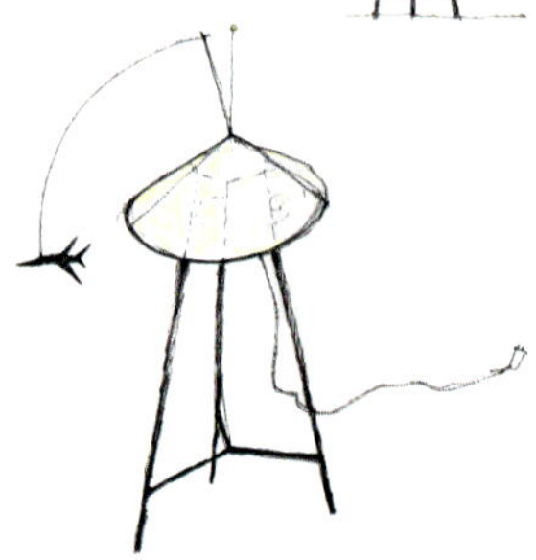

Already in Bill's graduate thesis project, *The Museum of Sand*, there was indisputable evidence of a fascination with light and birds. The two interests join here to form a flock of three lamps, each perched on skinny bird legs, some with feet, some curiously footless.

First there is moody Cloudy, her light dimmed by an aerial weather photograph. Towering over her is flirty Mamba Wazo, with a skirted rice paper shade and an arm holding out a come-hither collection of golden rocks and jewels. When the two lamps were alone together, the piece was titled *The Seduction of Cloudy by Mambo Wazo*. Here, the twosome becomes a threesome when Wazo Heights comes along, looking like a bird in leg warmers, illuminating the gathering through a fiberglass shade with embedded wood curls.

These bird-lamps are just one of many projects that demonstrate a desire to animate everyday objects. Chairs as humans, lamps as birds, a call message stand as a cherry tree. Here in this oeuvre, there are no arbitrary forms, and forms do not follow function, even if they accommodate it. Rather, the forms in Bill's universe draw us in by engendering accessible associations—some poignant, some silly—but all like little shared secrets.

PHOTOS: Bill Pechet • **SKETCHES:** Bill Pechet

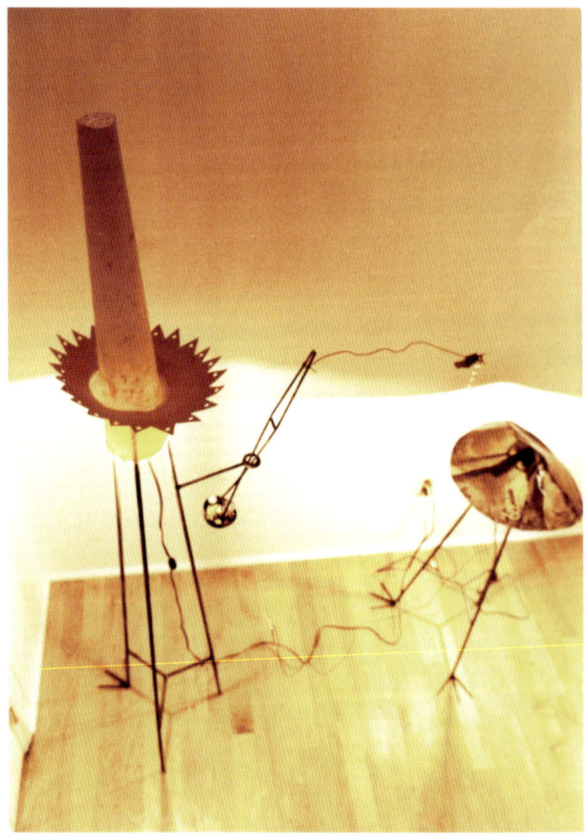

Colonel Mustard Upstairs

DEEP COVE PARK, NORTH VANCOUVER, BC • 2010

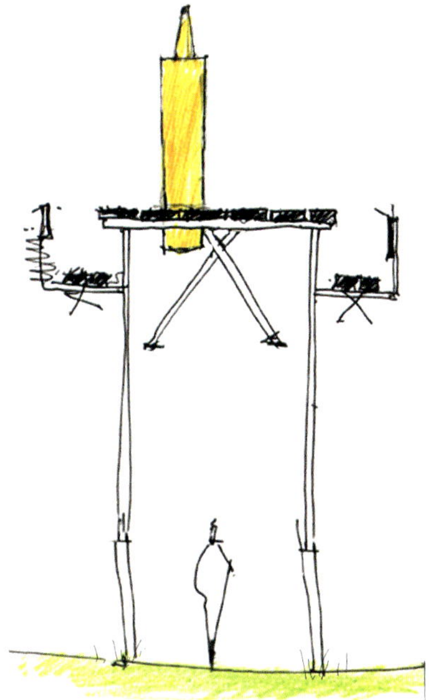

It would be an understatement to say North Vancouver is no stranger to bears. In the parks, picnic areas sport bear-proof garbage cans and sightings of black bears are all too common. When invited to propose a public artwork for Deep Cove Park, what could be more natural than to reference the precarious confluence of homines and ursī?

Colonel Mustard Upstairs is an ensemble of two parts, each rendered in mustard yellow: a picnic table perched high on a pole, safely out of reach of furry creatures and picnickers alike, and a garbage can atop a second pole that lights up the night. As in so many other projects in this collection, cross-references abound: the matching yellow of the picnic table and mustard bottle (French's Classic, not Dijon); mustard as both a condiment and the name of a decorated colonel in a popular game; Colonel Mustard, a fictional war hero and a protective night light standing at attention. So many points of resonance in such a simple proposal.

Pechet and Robb Art and Architecture

CLIENT: District of North Vancouver • TEAM: Bill Pechet and Stephanie Robb with Gabe Daly • SKETCHES: Bill Pechet • RENDERING: Gabe Daly • PHOTO: Stock • STATUS: Competition finalist

Dichroic Vancouver

980 HOWE STREET, VANCOUVER, BC • 2015–16

Every city has its dominant colours, an impressionistic blend of architecture and its surrounding landscape. Paris, with its stone fabric and overcast skies presents as many shades of grey. The pink stuccoed developments in Phoenix absorb the desert's dust and its overwhelmingly pink population. If Minneapolis is brown and green and San Francisco a palette of complementary pastels, then Vancouver must be grey-blue-green. Situated as it is in a temperate rainforest, surrounded by ocean waters and a backdrop of forested mountains, with clouds and rain and sunlight shifting by the minute, reflecting in towers clad in green and blue glass—the blend is dynamic. Sometimes brilliant blues dominate the sky, the water, the buildings; sometimes a cloak of grey blurs all distinctions.

Vancouver developers have noted a cityscape that can appear, at times, monochromatic, and some have taken to adding bright, static artworks on tower façades in order to stand apart. And stand apart they do, for better, or too often, for worse. When Manulife needed an artwork for their new office building in downtown Vancouver, they selected a dynamic installation, *Dichroic Vancouver,* one that alternately blends and contrasts with its context in response to everchanging weather and light conditions. The artwork engages the only site offered to the competing artists that was visible from a distance: four horizontal bands on the southeast and southwest façades between floors nine and twelve.

By day, the two building façades are animated by stripes of dichroic glass that change colour as our viewing angle shifts. By night, a concert of coloured lights, with a revolving program of twenty distinct (silent) songs—"Purple Rain," "Ping Pong," "Fireworks," "Laugh In," to name a few—further adds to the complexity of the material effect. Not only are the lights programmed to change colour and position along the four stripes, but as we shimmy up Nelson Street or along Granville, the lit glass shimmies with us. On weekends, when the area fills with revelers, the effect is downright disco!

PECHETStudio

CLIENTS: City of Vancouver and Manulife • **TEAM:** Bill Pechet with Gabe Daly, Ian Lowrie / Eos Lightmedia / Endall Elliot Associates / CEI Architecture • **FABRICATION:** Arbucomp (Germany) / Garibaldi Glass / Flynn Vancouver • **PHOTOS:** Michael Perlmutter (p. 30 top), Martin Tessler (p. 30 bottom, p. 31) • **STATUS:** Competition winner, built

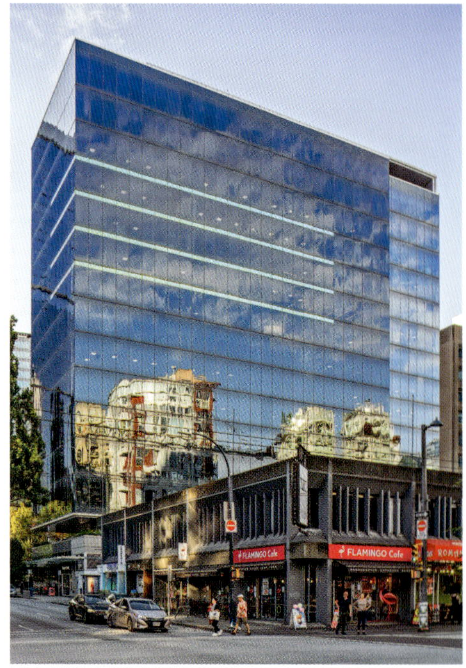

Double Digits

RCMP COMMUNITY SAFETY BUILDING, RICHMOND, BC • 2011

On October 1, 2011, a fully renovated and seismically upgraded RCMP Community Safety Building opened to the public. To prepare for the occasion, Richmond's Public Art Program put out a call to artists for a public artwork.

Double Digits proposed a sculpture consisting of two giant fingerprints, a "playful symbol" of police culture, that would sit off-centre in the forecourt of the main building entrance, allowing for unobstructed passage. The two waterjet-cut, aluminum plates, measuring 20′ by 10′ by 3/4″, would lean against one another for support and create a moiré pattern as people pass by. On a sunny day, the fingerprints would cast strangely familiar shadows on the pavement; by night, the lit sculpture would provide a visible marker from No. 5 Road.

The city selected a different proposal, *Child of the Fraser* by Glen Andersen, an artwork that took as its starting point the city of Richmond's unique coat of arms, steering clear of the politics of policing entirely. Perhaps some members of the jury did not find the idea of fingerprints playful in the context of policing.

PECHET and ROBB Art and Architecture
CLIENT: City of Richmond, Richmond RCMP • **TEAM:** Bill Pechet and Stephanie Robb with Gabe Daly • **RENDERINGS:** Gabe Daly • **STATUS:** Competition finalist

emptyful

MILLENNIUM LIBRARY PARK, WINNIPEG, MB • 2010–12

Passing through downtown Winnipeg, with its many shades of brown, it would be hard to miss *emptyful,* a half-full, stainless steel beaker profile standing 36′ high, emitting ethereal coloured light. Its form transforming from 2-D to 3-D as one's distance and perspective changes, the hollow vessel is an allusion to Manitoba's open, empty prairie. "The vastness of space which elicits this reading has a way of isolating figures such as buildings, producing silhouettes against the sky in a very particular way that is unique to prairie landscapes and cityscapes. It also produces a mental space which allows for the free flow of creation and the imagination. This fullness of emptiness is portrayed by the container as an abstraction of that idea." [BP]

During the summer months, *emptyful* emits rain and fog accompanied by cool coloured lights of blue and green, aqua and white, the artwork acting as a kind of vertical splash park to the delight of sweltering children and adults alike. Winnipeg can be as toasty in the summer as it is frigid in the winter when *emptyful* is animated with the colours of fire, yellow and orange, soft white, amber and red. "When the snow or rain is caught by these colours we imagine a sudden filling of the void with a giddy snow-globe effect, just once in a while when nature decides to collaborate with us." [BP] The public artwork—at times evoking melancholy, at times giddy joy—has become a local favourite and an iconic symbol of Winnipeg.

The backstory to *emptyful* started with the naming of Winnipeg as one of three 2010 Cultural Capitals of Canada. At the same time, Millennium Library Park was undergoing a sorely needed renovation following the 2005 transformative addition to the adjacent Millennium Library by Patkau Architects. The new park, actually a green roof atop a parkade, was conceived as a heavily programmed, urban oasis. During the planning for the renovation, three sites were identified for public artworks, including one funded by the Cultural Capital funding.

The call for "Expressions of Interest" read: "The Winnipeg Arts Council seeks a professional artist to create a permanent, contemporary artwork using the elements of water and light in downtown Winnipeg, Manitoba, Canada." The document went on to describe the rather heavy program for the artwork. It was tasked with terminating the view from the centre of the park while simultaneously drawing the public in from Donald Street. It was also required to create a screen using light and water that was "distinct and active" in every season. Finally, it needed to provide a buffer from the Donald Street traffic while safely attracting the attention of those driving by.

With a substantial history of successful public artworks under their belt, PECHETStudio was selected as one of five finalists, the only Canadian among four Americans, including artist Vito Acconci. The competing teams were invited to tour the challenging site, a 5′-wide sliver with a predetermined footprint along the wall shielding the Donald Street parkade ramp. Given the complexities of building in a sliver of a site atop a parkade, employing light and water in the extreme Winnipeg climate, the teams were required from the start to include structural, mechanical, and electrical engineers licensed in the province. They had just three short months to prepare detailed proposals, and given that the winning artist would be solely responsible for delivering the project on budget, unforeseen circumstances be damned, the proposal—actually a promise—had to be meticulously prepared. In February 2011, PECHETStudio was awarded the commission for *emptyful.*

Over the years since its grand opening, despite a detailed maintenance manual, the original programming of light and water effects has unintentionally been altered by a succession of maintenance personnel. It is now possible to experience fire light in the summertime and icy blues in the wintertime. Alas, the world is turning upside-down.

PECHETStudio
CLIENTS: City of Winnipeg and Winnipeg Arts Council • **TEAM:** Bill Pechet with Gabe Daly / CDm2 LIGHTWORKS / SMS Engineering / Crosier Kilgour / HTFC Planning & Design • **FABRICATION:** Parr Metal Fabricators / OB1 Contracting / Ful-Flo Industries / Mee Industries (USA) • **PHOTOS:** Gerry Kopelow (p. 34–35), Michael Perlmutter (p. 36, 38-39) • **DRAWINGS:** Gabe Daly, updated by Lőrinc Vass • **STATUS:** Competition winner, built

DELTA
emptyful

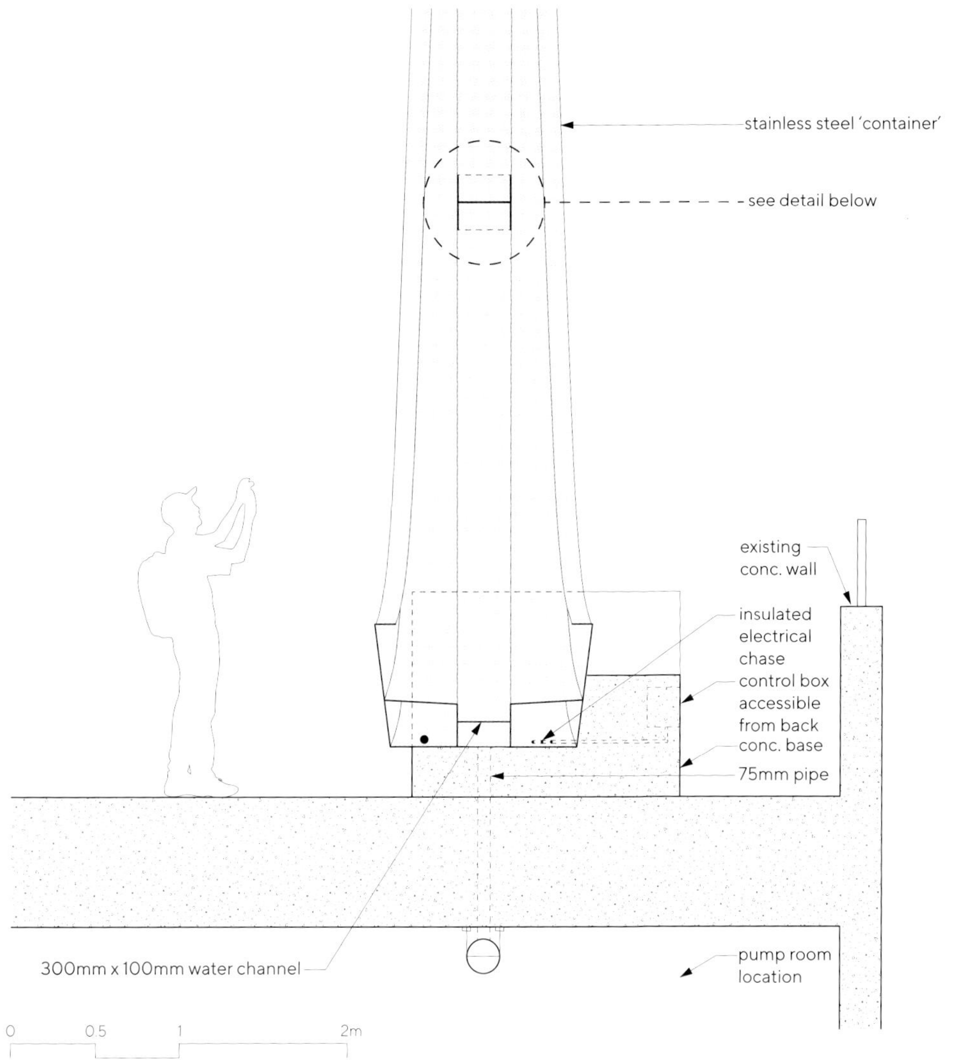
stainless steel 'container'
see detail below
existing conc. wall
insulated electrical chase
control box accessible from back
conc. base
75mm pipe
300mm x 100mm water channel
pump room location
0
0.5
1
2m

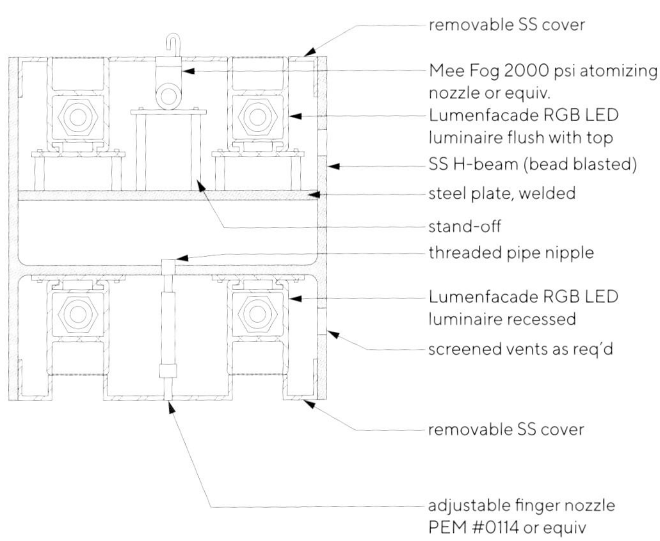
removable SS cover
Mee Fog 2000 psi atomizing nozzle or equiv.
Lumenfacade RGB LED luminaire flush with top
SS H-beam (bead blasted)
steel plate, welded
stand-off
threaded pipe nipple
Lumenfacade RGB LED luminaire recessed
screened vents as req'd
removable SS cover
adjustable finger nozzle PEM #0114 or equiv

Eternal Home Cemetery Gate

COLMA, CA • 2018–

As of the 2020 census, the deceased population of Colma, California—1.5 million—was 1,000 times greater than its living population. Colma, otherwise known as the "City of Souls," is a modern-day necropolis with sixteen to eighteen cemeteries, depending on the source, including four for Jews; one each for Catholics, Greek Orthodox, Italians, Chinese, Japanese, Serbians; and one for pets.

By the late 1880s, San Francisco's twenty-four cemeteries were full and cemetery owners needed to find expansion land outside the city. The southern end of Colma was deemed especially suitable for its easy access to the city by horse carriages, streetcars, and trains. In 1900, new burials were banned in San Francisco, and when, by 1914, every cemetery within the city limits was issued an eviction notice requiring the removal of remains and monuments, the little town of Colma inherited hundreds of thousands of new "residents."

By its own account, the Eternal Home Jewish Cemetery stands apart as the only cemetery in Colma with a dedicated Orthodox Jewish section and a certified space for green organic burials. Its Memory Garden is dedicated to the mourning of perinatal and infant losses. This is a noteworthy offering as in Judaism there is no traditional ritual for mourning fetuses or newborns who survive less than thirty days.

The commission, *Eternal Home Cemetery Gate*, was modest in scope: the design of a new pedestrian and vehicular gateway to better mark the entrance to the cemetery off the vast El Camino Real. The design borrowed its motif from the stained-glass patterns in the mid-century modern funeral hall that terminates the entry drive. The blues and aquas would offer a cool counterpoint to the arid climate, and at night, the lit sign would appear to float up towards the spirits of Colma.

PECHETStudio

CLIENT: Sinai Memorial Chapel • **TEAM:** Bill Pechet with Lőrinc Vass • **RENDERING:** Lőrinc Vass • **STATUS:** In progress

Everyday Evocations

Leslie Van Duzer

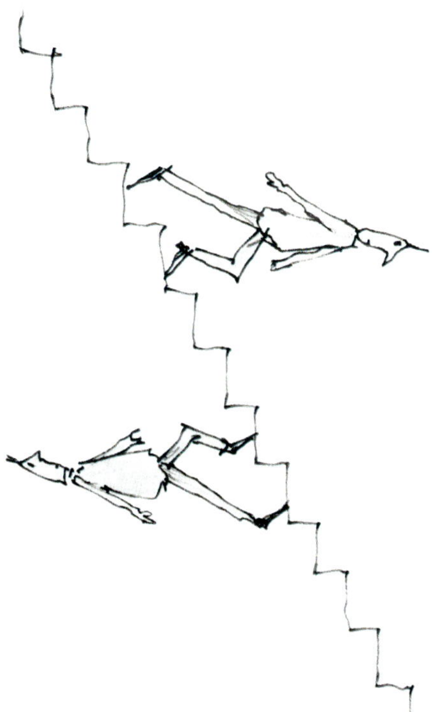

SKETCH: Bill Pechet

As you made your way through the ABC's, and are now well into the E's, you might have wondered about the decision to organize this body of work alphabetically. Faced with such a wide array of projects, surely it might make sense to form chapters by program types, sorting public artworks from residences, cemeteries from retail interiors. But if you understand program more broadly as agenda, rather than merely as functional categories conventionally defined, then things get very messy, very fast.

If a program/agenda can be, for example, to introduce humour into a public space, then you might find a giant bong-bridge and upside-down trash can light in the same chapter. Or, if the program/agenda is to explore subtraction as a design strategy, then the restoration of a historic Jewish cemetery and interventions in a public plaza would be found side by side. Since this body of work can be sliced and diced in so many meaningful ways, it seemed unproductive to organize it according to normative notions of function.

Another possibility, to show the progression of work by ordering the projects chronologically, might sound sensible as well, but Bill's ideas don't progress linearly over time, at least not in the sense of any meaningful distinctions between his early and late work. Rather, his projects continually circle back on themselves, often several decades later. The seeds of a project today may date back to his time in art or architecture school, and chances are, they do.

You might still think it would be helpful to create at least two, unambiguous categories, built and unbuilt work, but that would be very hard to justify as the unbuilt work is no less buildable, just less lucky. And besides, in some cases, what is today unbuilt, dormant, or even seemingly abandoned, can spring back to life at any moment.

And so, it was determined that the alphabetical order would be the most apt for this body of work. Roland Barthes argues convincingly for the benefit of this ordering system in his own autobiography, *Roland Barthes* (1977) by Roland Barthes, translated by Richard Howard.

> The alphabetical order erases everything, banishes every origin. Perhaps in places, certain fragments seem to follow one another by some affinity; but the important thing is that these little networks not be connected, that they do not slide into a single enormous network which would be the structure of the book, its meaning. It is in order to halt, to deflect, to divide this descent of discourse toward a destiny of the subject, that at certain moments the alphabet calls you to order (to disorder) and says: Cut! Resume the story in another way.

At the end of the day, it seemed far more interesting to "resume the story in another way." [RB] And indeed, the serendipity of projects separated by years and geography landing on pages side by side brought about happy accidents. As the titles of the projects were established long ago, any relationship between the flying whirligigs in *Acer Gigantis* and the flyway over *Air Borne* are new found treasures, not unlike the delightful discoveries of strange bedfellows in Bill's own *The Encyclopediette.* It is hoped that as you travel through these pages, apophenia takes hold, allowing you to imagine new relationships of your own making. Conspiracy theories welcome!

The title of this book, the ambigram *up / dn,* was intended as an early warning sign. You have entered, perhaps unknowingly, into a realm that invites you to stand on your head to see things clearly. In Bill's wonderland, delight comes from having your expectations upended, from finding your sense of agency compromised, from being ensnared in thick webs of references and puns. Case in point: *up / dn* also refers to the standard notational system found on stairs in architectural plans.

Finally, just one more thing about the construction of this book. You might ask why so many projects (88!) of such different scales and apparent significance have been included, when surely a cemetery for infants would displace an empty vessel and its twin filled with mini marshmallows. While projects of greater complexity have been allocated more space, all of the projects are Bill's children. He moves without qualifiers or favour between them, understanding that designing a cemetery to comfort grieving parents *(Little Spirits Garden)* does not diminish the importance of teaching architecture students how to think about positive and negative space *(halfsweet)*. Life is all that.

WEAVING

From the start of each new project, Bill sets out to construct a web of meaningful relationships, mining the physical characteristics, history, and sociocultural milieu of his appointed sites; investigating the inhabitants' stories, real and mythological; tapping into material associations and cultural references; connecting the animate to the inanimate. No matter the scale of a project, a thick network of relationships—think: Italo Calvino's invisible city of Ersilia—provides alternate pathways into the work without creating closed narratives. The coexistence of multiple overlapping threads, the more the better, keeps the work accessible and open to different interpretations. "Because I see myself between disciplines, most projects are in a dialogue with multiple audiences; each of whom have different worldviews, aspirations, histories and belief systems. Therefore, I am trying to think through their perspectives to allow many to participate. As a result, I guess I'm promiscuous, both inside and between each project, where meaning arises from a continuous loop of references, relationships, reflections." [BP]

For one trained in architecture who regularly collaborates with landscape architects, it is second nature to seek strong connections to the physical characteristics of a site, whether it happens to be along a major road, on a residential lot, in a park or plaza. Topography, vegetation, the adjacent context—all are major drivers for many of the works in this volume. In *Exeter House,* as in *Little Spirits Garden,* steeply sloping sites and unique vegetation inform not only their plans and sections, but also material decisions, such as the relationship between the colour of the Corten cemetery pavilion and the bark of the surrounding arbutus trees. With the redesign of the perimeter of *Ross Bay Cemetery* in Victoria, the relationship of the necropolis to the surrounding neighbourhood was altered with surgical precision. When one thing, an edge condition, becomes many things—a barrier, a gateway, an interment site, a bench for contemplation—the network of relationships grows ever thicker.

Elsewhere, the weaving starts from the history and inherited iconography of the site. Pechet and Robb's tribute to fallen soldiers, *Victory Square Lighting,* is an important early example. In Bill's subsequent public artworks, *Make West* and *Peeping Tom Thomson,* the stories of abandoned industrial waterfronts in Vancouver and Toronto ground the work. But nowhere have Bill and his collaborators celebrated the history of a place in such multifaceted ways as in the former working waterfront, *North Vancouver Shipyards*. Inspired by the resourcefulness of the shipworkers and their rich lexicon of materials, their stories are celebrated and brought to the fore through both conventional and unconventional means. Information boards relaying the history of the shipyards, the naming of "Shipbuilders' Square" and "Punch Clock Plaza", even the renovation of the pier—these were to be expected. But for a dedicated prospector, there are more treasures to discover. Located just inside the workers' traditional arrival gate, a giant file drawer with individual employee cards is backgrounded by a mural depicting the masses of shipbuilders *(x-files)*. Repurposed antique molds, now divorced from their original functions and arranged according to their formal properties, are similarly, if less overtly, commemorative *(Yardifacts)*. A specific yellow paint found in the original shipyards coats the landmark crane, the *infomoji* boards, and, most recently, the Minion-esque hoods of new recycling bins (*trashtalk*). The arcing, steel stage canopy, its form reminiscent of a ship's hull, and the lighting fixtures, trash cans, benches and pier details all tap into the material palette found on site. The remarkable success of this industrial-land-turned-public-space suggests this 25-year project has a long history in front of it.

This deep respect for the specificity of each place is, in many cases, intimately tied to the stories of individuals. In an early competition proposal by Pechet + Robb commemorating the hopeful immigrants who perished while awaiting admission to Canada, most of them quarantined on ships, *Grosse-Île Memorial* acknowledged the scope of the human tragedy by proposing 74,000 individual nameplates laid out on earthen "waves." Likewise, the stone portraits of, and drawn by, local children for *The Living Ruin* in *St. Andrew's Park*, are future commemorations of those who use the park today. In Bill's many cemetery projects, special care is taken to provide a variety of ways to leave mementoes in honour of individuals passed. Two especially poignant instances of this are the Little Spirits houses, designed to be positioned at will and fully personalized in memory of a lost infant, and the many scattered nooks provided within the ruins of *The Woods I*.

Relationships within a project are also established through material choices, such as the punny connection between stone patterning and a concrete wall poured against faux stone plywood in the *Southlands House,* plywood, which by the way, was borrowed from the faux finishes on the *Rec Room* dance floor, which themselves alluded to the rumpus rooms of suburban Canadian basements. There was the fictional repurposing of boards marking the scaling grid on the floor of the historic ship building hall as wooden benches seemingly held together by clamps along the waterfront at the *Shipyards.* A column capital of wooden spoons in *The Athinian* restaurant brought pots of Greek chickpea soup to mind, and orange fleece, already on its third life, got recycled again, tracing the material's history from plastic water bottle to fleece sportswear to gigantic sweater and back again to hats and scarves, jackets and leg warmers in *SweaterLodge.*

Further adding to the resonance of his work, there are countless cultural anchors. Some projects reference famous figures, real and fictional: Le Corbusier, Roger Penrose, Hokusai, and Colonel Mustard from the game of *Clue*. Many more reference quotidian objects: mustard bottles and picnic tables, honey bears, salmon, high school chemistry beakers, marshmallows, folded paper dolls, music boxes, suitcases, watering cans, keyholes, bongs, cigar rings, spoons, barns, bunnies, a hand with painted nails. Bill's illustrations for children's books have parents winking knowingly at one another, just as some project titles, which to his disappointment few ever query, "allude to the deployment of layered meanings and sometimes goofy puns." BP

Bill's early experience working with dancers sensitized him to the possibility that rituals and movement patterns could be reinforced through symbolism and spatial sequencing in the non-dance projects. Visitors to his cemeteries will find themselves in carefully staged processions linking indoor and outdoor spaces, passing symbolically in and out of the light. There are also deep connections to rituals, which may not be evident to the uninitiated. The "torn" corner of the funeral pavilion at Temple Shalom Cemetery in Surrey symbolizes the Jewish tradition of the *Kriah*, the tearing of one's clothing in mourning, while the provision of a beautiful, bronze basin supports ritual handwashing at the Jewish Cemetery in Vancouver.

Finally, at least finally here, there are the relationships between sentient beings and their inanimate counterparts. From his early *Souvenirs in the Museum of Sand,* where a face meets a vessel, to his recent design for recycling receptacles that offer garbage collectors a "hand-le" with a friendly shake, Bill regularly introduces anthropomorphism in his projects. In *Le Château*, designed in partnership with Stephanie Robb, human figures, flat like paper dolls, are set to fly away outside, while inside, others bend at the waist to take shoppers onto their laps. There are wandering, knobby human legs supporting *A Walking Table*, a giant hand with fingernails that change colour to reflect energy usage in *the False Creek Energy Utility Stacks*, and supersized, disembodied fingerprints marking the entry of an RCMP building in *Double Digits.* His lamps have skirts like flirts and helmets like soldiers; elsewhere, a garbage can with a light within takes on the persona of Colonel Mustard.

Perhaps one of the projects that best exemplifies the layering of relationships within a single work is the modest, unbuilt competition winner, *Bearing,* an early Pechet + Robb collaboration. The site is in Surrey, BC, near the perimeter of a large park, in a grove of cherry trees. The task was to add an art piece that would serve as a sign for an arts centre nearby. The neighbouring roadway is dotted with standard Cobra streetlamps. When this vernacular readymade was encouraged to go rogue and cluster within the grove, the roadway was linked to park, and Cobra lamps, with their trunks and branches, to the trees. Overhead, the constellation Ursa Major, or the Great Bear, dictated not only the location of the lampposts, but also their heights, with each lamppost's measurement determined by the distance to the corresponding star. And, it is certainly no coincidence that the Great Bear was the constellation of choice for a project in Bear Creek Park. Calling: earth to heaven.

TACTICS AND THEMES

While each project develops its own internal, highly site-specific network of relationships, there are recurring strategies—scale jumping, dislocating, material substituting, casting, perching, hiding controls—and motifs—waterworks and coloured lights, bunnies and birds, chairs and tables, circles like faces, oversized hands and skinny legs—that appear and reappear throughout this work. As Bill knows, a bag of tricks need not be exhaustive to allow for great variation.

Since art school, when Bill discovered the world in a sandbox, he has often used scale shifts to create uncanny work in the public realm. Consider *Big Chairs* and *GRANtable*, where one has to jump up to sit down. If oversized thrones are the stuff of kings and queens, their siting on a public waterfront trail and in a downtown neighbourhood park creates a delightful incongruity through both scale and dislocation. The word *incongruity* is key, as it is the momentary inability to reconcile a direct experience with an expectation that leaves us in a delicious state of bewilderment.

Some things are repurposed as they scale up, such as the humble soup spoon turned thirty foot-long public drinking fountain in *Spirit Square,* or a giant sweater that unlatches to become an interior space generous enough to accommodate Venice Biennale crowds and Vancouver museumgoers in *SweaterLodge.* In Victoria, the *Watering Garden,* a colossal watering can, much too large to pick up and pour, becomes a splash park when spraying water from the most unexpected places!

It should come as no surprise that Bill has been fascinated by casting since art school days; of course, a process that requires reverse thinking would be right up his alley. "I love the mental exercise of seeing the positive in the negative, not only for the making of solid things, but for seeing voids as solids in space." [BP] The aforementioned concrete sandboxes were the first of many casting experiments. Among the *Souvenirs from the Museum of Sand* were early casts of vessels, a spoon-shaped planter, miniature mountains and Bill's beloved honey bears. Later, there were Ductal casts of Little Spirit houses and bronze casts of donor nameplates, a sacred bell, and fragments of Vancouver's history. Inspired by the casting of curly wood shavings in fibreglass, a product he saw in an Arthur Erickson house and later used for a lampshade, Bill cast pine needles into fibreglass resin to create a canopy and guardrail for *Exeter House.* Casting—the transformation of fluids into solids and negatives into positives—is its own kind of alchemy.

The handcasting of hundreds of miniature concrete chairs (chairs that later grew up to become *Big Chairs),* each with slight imperfections, was an early embrace of the aesthetic of calculated roughness and Bill's interest in multiples. While this production might be considered rather obsessive, a still more extreme example of this interest in repetition with irregularities was another independent project, *Who's There.* Bill hired a painting factory in China to produce 500 copies of his original painting of a bunny (actually, a self-portrait). When the paintings were finally exhibited after a 10-year hiatus in his studio bathtub, the result could be compared to a photographic portrait shot in burst mode, the slight jiggle between images creating an unnerving reincarnation.

Bill also explores the potential of repetition variation when deploying multiples of industrially-produced readymades. In the transportation-related projects, for example, standard elements are dislocated and rearranged, multiplied to create surfaces, and/or, tweaked themselves. In *Chumway,* the ubiquitous road reflectors that divide lanes on the highway are lifted off the ground and up overhead, multiplied, and arranged side-by-side on a pedestrian overpass to create a surface that shimmers like the skin of a salmon. *roger that* rejigged solar-powered construction warning lights and clustered them into circular arrays on opposite sides of a highway and LRT station. Standard lighting fixtures appear as varied as a field of grass due to their arrangement on a gently sloping site in *Velvet Bent.*

"Witnessing the sublime effect of thousands of repeating Jizo statues in Japan, or experiencing the hypnotic and repeating rhythms of Steve Reich and Earth, Wind & Fire, produce, for me, a kind of transcendent experience that is as close as I get to meditating. They are visual and auditory mantras. My experiments in repetitions also allude to repeated actions and rituals that anchor our daily experience of life. This is why I have kept over 20 years of fruit stickers in a baggy, each one of them a record of a daily piece of fruit. Not only does it mark a repeated action, but it gives honour to the consumed delectable." [BP]

Things that glow in the dark have played a central role in Bill's projects from the earliest days of his practice. At times, custom light fixtures have been a focus. There was his charming trio of lamps, *Cloudy, Mambo Wazo and Wazo Heights,* and the repurposed light fixtures in *The Athinian* restaurant. In later works, the lampposts at *Victory Square* served as memorials, and the upside down *Trashy Lights* as a reference to the right-side-up trash receptacles.

In other public artworks, the fixtures recede and the focus shifts exclusively to light itself. In Winnipeg, *emptyful* radiates cool blue and green light into the summer night, come winter, warm red and orange light thaw the passersby. *Dichroic Vancouver* uses strips of programmed lights on an office building façade to mark occasions, some designed (i.e. disco lights on the weekends), some revised by the building owners (i.e. pink for Breast Cancer Month). Lights with hidden sources are also used to create the illusion of a levitated dome in *heaven between* and an entry sign in *Eternal Home Cemetery Gate*.

Proposals for lighting three downtown Vancouver streets illuminate the degree of site specificity in Bill's lightworks. For Davie Street, a festive strip with restaurants and bars and clubs, he designed a string of everchanging coloured lights, lurid and carnivalesque, while for the buttoned-up Alberni Street, with its checklist of luxury stores, he proposed light rings floating over the road, evoking diamond and smoke rings. And for Vancouver's entertainment zone, a parade of bright white lights creates a visual vortex as poles march down Granville Street in recognition of Vancouver's rich history of neon lights. "The nighttime is a magical, inverted space, where solid becomes void, where the subconscious wells up as a harbinger of dreaming, allowing us to reframe our understanding of what we think of the city, and by extension, who we are. The lighting projects are adornments to this altered reality, tapping into ancient associations of fireside and fantasy. I also love to make paintings that glow in the dark, revealing a surprise or unseen message." [BP]

When falling asleep as a young child, Bill often had the experience of flying out of body, down the hallway and out into the nighttime city. "I loved the freedom, release from gravity and perspective that these events gave me." [BP] His love of airplanes and flight were nurtured by his father, a flight trainer in WWII, who often took his children to the local airfield to see the small planes. "Probably the apex of my whole life was one trip where we flew Edmonton-Vancouver-Seattle-LA-San Diego ... four plane rides in a row. I was in absolute heaven sitting at the window and looking down at geographies and cities. Even now, I continue to take aerial views of cities and geographies. This is a prized collection that I occasionally show to students." [BP]

Bill's dream of flying, dreams which still recur today, his will to defy gravity, may begin to explain why the weightiest of cast objects are more often than not supported on bird-thin legs, spindles that incongruously appear too insubstantial to carry such a load. It helps explain why in project after project, we see space held tentatively—in the hinged roofs or "spatialized wingtips" of the *Little Spirits* pavilion, the *Southlands* and *Exeter Houses* and *The Woods*, "as if there was a kind of imminence of the possibility that they were only there for a second, folding as if about to take off and yet bound to the gravity of the earth, a kind of tension." [BP]

It seems Bill is always looking up. Who else would think to connect a stand of streetlamps to a constellation of stars (*Bearing*) or to tap into a flyway for inspiration (*MAMA* and *Airborne*)? Who else dreams of giant samaras flying through the sky, landing and petrifying as benches in a daycare (*Acer Gigantis*)? In the *Sound of Music,* the Reverend Mother might just as well have been singing about Bill as Maria when she articulated that great, universal poser: How do you catch a cloud and pin it down?

PHOTO: Michael Perlmutter

Exeter House

OAK BAY, VICTORIA, BC • 2004

It all starts with the site, a sloping .63-acre parcel in the Uplands of oak Bay, a landscape of over thirty Garry Oak trees and outcroppings of bedrock hillocks. Expertly navigating dense vegetation and a 13′ cliff, *Exeter House* embraces the site like a glove, both in plan and section.

In keeping with a West Coast modern tradition, the front face of the house is largely mute with minimal eyes on the street. An exquisitely landscaped front garden, an open carport, lightly stained cedar cladding, window mullions of anodized aluminum, an open stair to the main entry—these are all familiar elements from an earlier time. The house is not dated in its appearance, but rather more timeless, and more modest in demeanor than many of its contemporaries.

Despite the opacity of the front façade, the arrival sequence is more than generous. A stair with an extended covered porch welcomes the visitor past the lush garden to the front door of the upper, main level of the house. The stair begins as concrete, anchored to the island bedrock, then transitions into a floating steel set of treads that produce a change in the haptic and acoustic effects.

There is a humble grandeur to the sequence as one moves from outside in. The entire front entry, as well as the relationship of the house to the garden in the rear, was inspired by experiencing the *engawa* in Japan: a floor extension on one side of a Japanese-style house, usually facing a yard or garden and serving as a passageway and a sitting space. *En* refers to the indirect causes or relationships that make everything meaningful; *gawa* means connector or river. So, *engawa* could be translated as a river of affinities.

At the entry, the ceilings are unusually high as the plan splays open towards the rear garden, revealing a mossy mound of bedrock populated with ferns and oaks. Rather than minimize the space allocated for circulation, as is so often the case, here movement is celebrated, given thirty percent of the house's total 5,000 square feet. Perhaps this is not surprising when you learn that the owners are a choreographer and an athlete with an exercise studio on the lower level.

Building for a modest $180 CAD per square foot allowed for a spatial generosity, luxury of the best possible kind.

On the primary level of the house, there are three private zones—the master bedroom suite, an office/bedroom cluster, and the den/utilities—their walls and ceilings rendered in white drywall. A large roof and concrete floors sandwich the enclosed spaces and tie them to the open, connecting spaces—the foyer, living room, kitchen, dining room, and circulation—their lightly stained, pine-slatted ceilings drawing the eyes up and out to the exterior soffits. Despite the clarity of the concept, the house is much more than a built diagram that can easily be mapped in the mind. Rather, the house unfolds episodically, over time, like a good film whose organizational structure is never revealed.

The long curtain wall enclosing the rear of the house provides generous views onto the heavily vegetated garden, a garden whose limits are difficult to discern, leaving the imagination room to roam. This expansive, unfolding picture window floods the house with light and brings the colours of the changing seasons into the interior. Elsewhere, deeper in the house, strategically located windows and skylights offer subtle enticement. Come into the bedroom, come hither into the moonlight.

In good weather, the back garden is well used, with regular exercise classes on the open-air patio and dinners with friends and family in a large outdoor dining room sheltered by a fiberglass canopy embedded with pine needles. This crafted roof, like its matching guardrail at the front landing and the kitchen counters of aqua-coloured rice paper in plastic resin, are eye-catching moments seen against an otherwise quiet material palette. While these splashes of craft allow the absent hand of the maker to be ever present, this house does not foreground its designer. This house is rather a beautiful, spacious backdrop for the whims of nature and the lives that dance within it.

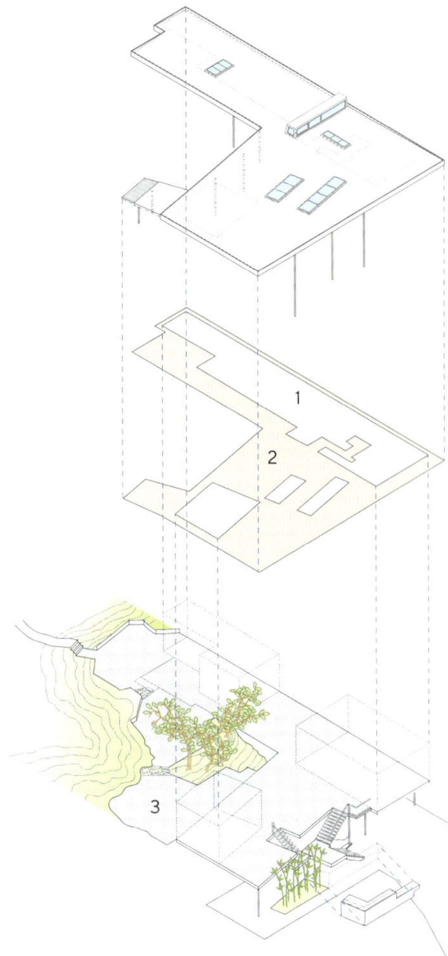

1. Enclosed spaces are untextured and white
2. Open spaces and those that connect to the outside are demarcated with stained pine ceilings
3. Indoor and outdoor circulation loop shown in grey

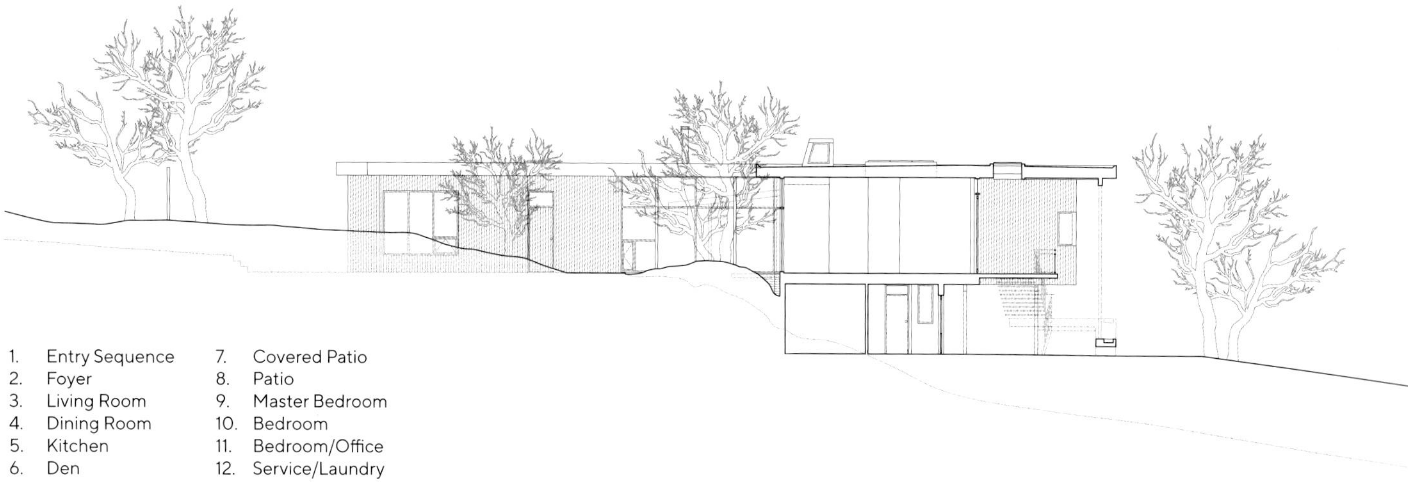

1. Entry Sequence
2. Foyer
3. Living Room
4. Dining Room
5. Kitchen
6. Den
7. Covered Patio
8. Patio
9. Master Bedroom
10. Bedroom
11. Bedroom/Office
12. Service/Laundry

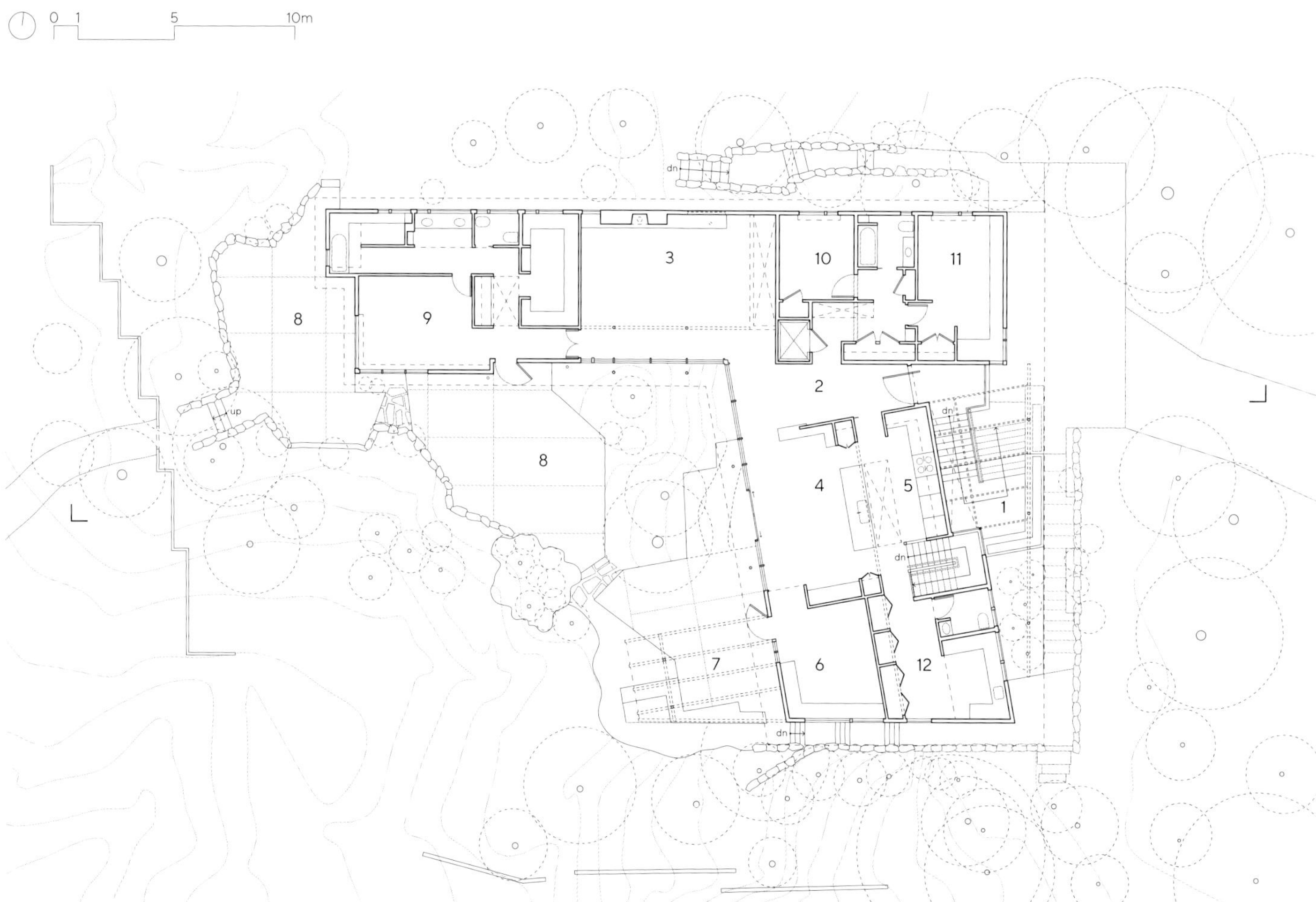

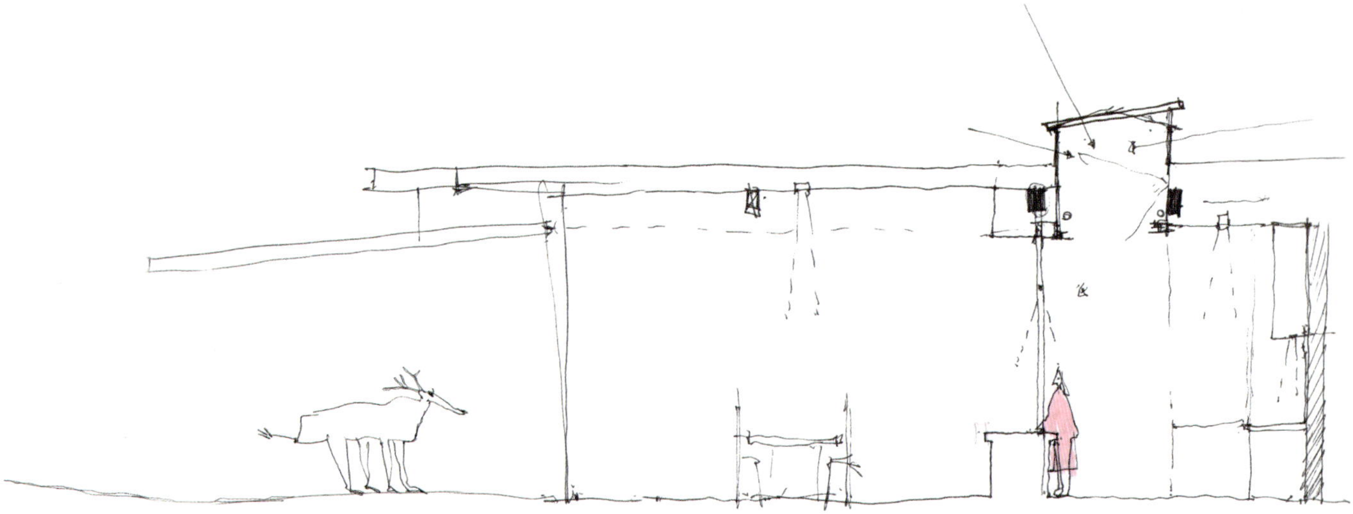

Pechet + Robb Studio

TEAM: Bill Pechet and Stephanie Robb with Maureen Kwong • **CONSTRUCTION:** W-2 Contracting Ltd. • **PHOTOS:** Michael Perlmutter (p. 49 top, bottom right, p. 51-53, p. 55 bottom), Martin Tessler (p. 49 bottom left, p. 54, p. 55 top)• **SKETCH:** Bill Pechet • **DRAWINGS:** Lőrinc Vass • **STATUS:** Built, no public access

False Creek Energy Utility Stacks

VANCOUVER, BC • 2009–10

In celebration of Vancouver's first renewable, energy-based, district heating system and the first wastewater-powered, heat-recovery system in North America—or, stated more plainly, the first successful conversion of poop to power on the continent—the city of Vancouver sought a public artwork that would interpret and make visible the functions of the new *False Creek Energy Utility Stacks.* Sited at the foot of the Cambie Bridge between Southeast False Creek and the new Olympic Village, the artwork also significantly marks an approach into downtown.

Coordinating with Frankl Architects, designers of the Centre, the requisite vent stacks were envisioned as a hand rising up from below the bridge, the raised hand a reference to the body heat processed within (and, however unconsciously, maybe a tribute to students everywhere.) The artificial fingernails, or reflectors, act out in response to the level of energy consumption at any given time, turning hottie red and orange during hours of highest energy usage and kool-kat blue at times with less demand. It is truly a unique gift to see in vent stacks fingers or to view nail polish as performative at the scale of a neighbourhood.

Pechet and Robb Art and Architecture

CLIENT: City of Vancouver • **TEAM:** Bill Pechet and Stephanie Robb (project coordinator) with Gabe Daly, Michael Fugeta, Matt Hessey / Sandwell Engineering Inc. / Walter Francl Architecture Inc. / Eckford + Associates / CDm2 LIGHTWORKS • **FABRICATION:** Westpro Constructors Group / Knight Signs

PHOTOS: Kristopher Grunert • **SKETCHES:** Bill Pechet • **STATUS:** Built

finding sudoku

HELEN PITT GALLERY, VANCOUVER, BC • 2007

Review by Robin Laurence, *Georgia Straight*, September 27, 2007

"A doodly, drifting, playful state of mind prevails in Bill Pechet's new installation. Finding Sudoku comprises more than 100 small objects assembled in a kind of conceptual cloud on the walls and floor of the Helen Pitt Gallery. These found, altered, or newly manufactured items range from a miniature moss garden, a cast-concrete sponge, and a line of pistachio-nut shells drawn on to resemble faces to floral decorations, painted pebbles, and a basket constructed out of toothpicks. Augmented with a charming little bookwork, Brancuzzi's Hope, and six of Pechet's notebooks, they reveal the teeming mental state that occurs somewhere between the full realization of a creative idea and the banal details of daily life.

"Pechet is probably best known as a designer and architect; he and his business partner Stephanie Robb represented Canada at the 2006 Venice Biennale of Architecture. His notebooks, which also function as sketchbooks, scrapbooks, address books, appointment books, teaching plans, and doodle pads, reveal other aspects of his lively intelligence. In between solving formal and structural problems related to his profession, he indulges in poetry, wordplay, cartooning, social satire, and drawings both serious and fanciful. Into this mix are injected the most prosaic details of daily life–doctor's appointments, ferry schedules, phone numbers, and dinner plans.

"An element of kitsch is introduced through the miniature music-box mechanisms attached to the wooden shelves on which the notebooks sit. Kitsch, cuteness, and intentional banality also inform the assortment of objects crowding the gallery walls, such as a Kleenex-box cover adorned with gold glitter, a teensy toy bunny, and a 'Minerals of Canada' sample sheet. The sweetness of childhood past resides in toys, miniature marshmallows, birthday candles, and especially in the recurring motif of plastic honey containers shaped like cartoon bears. Pechet's fascination with odd scale and unlikely materials is seen throughout the show, including in various castings of the honey bears in concrete and tinted resin. With the addition of an LED, a clear-resin version also functions as a wall lamp.

"The antiheroic and antimonumental aspects of Pechet's installation are not unusual in certain strands of contemporary art. They do, however, position him outside traditional architectural practice and constitute a subtle critique of his profession. This sweet contrariness is not entirely surprising, however, coming from the man who, with his partner, filled the Canadian pavilion at the Venice Biennale with an enormous, orange, polar-fleece sweater. Wraparound warmth and weirdness."

TEXT: Courtesy of Robin Laurence • PHOTOS: Bill Pechet

Funeral Hall and Administration Centre

GAN SHALOM CEMETERY, BRIONES, CONTRA COSTA, CA • 2022

A more peaceful setting for a final resting place one could not imagine. Gan Shalom Cemetery is set in a sublime, rolling landscape in Northern California, nestled between farms and ranches and regional parklands. When Sinai Memorial Chapel, guardians of several Jewish cemeteries in the Bay Area, had a vision of building a funeral hall and administrative centre worthy of these beautiful surroundings, they reached out to Bill, as they would later in Colma and Oakland.

The design for the new complex, from its siting and landscape design to its material palette, was subtly infused with meaning rooted in the place and the program. The new building would be located on the site of the current portable structure, still on axis with the arrival driveway but now oriented towards a great California oak. In Judaism, *Eitz Chaim*, the Tree of Life, is highly significant as a symbol of faith, familial relationships, community rootedness, and the continuance of life. Surrounding the new building, a borrowed landscape of berms, planted with native flora and anchored by large boulders, referenced the surrounding landscape and symbolized *Adama*: land, soil, the giver of life, the place to honour ancestors.

The distinct volumes of the funeral hall and the administrative centre were to be constructed of the same materials to create a whole from the parts. Plank-formed concrete, with wooden ceilings and screens, symbolized the physical and conceptual connection to the trees and the earth. "*Chomer*, material, refers to the physical realities of the tangible as a housing for the metaphysical." BP

The L-shaped entry courtyard, formed by the massing of the two adjoining programs, would offer shade under a grove of trees and polished boulders for resting. Before entering the funeral hall, mourners would encounter a small fountain and basin for the ritual handwashing. *Mayim*, water, is a precious life force for all living things. Once inside the main funeral hall, natural light would bring the presence of the spirit and compassion into the space. Above the coffin-dais, a double-height volume with a hidden clerestory was designed to admit southern light, casting a warm, diffused glow over the ceremonies. An expansive curtain wall at the front of the hall would frame a view of the great oak and open generously to allow the funeral procession to continue outdoors. Eternal light, or *Ner Tamid*, like *Mayim, Adama, and Chomer*, is an essential giver of life and the illumination of truth.

PECHETStudio

CLIENTS: Beit Olam of Contra Costa and Sinai Memorial Chapel • **TEAM:** Bill Pechet with Lőrinc Vass • **DRAWING/RENDERINGS:** Lőrinc Vass • **STATUS:** Unbuilt

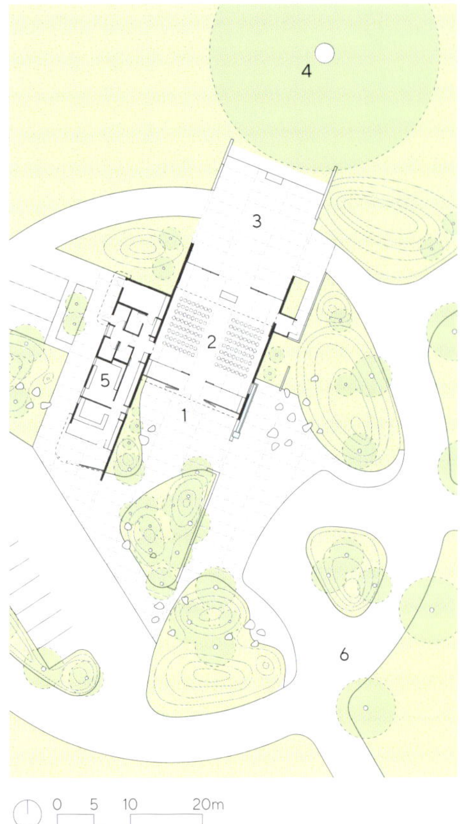

1. Entry Court
2. Funeral Hall
3. Outdoor Funeral Terrace
4. California Oak Tree
5. Office Wing
6. Existing Vehicular Route

Funeral Pavilion and Burial Ground Expansion

TEMPLE SHOLOM CEMETERY, SURREY, BC • 2023–

Temple Sholom Cemetery, situated among cedars and firs in Surrey, British Columbia, was designed by the late landscape architect, Cornelia Hahn Oberlander. The original site planning was exquisite, composed of sections of concentric paths lined with grave sites that saved the remarkable cedar, fir, and hemlock trees. When PECHETStudio was approached to expand the burial grounds, Bill respectfully extended the original pattern into three undeveloped sections of the cemetery, creating new sites for over 900 future interments.

In addition, Bill was asked to design a new entry gate, memorial walls, a new works yard with public restrooms, and, as a central focus for the cemetery, a funeral pavilion. The simplicity of the pavilion, a concrete podium with ramped access and an enclosure of cedar slats with three degrees of opacity, reflects the Jewish tradition of quiet humility that defines the funeral and burial rituals. The upper portion of each façade is opaque and weathertight, providing shelter from the rain. The lower portion allows for visual transparency and for the passage of breezes. Further reducing the opacity, on the east and west corners of the pavilion, every other slat is removed along a diagonal line to represent *Kriah*, the Jewish custom of tearing one's garment when in mourning. The pavilion visually floats above the podium, appearing to have been released from earth-bound constraints.

PECHETStudio

CLIENT: Temple Sholom • **TEAM:** Bill Pechet with Lőrinc Vass / Hemsworth Architecture (Architect of Record) / Aspect Engineering / Creus Civil • **DRAWINGS/ RENDERINGS:** Lőrinc Vass • **STATUS:** In progress

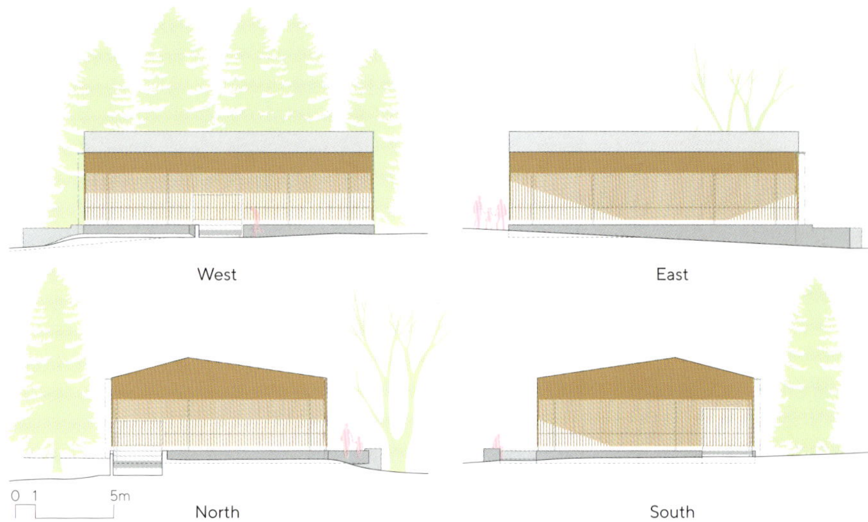

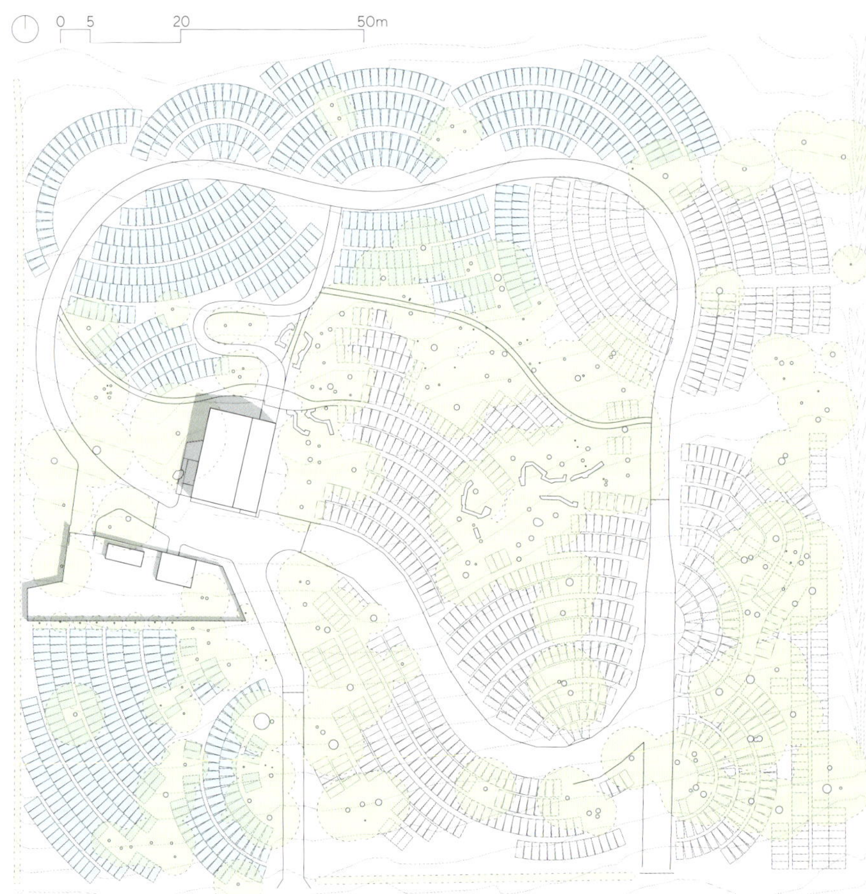

נֵר יְיָ נִשְׁמַת אָדָם

GRANtable

MAY AND LORNE BROWN PARK, VANCOUVER, BC • 1998

By 1998, Bill's big chairs and big tables were popping up everywhere: in the interiors of stores and offices, on stages, and on the Ambleside shoreline in West Vancouver. Now, there is big, as in the 16'-long table designed for *Savage Council* and *Big Chairs* that leave your feet dangling like Edith Ann on *Laugh-in*, but then, there is GRAN(D)!

GRANtable, with its imposing scale and symmetrical positioning, brings a whiff of grandeur to a small neighbourhood park in downtown Vancouver, one shadowed by looming towers and carpeted with a rag-tag lawn. A large oval of gravel, centred at the foot of an otherwise ordinary stair, sets the stage for a sixty-six foot-long concrete table with thrones at either end. Associations flood the mind: Vignola's great water table at Villa Lante (a source of inspiration) or meetings with paranoid Putin at the Kremlin, or perhaps scenes of decadence in *The Cook, the Thief, the Wife and her Lover*, or tense family dinners in *Succession*. Long tables have long associations with power, wealth, and debauchery.

But upon closer examination, there is a second, more subtle reading of this ensemble, one that is less aristocratic—or autocratic—and more democratic. At the centre of the long table, there is an embedded chessboard, flanked on either side by short concrete benches. Mere proletarians can sit across from one another, making strategic moves that run counter to the powerful throne sitters at the far ends. When the long sides are occupied—imagine a baby shower or Thanksgiving potluck—the noble table transforms into the people's table.

Pechet + Robb Studio

CLIENT: City of Vancouver • **STUDIO TEAM:** Bill Pechet (project coordinator) and Stephanie Robb with Nicolas Osenton / Phillips Farevaag Smallenberg / Yolles Group • **FABRICATION:** AE Concrete / Marc Bricault • **PHOTOS:** Bill Pechet (p. 64, p. 65 top centre, right), Courtney Healey (p.65, top left), Michael Perlmutter (p. 65 bottom) • **DRAWING:** Bill Pechet • **STATUS:** Competition winner, built.

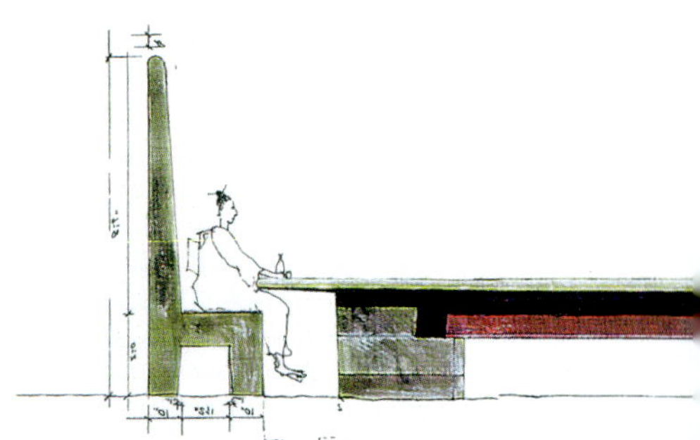

Granville Street

DOWNTOWN VANCOUVER, BC • 2008–12

It was 2010 and the Winter Olympics were coming to town. Granville Street in downtown Vancouver would be centre stage as the primary Entertainment Zone during the games. In anticipation, PWL Partnership with Pechet and Robb Art and Architecture were commissioned to refresh the beleaguered downtown street, one that had weathered over a century of booms and busts, numerous attempts at revitalization, and ever-shifting city policies.

The directive from the city of Vancouver for this round of improvements: "Design a street that reflects Vancouver's unique identity, character and sense of place." The scope of work included the addition of trees and lighting, sidewalk enhancements, bollards, benches, and bike racks. The design team set out to give the ten-block downtown zone of Granville Street, between the Granville Bridge and Waterfront Station, a coherent and refreshed identity while accommodating the unique conditions along its length. It should be mentioned, while this surface-level redesign was underway, eight of the ten blocks were torn up for the building of the underground Canada Line.

Surely Bill's most impactful contribution was the introduction of 380 LED vertical "lightbars" that run down both sides of the street, creating unified illumination alongside existing lighting and signage, and forming a vortex of illuminated convergence as one looks down the street. Appearing in television commercials and print ads even to this day, the bright white lights rekindled memories of the "Great White Way," as Granville Street was known in its neon heyday in the 1950s.

Modular seating of wood and perforated aluminum surfaces, strategically clustered from end to end of the zone, was designed to support a wide range of human interactions and postures. Pedestrians can stop and cuddle with a special friend side by side, sit kitty corner with a stranger on an L-shaped bench, rest alone or alone together on rows of single chairs.

Prior to 2010, the sidewalks were dotted with bronze stars honouring the luminaries of Vancouver's entertainment history. Previously scattered about, the design team proposed consolidating and aligning the stars in new basalt paving strips. The BC Entertainment Hall of Fame StarWalk now honours over 300 Vancouverites, many acknowledged since the Olympics.

The pedestrian realm of the streetscape was expanded with flex-parking zones that allow parking at the curb during the day and wider sidewalks to accommodate crowds in the evenings and on special occasions. The street is also designed to be closed to vehicular traffic, with the outdoor "rooms" providing the infrastructure to support festivals, street parties, art installations and all variety of performances. Thousands of people partied on Granville Street during the Olympics, and after fifteen years of use and abuse, the unifying interventions endure, save for a short-lived experiment in "bollard seats" that were unable to weather the alcohol-fueled vandalism of Saturday night partiers.

Pechet and Robb Art and Architecture

CLIENT: City of Vancouver • **PROJECT TEAM:** Bill Pechet (project coordinator) with Gabe Daly, Andrew McLean / PWL Partnership Landscape Architects (coordinating firm) • **FABRICATION:** City of Vancouver Public Works / Éclairage SDL / Valmont West Coast Engineering / Jacob Brothers Construction • **PHOTOS:** Maurice Li (p. 66-67 bottom, p. 68 top), Jonathan Carter (p. 67 top), Bill Pechet (p. 68), Michael Perlmutter (p. 69) • **SKETCH:** Bill Pechet • **STATUS:** Built

ORPHEUM
CAFE
VOGUE

Granville St
MEINHARDT

Grosse-Île Memorial

GROSSE-ÎLE, QC • 1998

Situated in the Isle-aux-Grues Archipelago in the St. Lawrence River, thirty miles from Quebec City, Grosse-Île is known as a botanist's paradise for its rare plants and wetlands, forests of balsam fir and red maple. Grosse-Île was also Canada's primary port of entry for immigrants until WWII.

From 1832 to 1937, Grosse-Île additionally served as a quarantine station for the Port of Quebec. As thousands of immigrants and sailors, many of them escaping famine in Ireland, had to be quarantined, the small island—just three miles long and one mile wide—was overwhelmed. While awaiting clearance, many had to remain aboard overcrowded and unsanitary ships. 74,000 immigrants, sailors, and local workers died due to epidemics aggravated by poor conditions.

The *Grosse-Île Memorial* proposal was ambitious. Every lost soul, all 74,000 of them, would be commemorated individually. Their names would be cast in brass and assembled by year in long boat-like forms. The boats would be cast out on earthen waves, mirrored in form to reference the long trenches, since collapsed, where the bodies were buried. A raised plate would mark each calendar year.

At the bottom of the escarpment, adjacent to the field, scattered fragments of shale and pottery would create a beach, a path. Concrete bunkers, embedded in the cliff, resembling ruins of a harbour settlement, would provide raised viewing platforms and seating for contemplation.

Pechet + Robb Studio

CLIENT: Parks Canada • **PROJECT TEAM:** Bill Pechet and Stephanie Robb with Nicolas Osenton • **MODEL:** Bill Pechet, Nicolas Osenton • **PHOTOS:** Bill Pechet • **STATUS:** Competition finalist

HALF and HALF not

In conversation with Lőrinc Vass

LV: Your lifelong relationship with Japanese culture and urbanism has profoundly shaped your creative practice. How did your connection to Japan begin and what influenced your decision to move to Tokyo in 1981?

BP: Growing up, we had a big book on the living room bookshelf called *Japanese Temples: Sculpture, Paintings, Gardens, and Architecture* (1964). It was filled with beautiful black-and-white images of what I later realized were the greatest temples and gardens in Japan. I remember being small and leafing through it, heavy on my lap. Somehow, those images of serene and layered spaces reached out to me as beautiful sirens, if you will, calling me to the shores of faraway places.

Years later, when we moved to Victoria, the Art Gallery had been bequeathed with a large collection of Japanese and Asian antiquities. They also offered Japanese calligraphy courses, and I enrolled at around fifteen or sixteen years old. The gallery shop had *raku* pottery for sale and I began to collect them, attracted to the imperfect nature of their surfaces and moody colouring. As a family, we periodically went to a Japanese restaurant in Bastion Square called Maiko Gardens, which, at least in my memory, had a beautiful little flowing river down the centre of the restaurant, tatami rooms, *shoji* screens, and waitresses dressed in kimonos. I loved the whole scenographic and tactile fantasy of it, feeling transported to an exotic place and time, just across the ocean.

While studying geography and art at university, I minored in Asian studies and began learning Japanese language and classical literature. A year or so later, I landed a job with Fuji World Trading Company, run by the enigmatic Mr. Takahashi, who, I think, assumed I spoke Japanese. Victoria was a popular destination for post-high school students learning English, and he paid me $800 USD to find housing for each student and handle any issues that arose. Meeting young Japanese people and gaining financial freedom (from the enormous fees I was paid), I was able to visit Japan for the first time around nineteen or twenty. I absolutely bonded with the food floor of the Ginza Takashimaya department store, and the rest, as you know, is history.

That history included eventually moving to Tokyo in 1981, after graduating from art school, to teach English while living in a *yojōhan* (four-and-a-half tatami mat room, almost 100 square feet). That teeny place was, perhaps, my most important lesson in living minimally and how a city as magnificent and complex as Tokyo offers many reasons not to stay in one's impossibly small apartment. Of course, the Japan I found was not the same as the interior of Maiko Gardens: it was a hallucinatory urban organism of ungraspable depth and complexity.

While studying at UBC, you returned to Tokyo to work at an architecture office and began developing your graduation project, *The Museum of Sand*. Located in the bustling commercial epicenter of Roppongi, the project explores the relationship between architecture and repose in an overstimulating urban environment. It transforms a parking lot owned by a Buddhist temple into a multi-storey museum-hotel complex that features sandboxes with sand from around the world, a suspended swimming pool, tearooms, courtyard gardens, and an interactive sand garden (the "raking room"). What aspects of Tokyo's urbanism, your experiences in Japan, and your architecture studies influenced the proposal?

I came to UBC Architecture after a year in Japan. At that time, the school was primarily invested in postmodern ideologies, such as using historical references on everything (but not the more sophisticated, ironic versions of this approach). We were also encouraged to use "pattern language," received praise for designing anything that looked like a Greek village, and were discouraged from being too monumental, showy, or conceptual. Having just arrived from Tokyo—a city in the throes of the country's "bubble economy," characterized by lavish, idiosyncratic and intense pile-ups of architectural experiments with complex, layered programming and no-holds-barred consumer environments—I wanted to explore other paradigms that were foreign to our school. I felt that everything should be a wonderland of spatial and sensory experience. Mourning my extraction from the hallucinatory magnificence of Tokyo, I sought to recreate it through imaginary environments.

A few years later, after a semester in Hong Kong and then working in Japan and the Philippines, I decided to investigate my relationship to Japan in *The Museum of Sand*. It was a fantasy that allowed me to return to Tokyo without getting on a plane and to explore ideas that liberated me to digest the last five years of my life, free from the familiar North American context in which most student work was grounded at the time. The project, while being a meditation on the place, has many secret messages that are also biographical, having to do with accepting my homosexuality and my body. But these messages are veiled, existing in the shadows and subtexts... some so obscure that I don't even know them myself. I am still, to date, in a state of arrested development working on that project, still in that sandbox, dodging some unknown demon called normalcy.

In the project, sand serves as both a literal and conceptual medium of play, with grains affixed to the pages of your research and project documentation. Another exuberant material, confetti paper, acts as the backing for the mylar presentation drawings and also appears throughout the pages of the book. What sparked your interest in these materials, and how did they intersect with your experiences in Japan?

In art school, I explored sensory boxes that contained different textures of things to touch such as sand (grainy), confetti (cool and tickly), flour, marshmallows, and more. I was interested in the haptic nature of our information receiving systems and the frisson that occurs during a sensory gap between seeing something and touching it—for the former leads to associative meanings. You can't look at confetti without imagining a wedding. Ironic, since my own parents' marriage was falling apart at that time. I also began to cast concrete mixed with unusual aggregates, such as the city of Victoria phone book, more marshmallows, and aquarium gravel. I loved the contrast between the "masculine," resolute nature of concrete and the fragile, spongy and goofy qualities of the other materials.

Also, my experiences with the *karesansui* (dry landscape) gardens of Kyoto, such as Ryōanji and the moon garden of Ginkakuj, were instrumental in shaping my ideas for *The Museum of Sand*. However, because touching is prohibited in those sacrosanct spaces, I cross-pollinated them with my experiential texture boxes from art school. I also found fascinating the tactility of ubiquitous building materials, like tatami, *kyo-kabe* (earth walls), or the smoothness of the sock floor versus the rougher materiality of the *genkan* (entryway). Food textures were similarly varied and consciously curated as part of a discourse on mouthfeel. For gosh sake, some candy bags featured exquisite diagrams illustrating the layers of textures you would experience as you uncovered the secrets of a lozenge! This hyperattentiveness to both aesthetic and bodily experience contributed to the programming and material interests of *The Museum of Sand*. I wanted to explore the range of experiential scales from fingertips to the whole body, from solitude to the collective, while flirting with dismantling the Western bifurcation of the sacred and the carnal. Fully out and queer by then, I envisioned a guy in a speedo, beckoning me to join him in a pool co-designed with Hieronymus Bosch. Perhaps, in my fantasy, after a refreshing swim, you'd ascend with him to the top floors of the hotel and find, if not love, then at least cross-cultural pollination....

I asked Sharyn Yuen, who ran a small paper factory on Granville Island called *Kakali*, to create backing sheets for the museum's transparent drawings and to incorporate confetti into the paper. I wanted to reference ancient Japanese paper-making techniques while also keeping it subtly campy, all too aware that simple nostalgia could come off as a one-liner, and mindful of my position as a Jewish boy from Western Canada appropriating the material of another culture. Setting the museum's brutalist shell against a soft and festively fruity backdrop was a simultaneous embrace and emasculation of convention.

Japanese design culture has continued to influence your work, some of which is humorously reflected in the sketch at the end of the interview. Could you elaborate on how these influences manifest?

The souvenir shop in *The Museum of Sand* gave me a future set of possibilities in the form of smaller domestic objects: sandboxes, glow-gardens, planters... votive honey bears. In terms of the built works such as *Little Spirits Garden*, *The Woods Columbaria*, and the outdoor spaces of *Exeter House*, the experience of seeing the moss gardens of Saihōji in Kyoto and the votive *Jizō* statues of Hasedera in Kamakura are all direct imports. These spaces attempt to recreate the original experiences, where choreography of movement, delineation of thresholds, the facilitation of repeated actions, rituals, and other temporal cycles are manifest. They are designed to encourage and accept the passage of time through the aging (mossing) of materials. Furthermore, the idea of the miniature as representing something larger plays out in both the mossy patches, which are like forests in themselves, and in the little houses, honey bears, and other tiny things that I enjoy making. They are small and self-deprecating, yet potent in their diminution. When you change the scale of something, an enchantment is implied. I often find myself resisting (or avoiding) scales that fit just right, and rather prefer to fiddle around with the size of something so that viewers or participants are cajoled into questioning their own position in the physical world. These techniques of scale manipulation are found again and again in Japan, manifesting in many ways.

Another way to answer your question is by considering the condition of contemporary Japan and its influence on some of my more urban, electric projects. *Granville Street*, *Dichroic Vancouver*, and *emptyful* were directly inspired by the experience of Tokyo at night, where, during my youth, I witnessed and fell in love with the spectacle of the illuminated city. I suppose this is reflected in the polarized nature of my work, which, on one hand, is deeply inspired by the marching progress of time—an "old-soul" kind of thing—and, on the other, by a simultaneous "new-soul" fascination with things that glow and pulse.

How did your experiences as a foreigner in Japan, particularly in encountering forms of otherness, shape your self-discovery during your many visits?

The period from 1981 to 1987 was one of personal growth and transformation, so each time I visited, I was evolving, and my relationship with the country varied. During my year teaching English, I was so accepted by my students—who came from various backgrounds—that I truly felt embraced, without any sense of otherness. However, one exceptional occasion changed my perspective: I attended the birthday party of an older woman who had ostensibly picked me up at a museum. Nothing sexual took place, but she would give me free museum tickets and take me out for lunch. When I arrived at her party, held at a super-fancy restaurant, the table was surrounded by Caucasian fellows around my age, and I realized that I was part of a collection. It became even stranger when her husband, a wealthy industrialist, arrived with his mistress. In that moment, I understood that I was, indeed, in a culture with rules I did not fully understand, where being a foreigner could represent an objectified condition.

During a subsequent stay in Tokyo, a gay co-worker took me to a nightclub in Akasaka that catered to men who are attracted to trans women. All the servers were transgender and the floor show—featuring "famous women from history"—was like a mini Las Vegas musical revue performed by the servers, complete with period costumes specifically tailored to reveal trans bodies. Later, my friend tried to get me into a bar with a backroom, but I was denied entry as a foreigner. This was not the Japan that I thought I knew, and it prompted me to reassess my somewhat naive understanding of the place. It reinforced the idea that there are layers of understanding and experiences that may never be fully accessible.

With each visit to the country—once with George Yu (RIP), several times with George Wagner (also RIP), and most recently with you, my friend Lőrinc—I have encountered a different place and a different me. For some, relocating opens up aspects of our latent selves that somehow don't emerge within our own place or home. For me, oddly, this happened in the Philippines in terms of my personal, sexual self. Japan, on the other hand, gave me a chance to find a voice. One thing is certain: the chaotic and cacophonous environment that I first encountered in my youth, and which informed *The Museum of Sand*, has metamorphosed into something different, where I now see repeating patterns and systems instead of chaos. It is no less magical, however, as part of my soul lives there.

These anecdotes on the evolution of your perspective on Japanese urbanity are all the more fitting given your pivotal role in establishing the tradition of study abroad trips to Japan at UBC's School of Architecture and Landscape Architecture. These excursions have enabled many students to engage in a similar process of discerning organizational patterns beneath Tokyo's seemingly indecipherable complexity. On two recent tours, where I joined as an accomplice, you brilliantly distilled each day's theme—what we called traverse "noodles"—into witty and humorous titles. A few examples include "Layer-Cake" (introducing Tokyo's stratified urbanism), "Erections of Planning & Alleys of Pleasure" (traversing Shinjuku's skyscraper and entertainment districts), and "Moss to Munch" (savouring moss-covered temple gardens and a vegetarian *shōjin ryōri* meal in Kyoto). Could you speak more about how you detect and interpret patterns and themes across different scales and media?

Yes, I love those "noodle" titles, and we had a lot of fun concocting them. The "erections" one certainly stands out as a giggle-fest, but beyond the joke, it attempted to distill the bifurcated yet mutually contingent nature of Shinjuku: the corporate, authoritarian west side, with its vertical expression of masculine power structures, against the east side, characterized by its more idiosyncratic morphology of street patterns and programs—restaurants, bars, entertainment, and the sex trade. The west side is "day" and the east side is "night," and they are codependent: the sobriety of the business and institutional world on one hand, and the zany, inebriated counterpoint to it within Kabukichō and environs. And through design and artifice, this dichotomy beautifully reveals the culture of the place—its mores, protocols, and collective psychologies. Whether or not the students grasped our more sophomoric titles, the "noodles" reflected our desire to introduce thematic structures that added a sense of ordering, helping to ameliorate the typical perception of Tokyo as an ungoverned mega pile of phenomena.

Alongside this, I have always been acutely aware of patterns in cities. This includes the cadence of building types, the deployment of material and formal strategies in buildings from different eras, the repeating occurrences of manufactured elements that make up our urban experiences, as well as the associated ideological, economic, and cultural contexts that produced them. Projects like *Who's There*, *Granville Street*, *roger that*, *Closer Than*, *Hundreds of Little Chairs*, *The Encyclopediette*, and even the built cemetery projects all, in one way or another, participate in, or are informed by, the construction of repetition that is so emblematic of our modern lives.

Returning to the notions of "arrested development" and playing in a sandbox, queerness in your work manifests as childlike play—not a confrontation or critique of norms, but an embrace of a prior state, of being "not-yet-straight," open to possibility. This manifests through the destabilization of familiar motifs and the engendering of playful, often humorous, associations, as seen in *Victory Square Memorial Lights* (designed with Stephanie Robb) which resemble soldiers' helmets but are also slightly flamboyant, or in the "eyes," "hands," "fingers," and "fingernails" animating urban furniture and infrastructure in *Trash Talk*, *Infomoji*, *GRANtable*, and *False Creek Energy Utility Stacks* (also with Stephanie), among others. The permutation of possibilities is also hinted at by the title of this book. How do you see your practice engaging with norms, both in terms of social conventions and canons of design?

Growing up in a household where arguments and conflicts were daily occurrences, I was formed (or farmed) in a context where non-consensus was the norm. Being exposed to disparate views on politics, aesthetics, ethics, and more personal issues, I somehow became the Switzerland of the Pechet household, often using humour as an ameliorative device. While this was perhaps a bit too much for a little kid to handle, it led me to understand that there is not one truth: that all is subjective, open to interpretation, and that there is a middle ground. To top it off, being Jewish in a non-Jewish world and, even though I didn't have the language for it yet, gay, created a feeling of being an outsider, allowing me to observe the tropes, ironies, contradictions, beauties, and sadnesses of situations from a distance. This prepared me to have a kind of chameleon-like agility as an adult, with skills that are helpful in both my personal and professional life.

To answer your real question, given these origins, I often use slight strangeness, distortions, humour, and puns as a tactic to provide an inroad to deeper, more reflective and serious ideas. I am very trope-aware, therefore I am often quoting the canon, but in an astigmatic way. I suppose that disarming the conventional reading of a thing or place is a political act; different voices should constitute a healthy society, where freedom is given to see the world a little differently. Truthfully, my happiest place is in trying to bring a bit of a smile to the public realm—or at least to remove a frown. I know it's a bit much to ask someone entering a cemetery to do the Macarena, but at least you can offer them a pool of water to see the reflection of the sky.

This disarming yet non-innocent, queer play in your work often operates through perception. In the short essay "Mossy Japan," published in *Tokyo from Vancouver* vol. 1, you discuss the technique of *mitate*, or "reseeing"—the reuse of an element or motif by seeing it anew. Projects such as *roger that*, *Closer Than*, *36 Views of Sulphur Mounds*, and *Peeping Tom Thomson* probe the relationship between vision and cognition, or disrupt a singular viewpoint in favor of multiple perspectives. Can you describe your own approach of "reseeing" the world and how you translate these observations into your work?

My witnessing of *mitate* in many constructed conditions resonated with my own way of looking at the world with benevolent askance, where quoting something out of context—through scale change, distortion, material manipulation—would, I hope, bring a simultaneous familiarity and strange newness to a situation. *Mitate* allows one to imbue small spaces with references beyond their physical boundaries, such as miniaturizing known landscapes and making allusions to literary and imaginary worlds. Gardens designed this way originally served a select audience of aristocrats and the other cognoscenti, so I relish the idea that my work is a bit downmarket and available to all.

Many of my projects are also about contradictions and repositioning, both physical and cerebral. In *roger that,* the revealing of more than one truth is achieved through movement and subsequent reflection. The two clusters of repurposed highway safety lights, assembled into giant celestial orbs and facing each other across a freeway, challenge the notion of two sides by being mirror reflections of one another—completely equal and carefully aligned to the same datum. Their weirdness of sending signals to each other (hence the title) verges on the ridiculous, because the message is the same—why even send it?

36 Views of Sulphur Mounds references Hokusai's *Thirty-six Views of Mount Fuji,* which depicts the sacred mountain from multiple points of view while revealing cultural vignettes of the time. The sulphur mounds, by comparison, are generally seen as a visual pariah within Vancouver's scene-obsessed culture; their acrid yellow chromatics disrupt the myth of the city's harmonious relationship with nature and reminds us of an economy rooted in resource extraction. I actually love the color and get a giggle out of how transgressive it is as a visual and symbolic pile of chemicals. So the series, in a way, opens up a discourse on how we choose to see things.

Your studio feels like a miniature landscape in itself, filled with quirky objects: birds' feet, bunnies, honey bears, mirrors, dichroic glass, marshmallows, ... How does this space and its "carefully curated clutter"—a reference to the tiny domiciles brimming with idiosyncratic collections depicted in the 1993 book *Tokyo Style*—influence your creative process?

I suppose the plethora of stuff—some of it residue of past projects, some of it just being "things"—helps stimulate my curiosity. A weird pink funnel, my mom's small collection of miniature *netsuke* sculptures, a *SweaterLodge* button (and you know the list is endless) serve as reminders that the world is a bottomless universe of oddness, of junk that can be revisited. Once in a while, I rearrange some of them, examining how stacking or abutting them creates new relationships out of ordinary objects. The studio is one of my two Shangri-Las, the other being my apartment, where I paint. In both spaces, there is a constant flow of human and non-human flotsam and jetsam: rocks, plants, domestic objects, material samples, souvenirs, model fragments, and more. It's like being in a sandbox with my toys.

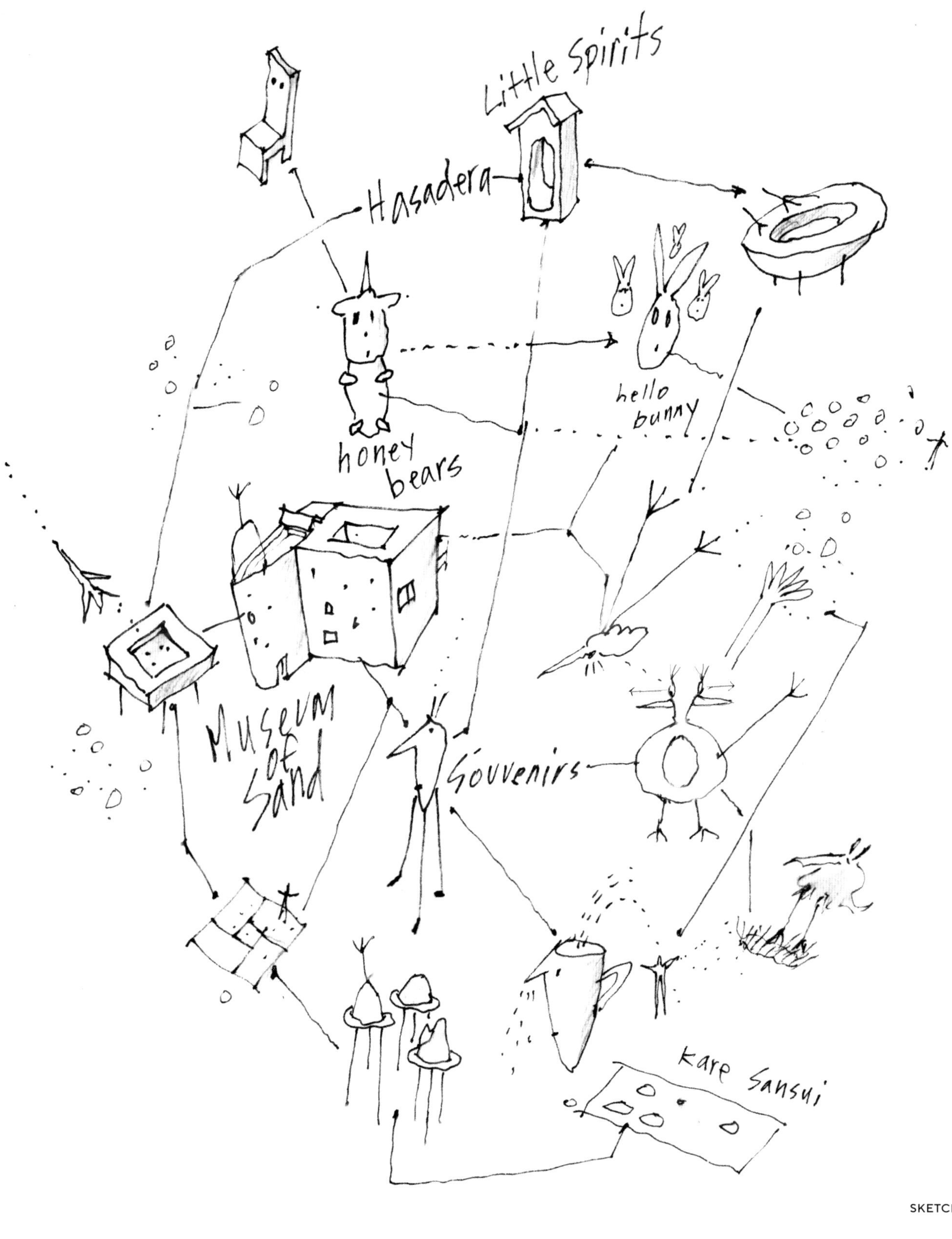

SKETCH: Bill Pechet

halfsweet

WEE GALLERY, LASSERRE BUILDING, UBC, VANCOUVER, BC • 2011

ASSIGNMENT (SELF-IMPOSED): Design an installation that demonstrates architecture's primary actions: the filling or voiding of space.

COMPONENTS: A box divided in half, two identical glass vessels, mini marshmallows.

SITE: Wee Gallery, Lasserre Building, third-floor studio, University of British Columbia.

DESIGN SOLUTION: In one half of the box, the first vessel is filled with marshmallows, becoming a solid figure in a voided field. In the other half of the box, the same quantity of tiny marshmallows fills the space *around* an empty vessel. The figure becomes a void, the field (of marshmallows), the solid.

LEARNING OBJECTIVE: Students should gain an understanding of two distinct ways of thinking about space.

PHOTOS: Bill Pechet • STATUS: Petrified

Hare B&B

2021

Although written for kids, *Hare B&B's* funny-serious story explores ideas of survival and morals, where good and evil rely on each other, something often entwined in storytelling made for children and adults. To illustrate this codependency, I drew fronts that are different than backs, masks, and farcical disguises that affectionately depicted a villain who is as goofy as she is roguish. These illustration tropes try to build sympathy for what is going on behind the scene, as much as what the official story is telling us. – Bill Pechet

STORY: Bill Richardson • **ILLUSTRATIONS:** Bill Pechet • **PUBLISHER:** Running the Goat Books & Broadsides • **STATUS:** In print

heaven between

BROADWAY STREET AT EDMONTON STREET, WINNIPEG, MB • 2016

The Winnipeg Arts Council had long envisioned commissioning a public artwork for Broadway, and the Downtown Winnipeg BIZ was interested in creatively lighting the street. This confluence of interests set the stage for a competition calling for a light-based sculpture on the median strip of a historic street that predates the city of Winnipeg.

For those unfamiliar with the site, the Manitoba Legislative Building anchors one end of Broadway, Union Station the other. While the site selected for the new artwork at the intersection of Broadway and Edmonton was prominent, it also posed serious challenges. The 100-year-old elm trees lining the boulevard were dying of Dutch elm disease, and underground electrical conduits precluded digging in the center of the median.

In dialogue with the two neoclassical domes of the monumental buildings at either end of Broadway, *heaven between* offers a third, very different kind of dome, a non-structural dome, one suspended in mid-air. Connecting heaven and earth, the perforated dome is conceived as a mandala of elm leaves based on a Penrose tiling, an elegy to the dying trees along Broadway. When standing outside the dome, the leaf pattern appears random, but standing within, one discovers the order. By day and night, the intricate cut-out pattern alternately casts shadows and then a warm, flickering light, like a flame, onto a small plaza below.

Due to site conditions that prevented digging under the dome, two massive flanking columns with 30′ footings (requiring 1/5 of the total budget), were required to suspend it. The columns were initially planted with climbing vines to minimize their visual impact, but without proper nurturing, the vegetation did not survive, leaving the structure naked by day. After dark, when the supports fade into the night, the glowing dome comes into its own, appearing to hover magically.

The title of the artwork, *heaven between*, begs some questions. Why *heaven*? Well, the sky vault is sometimes called a dome and the sky is commonly envisioned as heaven. Then, a suspended dome might seem to reference the heavens *above*, so why *between*? Between the two monuments and their domes at either end of the boulevard? Between two roads? Between night and day, earth and sky? Sure, all readings are welcome, but for Bill alone, *heaven between*, between life and death, memorialized the recent passing of the elm trees and his mother.

PECHETStudio

CLIENTS: City of Winnipeg and Winnipeg Arts Council • **TEAM:** Bill Pechet with Gabe Daly, Thomas Gaudin, Sam McFaul, Shizuka Sasaki / CDm2 LIGHTWORKS / Crosier Kilgour / SMS Electrical Engineers / Dyregrov Robinson Geotechnical Engineers • **FABRICATION / CONSTRUCTION:** Parr Metal Fabricators / OB1 Contractors / Control Electric • **PHOTOS:** Michael Perlmutter • **RENDERINGS:** Thomas Gaudin • **STATUS:** Competition winner, built

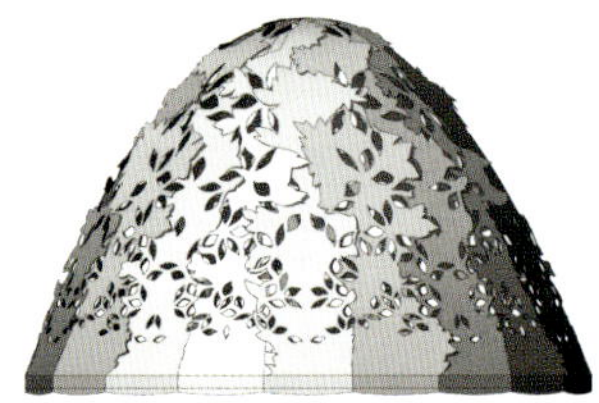

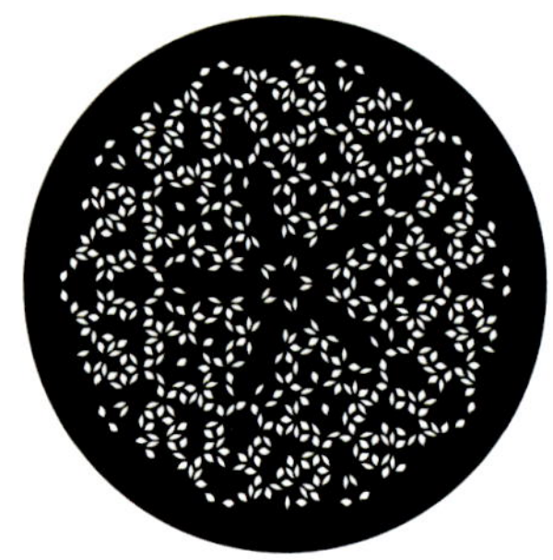

Hebrew Cemetery of Reno

ANGEL STREET, RENO, NV • 2017, 2020–

According to the Jewish Virtual Library, it was the discovery of gold on the Comstock Lode in 1859 and the Silver Rush around Virginia City in 1862 that first attracted Jews to Nevada: prospectors, as well as lawyers, engineers, shopkeepers. While the population of Jews in Nevada never exceeded one percent during that period, a dedicated Jewish cemetery was a priority for the early settlers.

The original two-acre plot for the Hebrew Cemetery was purchased in 1877, and in an article published a few years later, The *Reno Evening Gazette* offered an assessment of the site selection. "The location is good and… the Hebrew Cemetery will be a delightful suburban retreat from the cares and sinfulness of the world." The cemetery is bound by Angel Street to the east, and an apartment complex to the west. To the north it is bordered by a laneway flanked by single family houses, and to the south, a decommissioned road adjacent to a neglected cemetery for Union Soldiers.

Given the need to expand, the Hebrew Cemetery of Reno purchased the decommissioned road and subsequently hired PECHETStudio to reimagine this abandoned space. The original cemetery was built as a grassy, picturesque burial ground at a time when water conservation was not front of mind. In contrast, the proposed expansion would be a landscape of stone and rock with minimal and strategically placed vegetation. The burial sites would be punctuated midway by a restful oasis, a landscaped garden built up over time from the excavation of grave sites.

In addition to adding new space for interments, the design included two new structures bracketing a walled garden for cremation interments: a service building with a recessed, ceremonial handwashing basin and a covered, open-air funeral pavilion, each with a round oculus illuminating the sacred ground.

The programming for a Jewish cemetery can be complicated; each community has its own requirements. The Orthodox would be buried at the west end of the decommissioned road and they would require their own gate. A columbarium would be near the entrance on Angel Street, but there won't be any Orthodox Jews interred there. Within one community, many distinct communities, each with their own culture and burial rituals.

PECHETStudio

CLIENT: Jewish Community of Reno • **DESIGN:** Bill Pechet with Gabe Daly, Jeremy Schipper, Lőrinc Vass, Sara Zonouzi / CFA • **DRAWINGS:** Lőrinc Vass **RENDERINGS:** Jeremy Schipper and Lőrinc Vass • **STATUS:** In progress

1. Existing Cemetery
2. Hearse Turnaround and Entry Court
3. Storage Building and Ceremonial Handwashing Area
4. Columbaria Court
5. Covered Ceremonial Court
6. Burial Plots
7. Oasis
8. New Access Gate and Service Vehicle Parking

hi-bye

7TH AVENUE TRANSIT MALL, CALGARY, AB, CANADA • 2011

Thousands of commuters flow through the windy corridor of Calgary's 7th Avenue transit mall each day, hair and jackets afloat. *hi-bye* proposed gleefully acknowledging their comings and goings, their arrivals and departures, with a friendly wave of welcome, or as the case may be, farewell.

Along 1.25 miles of the downtown corridor, between the gateway LRT stations City Hall and Kerby, *hi-bye* proposed installing 900 rotating arms, using repetition to emphasize the physical and programmatic continuity of the corridor. The aluminum arms would be engineered by aviation specialists and fabricated to the highest of standards. One third of the arms would be mounted on each of the station canopies, while the remaining third would be installed on existing poles between the stations. All 900 would be supported on existing infrastructure. Each was designed as a kit of parts intended to attach into existing holes and beams with galvanized steel plates, gaskets, and hardware.

Hundreds of arms with hands would wave in succession as the wind gusts with the passing of a train, not unlike the human waves at a Flames game.

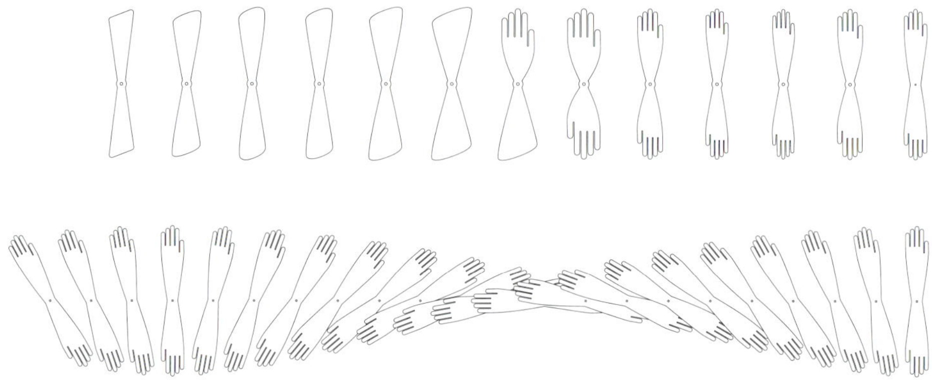

PECHETStudio

CLIENT: City of Calgary • **DESIGN:** Bill Pechet with Gabe Daly • **FABRICATION:** Toby's Cycle Works (prototype) • **PHOTO:** Bill Pechet (of Gabe Daly) • **DRAWINGS/RENDERING:** Gabe Daly • **STATUS:** Competition finalist

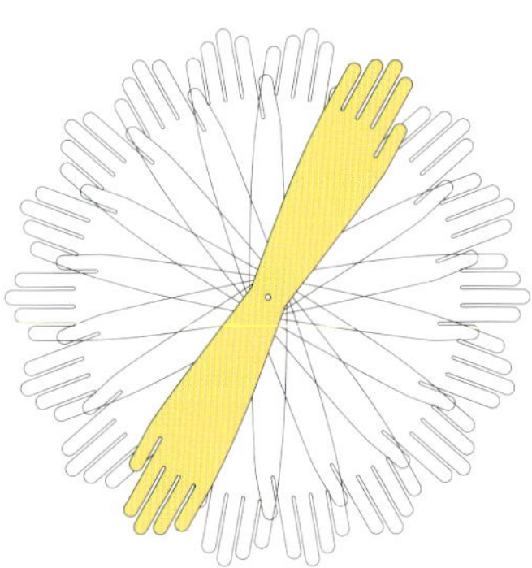

Hjørring Water Park

HJØRRING, DENMARK • 2018

A decade after the opening of *Watering Garden* in Victoria, the Danish city of Hjørring reached around the globe to request a design for a water-park featuring a giant watering can. One has to smile thinking of the possibility of that quotidian, scaled-up object becoming a Pechet trademark, like Frank Gehry and his giant fish.

The *Hjørring Water Park* was to be sited in the Folkparken, a linear greenway connecting the city centre of Hjørring to its agricultural surrounds. The city had recently diverted their stormwater system into a string of naturally draining filtration streams and ponds. The site designated for the spray park would be near the daylit source of the water, becoming a symbol of the city's environ-mental stewardship.

The proposed giant watering can was to emit water in its many forms—fog and mist, streams and gushes, squirts and gurgles—then to travel through a sand-and-boulder "estuary playground" before draining into an adjacent pond.

While this project never came to fruition in Denmark, several projects productively channel-ing water have been realized in British Columbia. The runoff from the *Watering Garden* in Victoria, for example, replenishes the lakes in Beacon Hill Park, while an overflowing basin in *St. Andrew's Park* drains into a sandbox encouraging sand castles in the middle of the city. *Ponte Bong* entices children to follow a channel of water, from a faucet at the top of a mound, down the hill, and into the wetlands of Hinge Park. *The Big Dipper* in Spirit Square in Victoria takes runoff from the bowl of the giant spoon, the drinking fountain proper, and channels it down a looooong spoon handle to irrigate the Spirit Garden. As with so many projects between these covers, flow—whether of water or wind, goods or people, birds or planes—is a cause for celebration.

PECHETStudio

CLIENT: Hjørring Kommune Planning and Engineering Departments • **TEAM:** Bill Pechet with Gabe Daly, Jose Gonzalez, Warren Scheske • **DRAWINGS:** Warren Scheske, updated by Lőrinc Vass • **RENDERING:** Warren Scheske • **STATUS:** Unbuilt

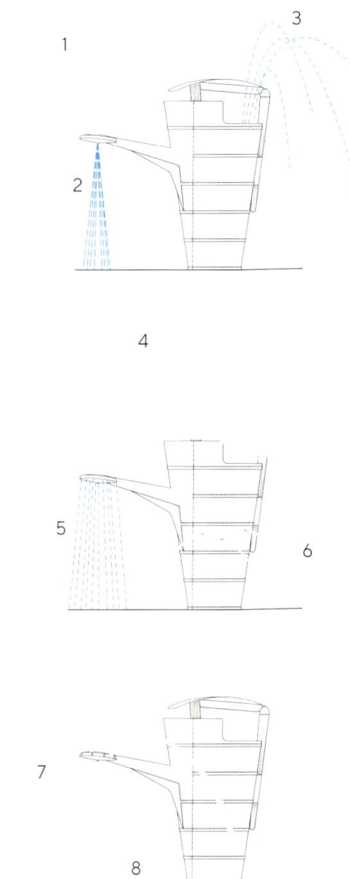

1. Mist
2. Narrow Shower
3. Rooster Tail
4. Fog
5. Wide Shower
6. Spouts
7. Streams
8. Ground Flush

Homewerk Set Concepts

MULTIPLE SITES • 2002–10

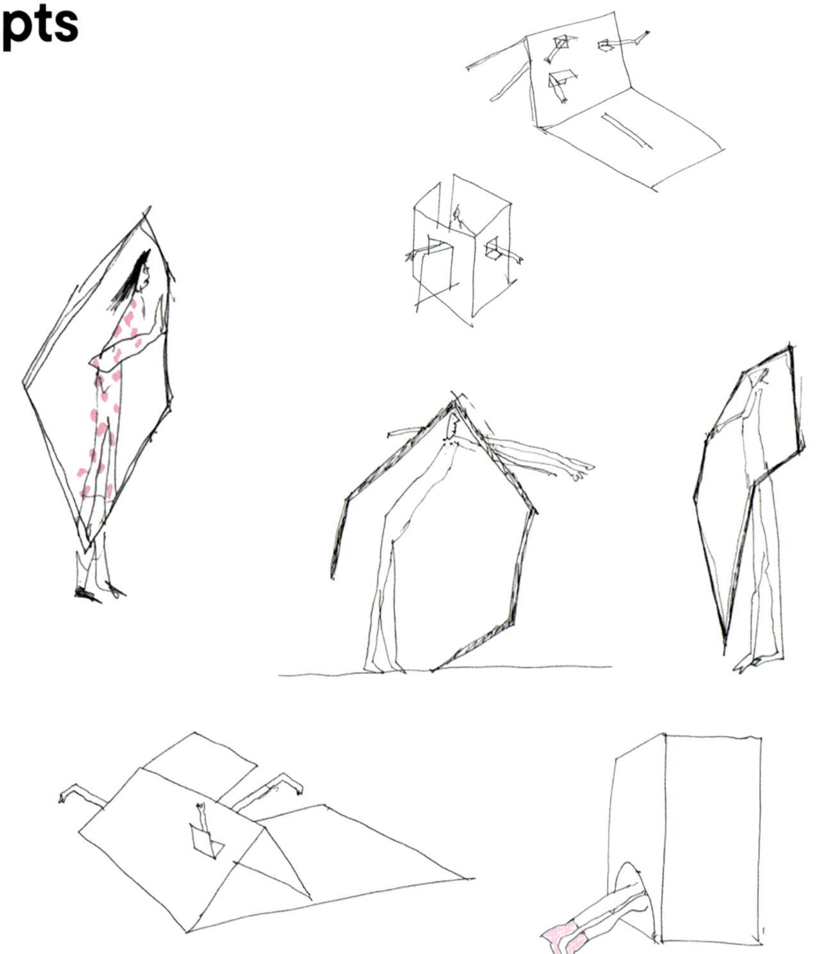

Choreographer Jennifer Mascall's project began with an invitation to Bill to sketch the spontaneous movements of four dancers interacting with 4x8 sheets of cardboard, box cutters, and tape as they explored the meaning of home. "Dancers are like children. If you give them a prop, they are going to start experimenting with it in ways you cannot anticipate." BP

Mascall typically works on pieces over several years and *Homewerk* was no exception. In this case, the project had an eight-year duration, including a seven-year tour. The sketches from the preliminary session were further explored during residencies in elementary schools in a collaboration between the Mascall dancers, Dalhousie architecture students and the illustrator. The performance was further developed with the addition of text and music by Noah Drew.

CHOREOGRAPHY: Jennifer Mascall, Mascall Dance • **SKETCHES:** Bill Pechet

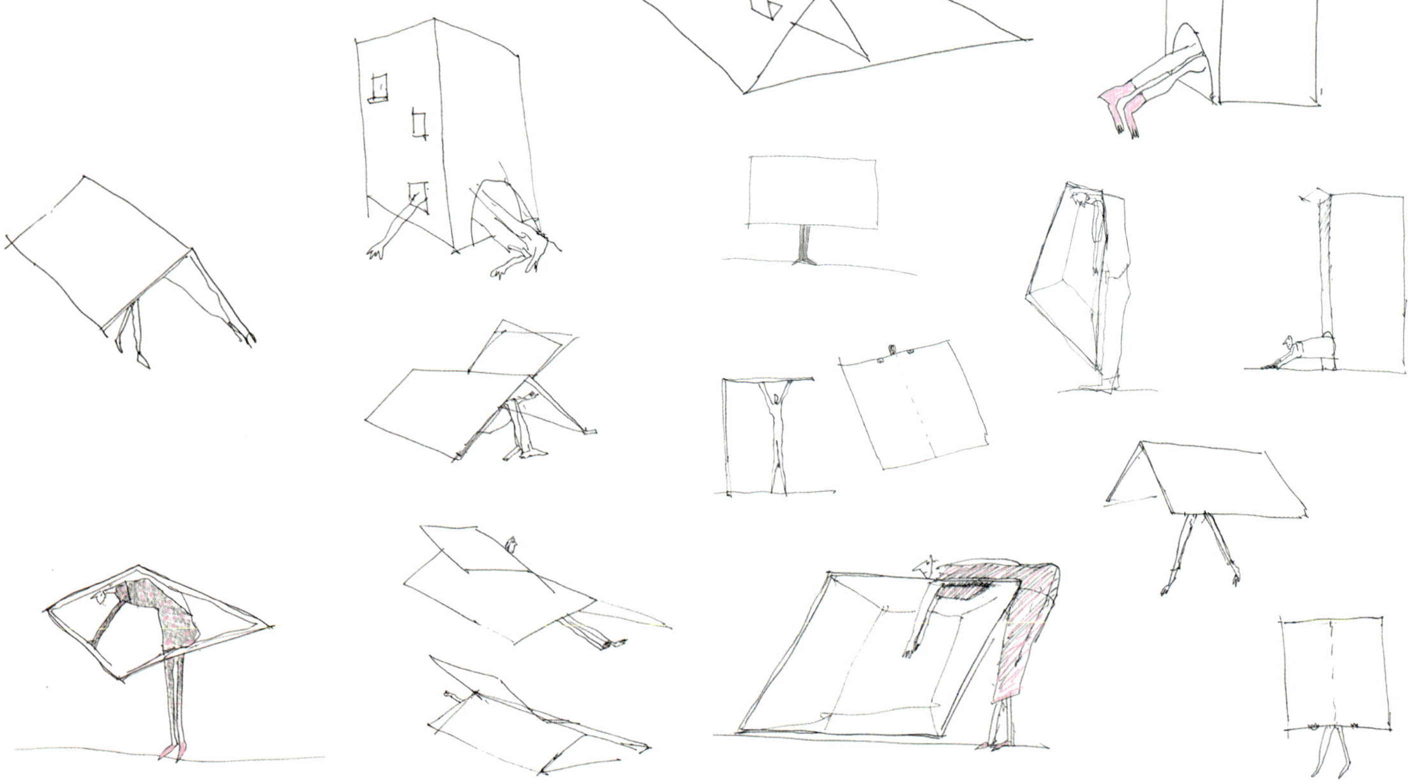

In the Course of Sleeping

LES BALLETS DE MONTE-CARLO, MONTE-CARLO, PARIS, NEW YORK, AND BALLET BC, VANCOUVER • 1996

John Alleyne, Artistic Director of Ballet BC (1992–2009), envisioned a new ballet about time, specifically, the time it takes for a dewdrop to fall. In the tradition of storybook ballets, he set *In the Course of Sleeping* in an airport for fairies.

Alleyne assembled an international team for the production. Bill was responsible for the props, sets, and in collaboration with the French lighting designer, Dominique Drillot, the projections. A giant dewdrop, lit from pearl-white to fire-red, was suspended from a long stem and lowered very slowly over the course of the performance, its movement nearly imperceptible. The 40′ backdrop, with Bill's drawing of a giant bird's wing enlarged and painted by a specialty painter in the Netherlands, received an overlay of projections portraying the passage of time: a bird beating its wing, a jet gliding overhead, a cloud drifting, the eye of the surrealist artist Jean Cocteau surveying.

In the "airport," a self-propelled luggage cart resembling an oversized walnut shell carried the fairies' translucent suitcases, each filled with gossamer clothes and lit from within. Nancy Bryant, a close Vancouver friend, designed costumes that interpreted the weightlessness of both fairies and ballet dancers.

CHOREOGRAPHY: John Alleyne • **TEAM:** Bill Pechet (sets, props, projections) / Dominique Drillot (lighting) / Nancy Bryant (costumes) • **PHOTOS:** Bill Pechet

Jewish Cemetery Restoration

MOUNTAIN VIEW CEMETERY, VANCOUVER, BC • 2015

In 1886, Vancouver established its first and only cemetery, aptly named Mountain View Cemetery for its sweeping views of the North Shore Mountains. Six years later, a small Jewish cemetery was consecrated within its boundaries, and since then, 450 Jews have been interred there. As other Jewish cemeteries were established in the region, this sacred space slowly succumbed to entropy and neglect.

It was acts of vandalism in 2012 that brought the cemetery back to the attention of the community. Local philanthropist and community leader, Shirely Barnett, and the Schara Tzedeck Cemetery Board spearheaded an initiative to restore the cemetery in partnership with the Jewish Museum and Archives of British Columbia, other community organizations, and the city of Vancouver. The late landscape architect, Cornelia Hahn Oberlander, a prominent member of the Jewish community, and Bill Pechet, were hired to design the restoration and introduce new amenities to enhance the visitor's experience.

A new entry court interrupts a long hedge-lined path on the perimeter of the Mountain View Cemetery. A change of paving slows the casual passerby and welcomes visitors to enter the Jewish Cemetery. A bench, nestled in the slope directly opposite the beautifully rebuilt historic gate, offers a peaceful place to rest and reflect. From the outside, the arch of the gate announces the "Jewish Cemetery." Once inside, the message speaks to those housed within, reading from right to left: "תומשנ םכילע םולש תורוהט" or "peace be upon you, pure souls."

The gate is anchored by a low, stone-faced wall. Its elegant cladding is andesite from Haddington Island near northeastern Vancouver Island, the same stone found on Fairmont Hotel Vancouver and the BC Legislature. The symmetrical configuration of the wall provides on either side of the gate a recessed space embracing a bench. At the far ends, left and right, are niches with bronze plaques honoring donors, and closest to the gate, two niches house a bronze memorial stone container and a handwashing basin.

One of the most important early moves in any restoration project is subtractive. In the *Jewish Cemetery Restoration*, stone curbs lining the paths were literally unearthed, allowing visitors to experience anew the original recessed paths once found throughout the Mountain View Cemetery. The curbs, and the gravestones, some tucked away in niches in the border hedge, were cleaned and stabilized.

Much research was conducted for the restoration of the cemetery, and in the process, historical documents came to light. Not only was the cemetery restored, the deep history of the Jewish community in Vancouver was further illuminated.

PECHETStudio

CLIENT: Schara Tzedeck Cemetery Board and the City of Vancouver • **TEAM:** Bill Pechet with Gabe Daly, Jose Gonzalez / Cornelia Hahn Oberlander Landscape Architect / C.Y. Loh / Jansson Structural Consulting / GeoPacific Consultants / Bartlett Tree Experts / O-Bronze / J.B. Newall Memorials **CONSTRUCTION:** North by North West Ventures **PHOTOS:** Michael Perlmutter • **DRAWING:** Gabe Daly, updated by Lőrinc Vass • **STATUS:** Built

0 1
5
10 m
existing curbing
new curbing
unoccupied graves

JEWISH CEMETER

Ritual Washing Basin

שלום עליכן, נשמות טהורות

Kakali Paper Factory

KAKALI PAPERS, GRANVILLE ISLAND, VANCOUVER, BC • 1990

The Story of Bill is populated with recurring, shapeshifting characters, in this case, a college classmate turned material supplier turned client. Sharyn Yuen and Bill first met as students in the Visual Arts program at the University of Victoria, before they both left Vancouver Island for the mainland. As Sharyn set up the Kakali paper-making factory on Granville Island, Bill embarked on his graduation thesis, *The Museum of Sand*, at the School of Architecture (now SALA) at the University of British Columbia. For his project, he commissioned handmade paper sheets from Kakali to serve as backdrops for his translucent drawings.

One year after his graduation, Sharyn became Bill's first client when she commissioned him to design the interiors of her second space on Granville Island, Kakali Papers. Sharyn had studied papermaking in a tiny village in Japan, further deepening their shared affinities. Housed in one of the original industrial buildings, Bill's design was minimal: a simple stud wall separating the paper factory from the showroom, a thin white surface, gypsum-like paper, with apertures revealing wood studs wrapped in grass. The skeleton of the industrial building remained exposed, the concrete floor, untouched. A cantilevered wood plank with a flower arrangement and paneled doors of bamboo mats were unmistakable signs of their common fascination with Japan.

CLIENT: Kakali Papers • **PHOTOS:** Bill Pechet • **SKETCHES:** Bill Pechet • **STATUS:** Partially dismantled

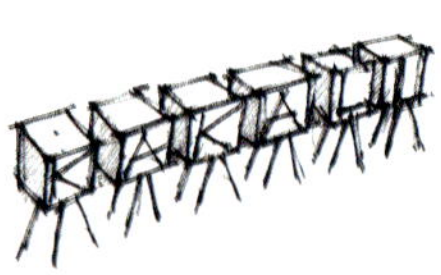

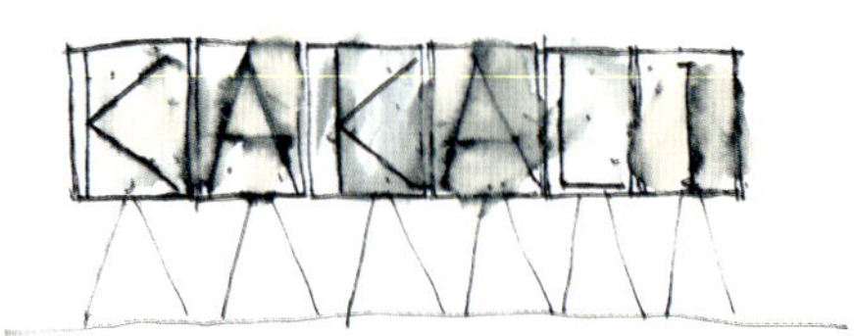

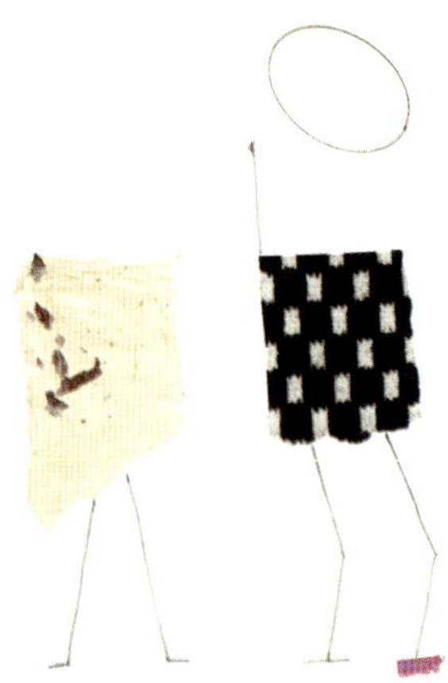

Le Château

BURRARD STREET, VANCOUVER, BC, CANADA • 1996

Six figures flying, arms outstretched, hovering over the Burrard Street sidewalk announced the flagship Le Château store like so many gargoyles luring parishioners. The cantilevered steel figures, with glowing eyeballs of changing colours, appeared evermore menacing as they leaned precariously over a delicate glass awning. Three in skirts, three in pants, the figures announced the men's and women's apparel sold within. In a crowded retail area in downtown Vancouver, the shoutout could not be missed.

Inside the shop, the figures reappeared, now grounded and bending at the waist to serve as chairs. How delightful it must have been to sit on their laps while waiting for a friend to make a purchase. The changing room walls and the moveable counters were clad with stripes of Formica of different colours and patterns, like so many bolts of fabric. The playful design of the interior's furnishings was replicated in stores across Canada.

In 2016, executive vice-president of Le Château, Franco Rocchi, told the *Georgia Straight*, "In the '90s before there was e-commerce, brands would try to get as close to the customer as possible physically—the more *[sic]*, the better. In today's digital world, that business model no longer holds water." And so, after a respectable twenty-year run, the Le Château flagship store on Burrard Street was no more.

Pechet + Robb Studio

TEAM: Bill Pechet and Stephanie Robb with Nicolas Osenton / Allan Diamond Architect / JM Engineering • • FABRICATOR: Spacan Metalshop • CONSTRUCTION: Kindred Construction • PHOTOS: Martin Tessler (p. 93), Bill Pechet (p. 94-95) • MODELS: Bill Pechet, Nicolas Osenton • STATUS: Dismantled

le château
hâteau

Little Spirits Garden

ROYAL OAK BURIAL PARK, DISTRICT OF SAANICH, VICTORIA, BC • 2013

There among the arbutus, firs, and hemlocks on the eastern edge of the Royal Oak Burial Park, lies a tiny village, *Little Spirits Garden*, of wee souls and a secluded space for families who wish to memorialize an infant lost, whether by miscarriage, stillbirth, or abortion; whether recently or long ago; whether locally or in a distant land.

Reminiscent of hill towns, the garden paths follow the topography, creating a meander conducive to contemplation, an unfolding, episodic path that resists mental mapping. As one wanders through this serene and sorrowful space, the air is bittersweet—fragrances of damp forest and ocean and fog mingling with the delicate sound of windchimes. Hanging from tree branches, they were cedar remembrance flags, with messages, anchored by small copper bells.

While living in Asia, Bill encountered the Buddhist tradition of commemorating children with statues of Jizo Bodhisattva, guardian escort to the afterlife. The votive statues are adorned by grieving parents with red bonnets and bibs to ward off evil spirits. "I found this inspiring, so tender and beautiful to see these creations. I was struck by the sense of magnitude when these were displayed together on special occasions, showing a collective loss in society." [BP] This inspiration is evident in *Little Spirits*, with rows and rows of small Spirit Houses, each memorializing an infant lost, arranged on concrete terraces like so many Jizo statues in Japan.

Back in British Columbia there was initially resistance by some to the idea of embracing a Buddhist tradition for the new infant memorial, but the concept was finally accepted. "My inner monologue at the time told me our entire country is based on immigration and adopting ideas from the rest of the world." [BP]

Families were invited to personalize the interior of their Spirit House. Had the aesthetic of the Jizo statues in Japan prevailed—uniformity with limited variation allowing for both personal and collective remembering—the exteriors would have remained a uniform white. But without any common tradition to follow, Canada's diversity was soon apparent in the great assortment of additions that "coloured outside the lines." The Spirit Houses were painted bright colours, inside and out, with sentimental trinkets spilling onto the terraces. Miniature dreamcatchers, crosses, and angels. A gold-leafed sea urchin here, a butterfly there. Bunnies and princesses and rocks painted by siblings. The evidence of multicultural grief was best left unbounded.

It took the casting of many prototypes to arrive at the elegant form of the Spirit Houses, their soft, embracing interior contrasting with their rectilinear exterior, womb meets house as commonly drawn by a child. "I realised that the Spirit Garden would have to be an ecumenical space, because we are a pluralistic society in Canada. I would need a symbol that was inclusive, and the house is a universal symbol of protection, and non-denominational." [BP] A womb-shaped window, complete with a shutter operable only from the inside, allows the little spirits to make their escape, or, to stay at home. A recess in the same shape on the bottom of the house sits like a piece of Lego onto a matching peg on a concrete terrace. Houses can easily be added, or moved. There is currently room to honour 3,000 little ones, but the loosely defined edges of the garden allow for additional concrete terraces in the future, like the *torii* gates at Fushimi Inari-taisha in Kyoto that dissipate into the surrounding landscape.

In a clearing, a garden for scattering ashes is marked by a birdbath cast in the shape of a womb. Polished basalt spirit stones with plaques of bronze offer another form of memorial. The central pavilion of the *Little Spirits Garden*, located on a high point of the site, hosts the funerals. Its Corten roof echoes the colours and shapes of the surrounding arbutus, its precast concrete and bronze altar inspired by the shape of a heart offers "a comforting, maternal anchor." [BP] A brass bell sits atop the altar on a brass plate that protects a communal ossuary within. When the bell tolls, one more little spirit is released.

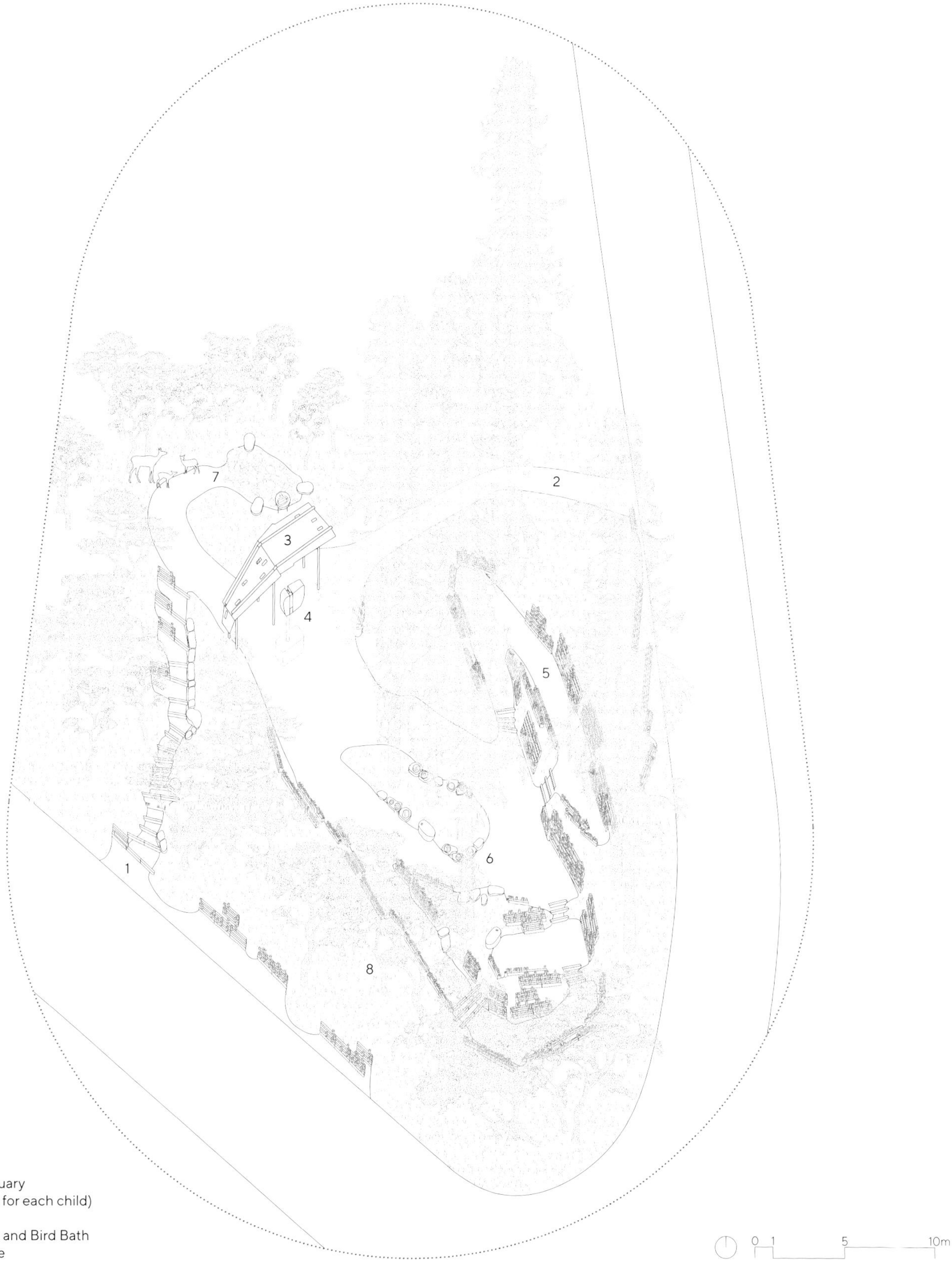

1. South Entry Steps
2. East Path Entry
3. Funeral Pavilion
4. Subterranean Ossuary
5. Spirit Houses (one for each child)
6. Memorial Stones
7. Scattering Garden and Bird Bath
8. Arbutus Tree Ridge

PECHETStudio

CLIENT: Royal Oak Burial Park • **TEAM:** Bill Pechet with Gabe Daly / DALY Landscape Architecture (project coordinator) / C.Y. Loh Associates • **FABRICATION:** Szolyd Development / Paradise Cityscapes **SKETCHES:** Bill Pechet • **DRAWINGS:** Lőrinc Vass • **STATUS:** Built • **PHOTOS:** Gabe Daly (p. 96), Lőrinc Vass (p. 98-99), Michael Perlmutter (p. 100, p. 101 left and middle), Bill Pechet (p. 101 right)

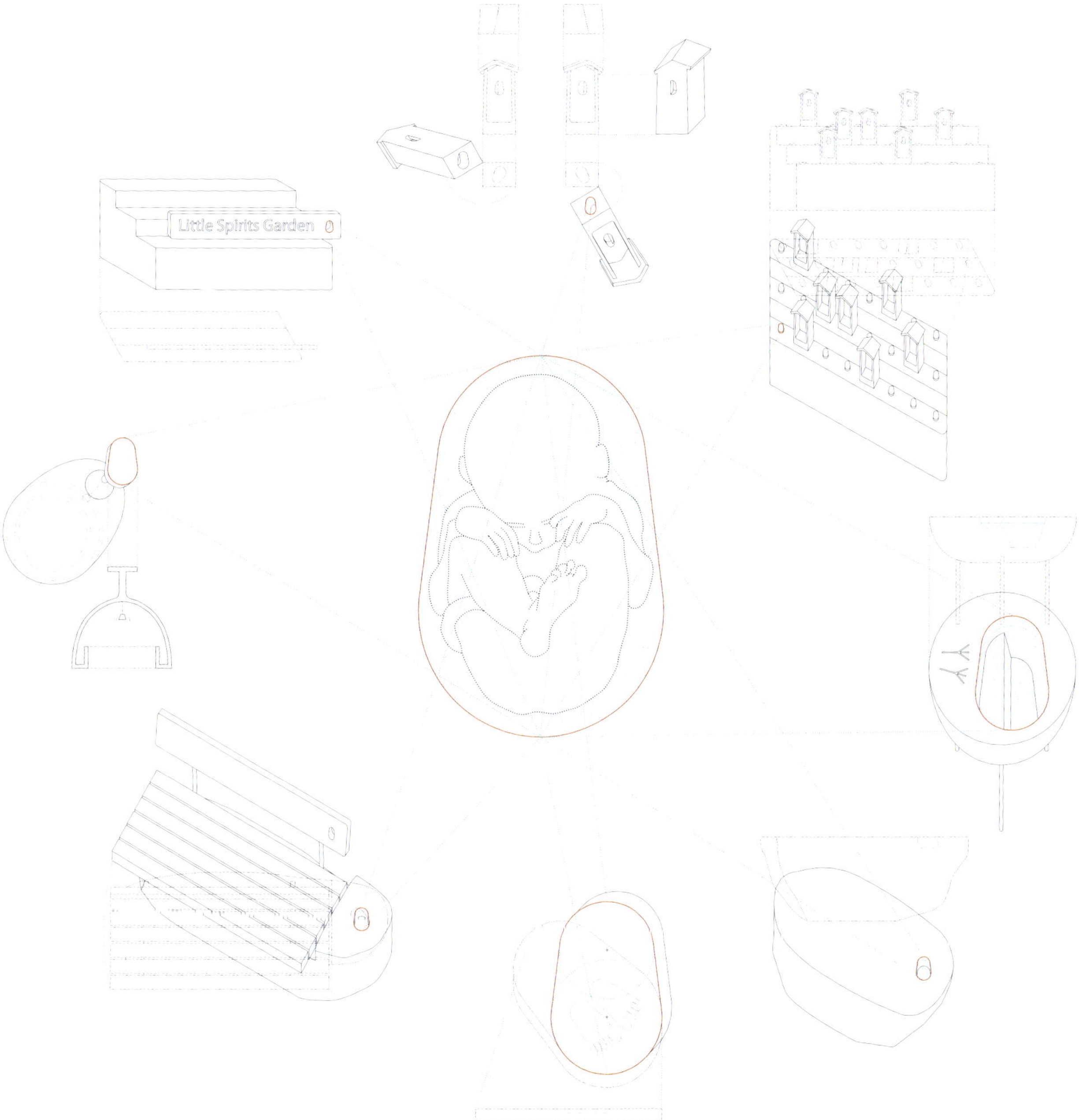
Little Spirits Garden

Lola Flies Alone

2022

Dream-like washes of floating objects and ephemera release a little girl from the claustrophobic confines of the interior of a jet into a fantastical world of her imagination. Is the flight attendant, Arshbir, just a flight attendant, or is he the "God of the Sky" (as is the translation from Punjabi)? Hint: his tie and turban are made from clouds. – Bill Pechet

STORY: Bill Richardson • **ILLUSTRATIONS:** Bill Pechet • **PUBLISHER:** Running the Goat Books & Broadsides • **STATUS:** In print

Lottikon

GRANVILLE ISLAND, VANCOUVER, BC • 2000

Forests, rocks, rivers, rain… all that is the landscape of British Columbia encapsulated within a small shop in an industrial building on Granville Island. With fir plywood walls and a cracked tile river mosaic floor, with clusters of lights like so many raindrops, *Lottikon* turned the outside in.

Collaborator James Koester, a welding artist, added freestanding steel trees, shelving supports, a chair and legs for displaying props: giant woks and Bill's cast concrete tabletop in the shape of a saw that could cut down the forest. A big chair rendered in plywood was brought in to watch over customers on the river banks.

CLIENT: Maiwa Handpainted Fabrics • **TEAM:** Bill Pechet and James Koester • **FABRICATION:** Bill Pechet and James Koester • **PHOTOS:** Bill Pechet • **STATUS:** Partially dismantled

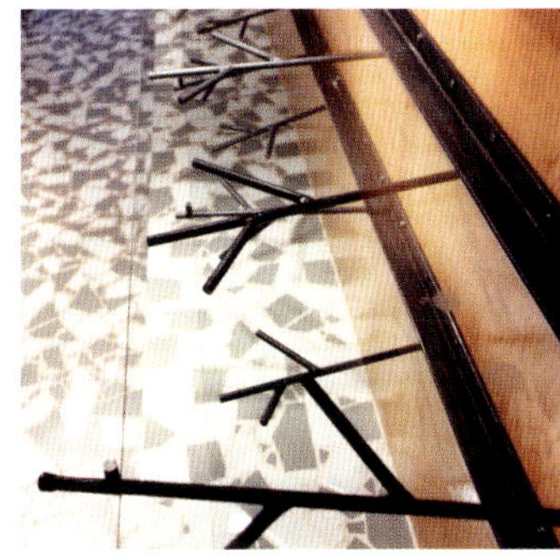

Make West

BAUHINIA AND AVILA RESIDENTIAL BUILDINGS, COAL HARBOUR, VANCOUVER • 1997

Imagine the history of Western Canada as a vase dropped from the twenty-seventh floor of a Coal Harbour tower, its shattered fragments scattered about. Upon close examination, a complex story of the original construction of the site as the terminus of the Canadian Pacific Railway emerges, alongside references to the nature displaced. A partial map, railroad plans and track details, a periodic table, a tree inventory, instructions for topographic surveying equipment and various other tools... these shards conspire to provoke questions about what came before luxury condos.

But it is not a complete story. Even with great patience, it is impossible to reconstruct a single narrative from the fragments. Some pieces appear to be missing. But a question posed by the history's narrator, a Dr. Elizabeth J. Leclip, or Beth Leclip, is still legible: "What systems, both major and minor are complicit in this symphony of locus-motion?" Those with a penchant for anagrams might discover a harmonic link between the names of the artist and his narrator. Of course, all histories are part fiction and we are complicit in their retelling.

Make West offers a case study in the challenges of installing public artworks on private property. After the units in a residential tower are sold, the owners are trusted to respect and maintain artworks installed by the developer. But the owners did not commission the artworks, and in some cases, may not even appreciate them. There is little incentive for a Strata to preserve an artwork and assume responsibility for its ongoing maintenance in perpetuity, all the while maintaining public access to their private property.

In the case of *Make West* and the Avila Building, the Strata rearranged the original installation of 6,000 square feet of slate slabs and 120 cast bronze shards without consulting the artist, and added a spray of "no trespassing" signs limiting access to what is a public artwork. More recently, piles of gravel were thoughtlessly poured over the artwork without concern for its integrity. No doubt there are many similar examples of public artworks on private property that have been altered, neglected, even removed. We should question the wisdom of offering developers the option of locating their percent for art contributions on private property.

"Thankfully, given that history has shown that bronze material outlasts generations and epochs, the shards will always be 'somewhere,' quixotically referring to a strange game of historical and mythical invention." [BP]

PECHETStudio

CLIENT: ASPAC Developments Ltd. • **TEAM:** Bill Pechet with Nicolas Osenton, Jill Anholt • **FABRICATION:** Ornamental Bronze • **PHOTOS:** Michael Perlmutter • **STATUS:** Built and reconfigured by Strata

Make West
"Chase not the goose but find solace
in the downy underlay of her
migrational desire. While we, earth-
bound (in the gravity of progress)
continue to segment our greatest of
mothers into cartesian nomenclature,
her wings cast after-images on our
rails, roads and ports.
What systems, both major and
minor are complicit in this
symphony of locus-motion?"

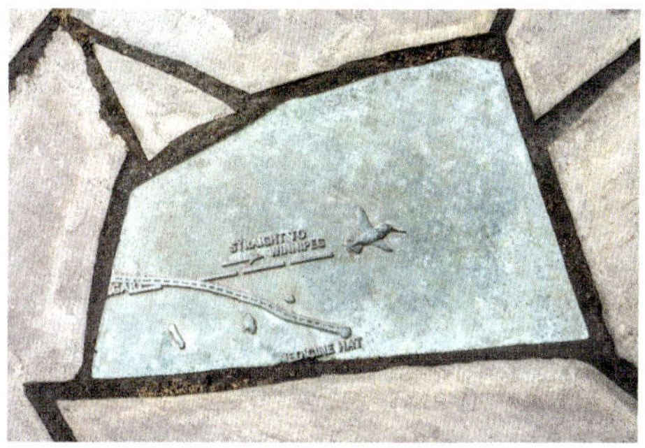

Pier

uld be fun to act
in this chapter.
ght be acted.
ne, the rest

MAMA

CITY HALL PLAZA, RICHMOND, BC • 1999

Richmond's new city hall was built on the 49th parallel, under the Pacific Flyway, a great migration route stretching from Alaska to Patagonia. A billion birds, hundreds of species, pass over the site twice a year, along with twenty-five million airline passengers flying in and out of YVR annually. Coming and going, going and coming.

In response to this spectacular air show of so many warblers and snow geese, hawks and swans, Uniteds and WestJets overhead, *MAMA* proposed a nest, an intimate gathering space in the plaza for humans and the occasional bird. Like the best of nests, *MAMA* was to be built out of scavenged materials, in this case remnants from the new city hall construction site. Railings would create the grass-like container and two bent streetlights would serve as *MAMA's* watchful eyes.

Pechet + Robb Studio

CLIENT: City of Richmond • DESIGN: Bill Pechet and Stephanie Robb with Nicolas Osenton • SKETCHES: Bill Pechet • STATUS: Competition finalist

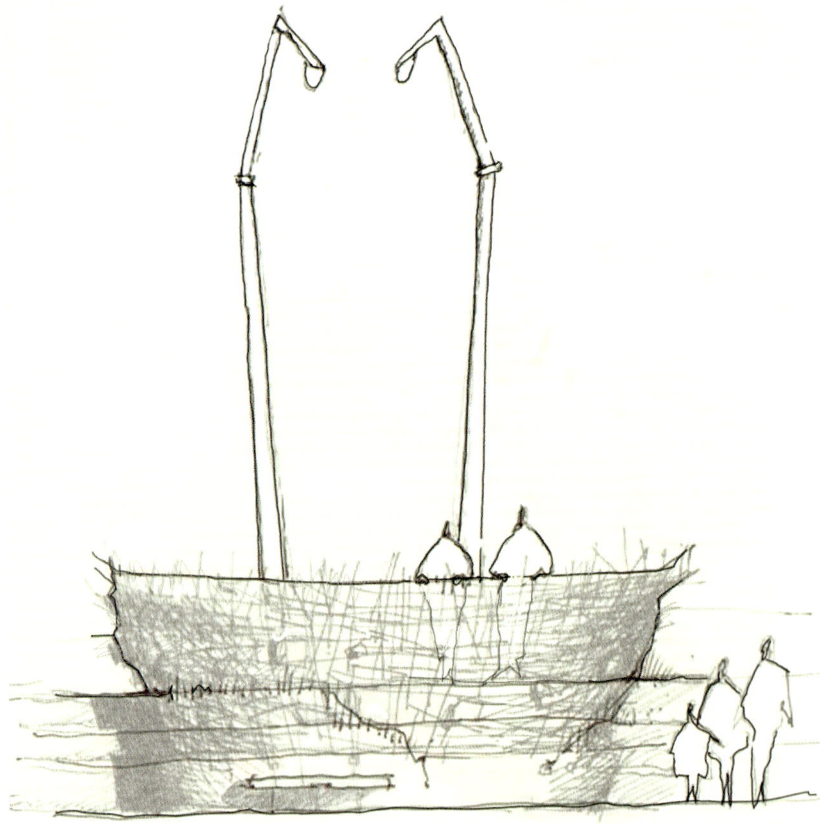

Motorless Marina

FALSE CREEK, VANCOUVER, BC • 2002

Tucked into the northeast corner of False Creek, *Motorless Marina* is a proposal for a public marina dedicated to hand-powered craft. The marina would provide a 980-square-foot building for vessel storage and office space on a 4,000-square-foot float. The humble, playful character of the architecture, with readymade circular skylights that appear like bubbles at night, was meant to invite a curious public to try their hand at dragon boating, or perhaps canoeing and kayaking.

The brainchild for the idea came from an entrepreneur who was making an unsolicited proposal to the city. He suggested that the *Motorless Marina* would not just be for recreational use, but that it, being close to the Main Street-Science World Station, could actually augment the city's public transportation system. "Transit meets lifestyle in this hybridized program." BP

The project has not proceeded past the conceptual stage, but now and then, the idea floats to the surface as a component of various proposals for this "unfinished" area of False Creek, a part of Vancouver still unresolved due to the tidal surges of development and public space proposals that bob in and out of the news.

Pechet + Robb Studio

CLIENT: William Harvey • TEAM: Bill Pechet and Stephanie Robb with Nicolas Osenton / Hay & Company Consultants • DRAWINGS: Bill Pechet • STATUS: Unbuilt

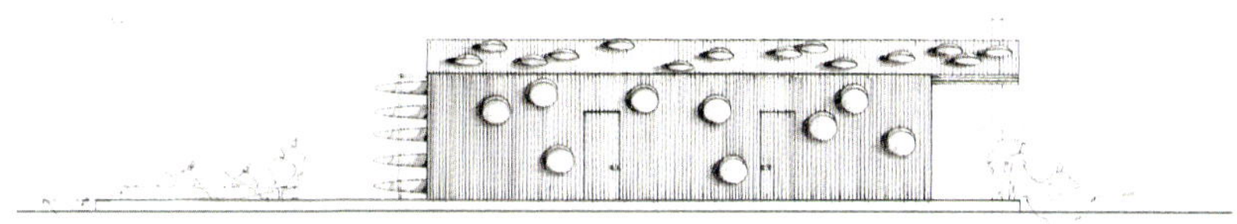

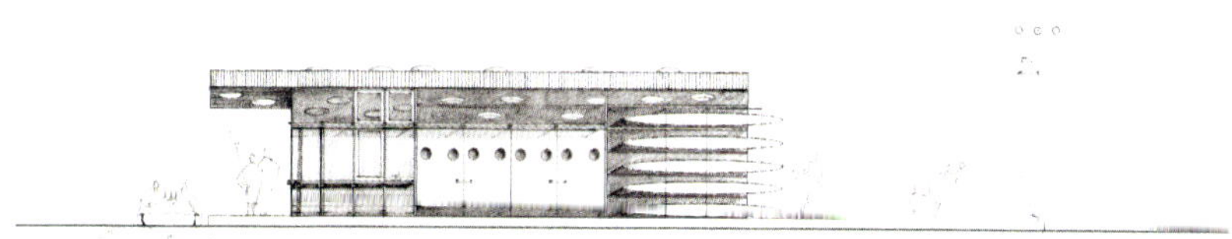

Mountain View Masterplan and Necessaria

MOUNTAIN VIEW CEMETERY, VANCOUVER, BC • 2000—17

Vancouver's first and only cemetery ran out of space for new interments ninety-nine years after its founding. For fourteen years, from 1986–2000, Vancouverites were shut out of the city's sole burial site. With no new revenue and annual maintenance expenses at over a half million dollars, the city of Vancouver needed to act.

PWL and Pechet + Robb Studio were commissioned to create a 100-year masterplan with the aim of designing a more unified and beautiful cemetery with enough new interment space to become self-supporting. It was an ambitious undertaking with a broad scope and many stakeholders.

By filling in the gaps along the periphery with in-ground burial sites, aboveground mausolea, and new columbaria for the vast majority of Vancouverites who choose cremation, the team was able to double the cemetery's capacity of 160,000 interments. Memorial walls and a scattering canal further addressed the public's desire for memorialization options.

One of the most important strategies in the plan was to "resurface" Brewery Creek, the culverted stream that flowed through the site in pre-colonial times. A full-scale revival of the waterway was impossible because of buried remains so the team proposed a network of landscapes, pathways and surface water to signal its historic and subterranean presence. This ten-block-long idea would allow visitors to walk from tip to tip of the cemetery while adding tens of thousands of new interment spaces along the way. The most ambitious part of this plan was the aforementioned canal, that could be created along the unused shoulder of a road.

The scope of improvements further included the closure of unnecessary roads, the acknowledgement of historically significant neighbourhoods within the cemetery, a new chapel and the consolidation of maintenance, administration, and caretaker facilities on a single site.

In the summary report presented to Vancouver City Council on March 7, 2000, written by the Director of Non-Market Operations and Manager of Mountain View Cemetery: "By responding to the changing needs of the public for memorialization options and services; by more efficient use of scarce land resources; and by reclaiming unused plots for resale, the Cemetery could reopen for business and become financially viable. Mountain View Cemetery could then begin fulfilling the public's demand for memorialization opportunities within the City's boundaries."

In addition to the masterplan, in 2017, PECHETStudio designed *necessaria* that included a suite of new site furnishings—benches, recycling receptacles, flower-watering stations and signage—"inspired by buoyant forms to evoke a feeling of flotation within the vast landscape of this large metropolitan necropolis." [BP] Levitations are a recurring phenomenon in cemeteries where Bill has played his hand.

Pechet + Robb Studio

CLIENT: City of Vancouver • **TEAM:** Bill Pechet (project coordinator) and Stephanie Robb with Nicolas Osenton, Rochelle Bacigalupo, Steve Suchy, Herman Kao / Philips Wuori Long Landscape Architecture (co-coordinating firm) / Harris Hudema Consulting Group / Cityspaces Consulting / LEES + Associates • **MODEL:** Steve Suchy, Herman Kao • **PHOTO:** Steve Suchy • **SKETCH:** Bill Pechet • **DRAWINGS:** Bill Pechet, Rochelle Bacigalupo, Nicolas Osenton • **STATUS:** Masterplan completed, Necessaria prototype only

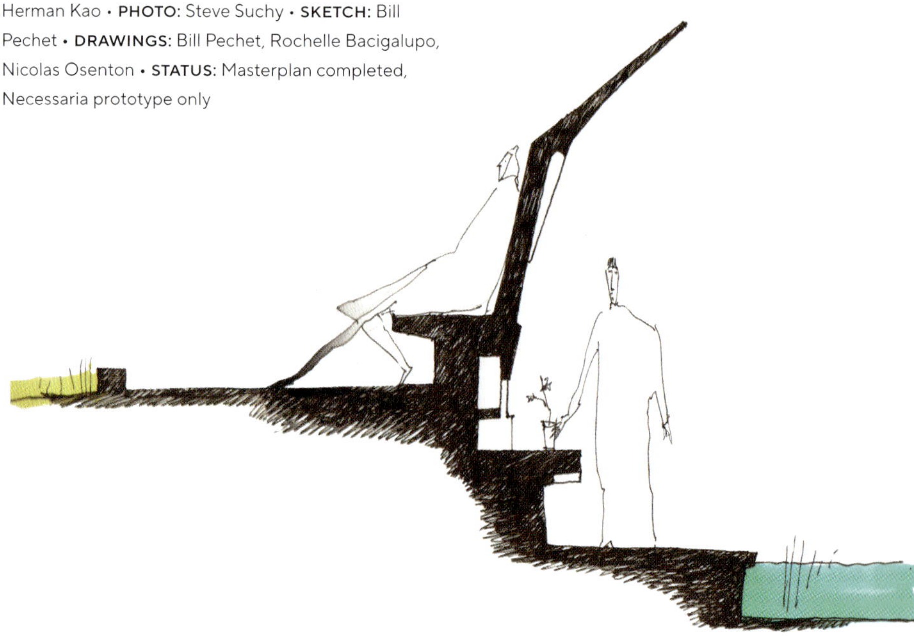

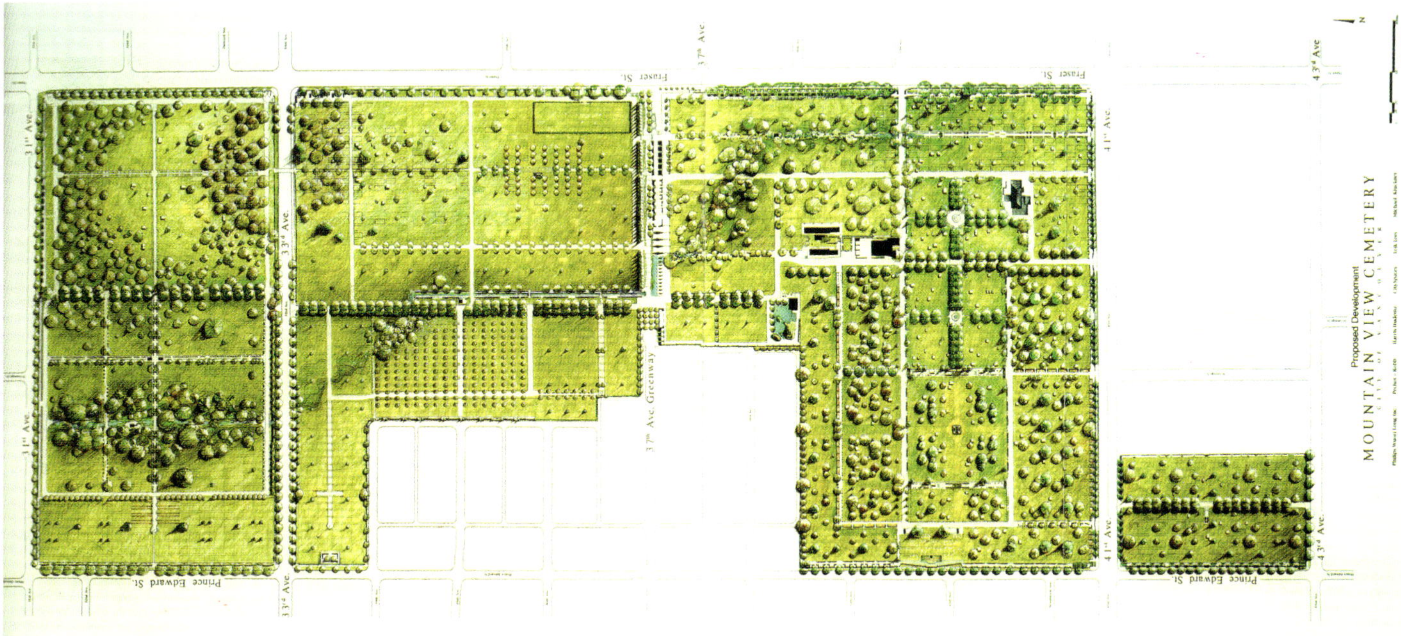
Proposed Development
MOUNTAIN VIEW CEMETERY
31st Ave.
33rd Ave.
37th Ave.
Fraser St.
37th Ave. Greenway
41st Ave.
43rd Ave.
Prince Edward St.
N

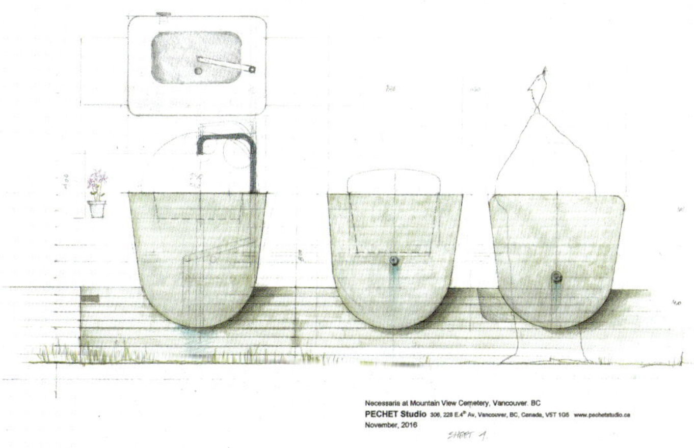
Necessaria at Mountain View Cemetery, Vancouver. BC
PECHET Studio 306, 228 E.4th Av, Vancouver, BC, Canada, V5T 1G5 www.pechetstudio.ca
November, 2016
SHEET 1.

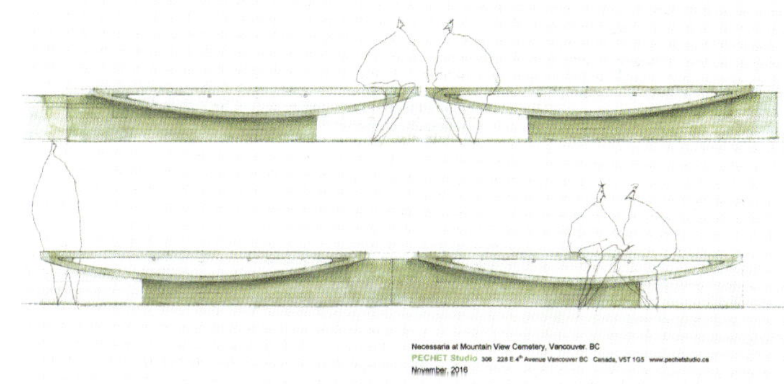
Necessaria at Mountain View Cemetery, Vancouver. BC
PECHET Studio 306 228 E.4th Avenue Vancouver BC Canada, V5T 1G5 www.pechetstudio.ca
November, 2016

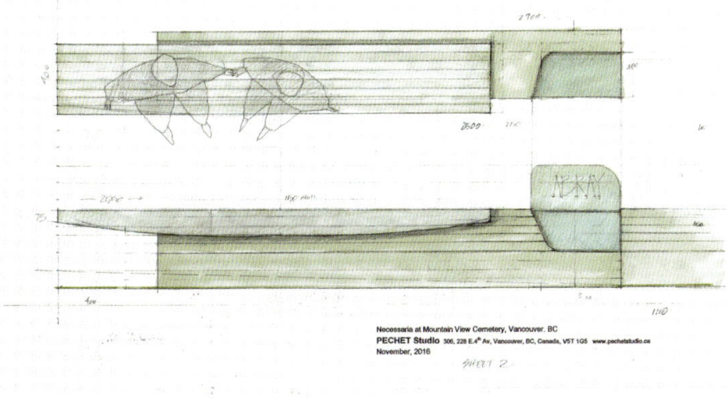
Necessaria at Mountain View Cemetery, Vancouver. BC
PECHET Studio 306, 228 E.4th Av, Vancouver, BC, Canada, V5T 1G5 www.pechetstudio.ca
November, 2016
SHEET 2.

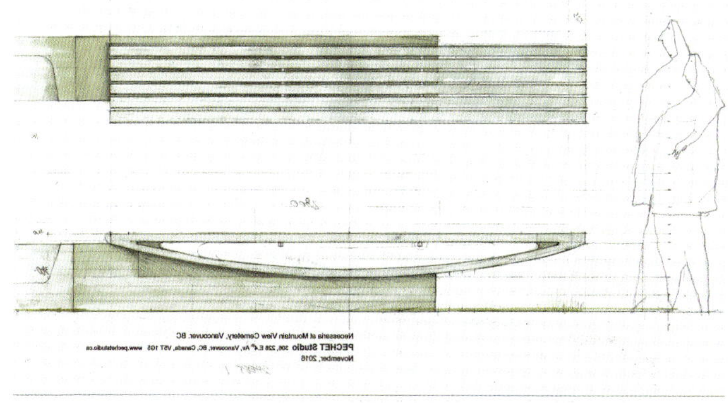

My Bunny Lies Over the Ocean

2024

In these drawings, I explored an idea that wasn't explicit in the writing, proposing that, even though the bunny was victimized by being abandoned, it did have a grand and exciting adventure along the way.

The cover challenges the "depth of a drawing" by placing a drawn "hole" for the "O" of "Ocean." It also puns on the words "lies over" by creating a lagoon on the back cover that looks like a bunny lying over the ocean. — Bill Pechet

This sung picture book by Bill Richardson is set to the old Scottish folk song, "My Bonnie Lies over the Ocean." The QR code on the next page (also found in the book) allows the reader to join the Barbershop Bunnies in singing this delightful book.

STORY: Bill Richardson • **ILLUSTRATIONS:** Bill Pechet • **PUBLISHER:** Running the Goat Books & Broadsides • **STATUS:** In print

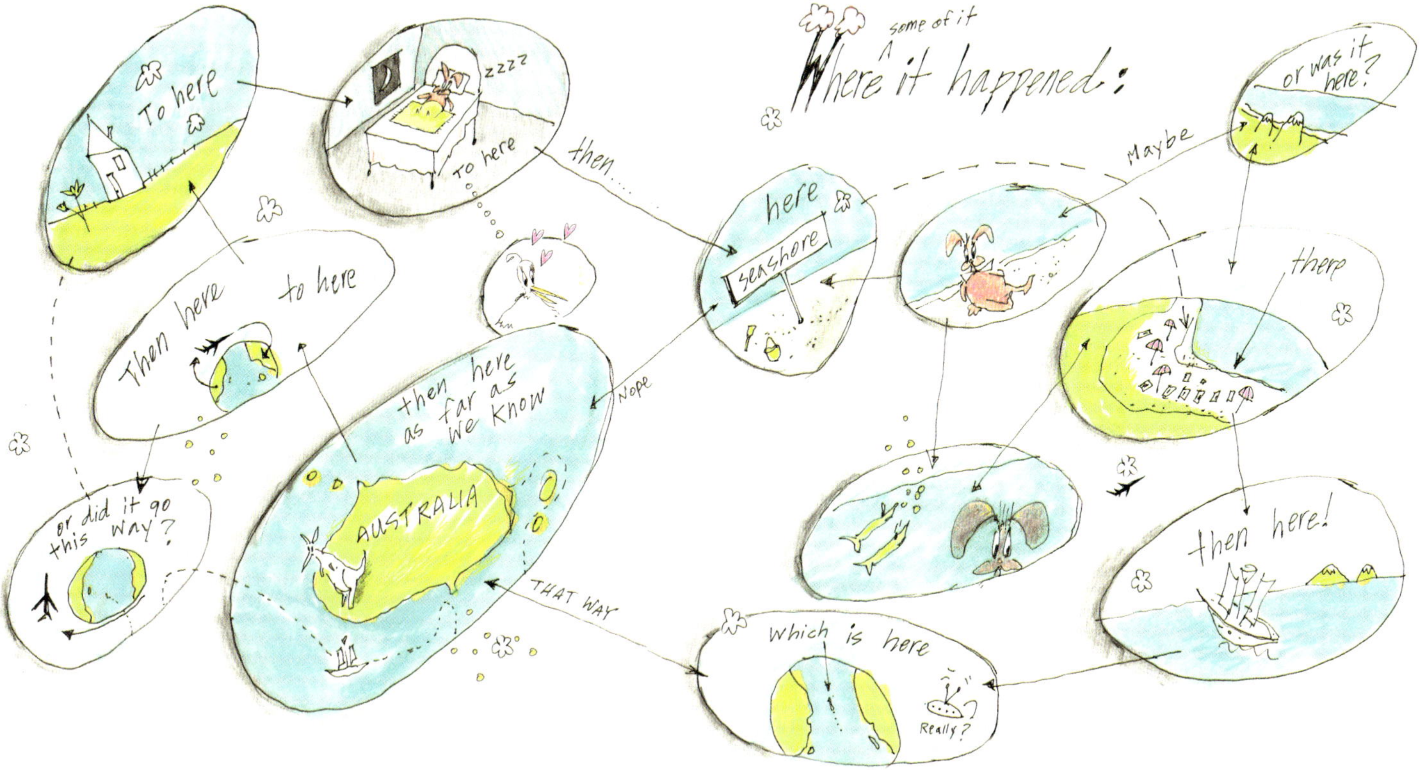
Where some of it it happened:
To here
zzzz
To here
then.....
Then here
to here
here
seashore
Maybe
or was it here?
there
then here as far as we know
AUSTRALIA
Nope
or did it go this way?
THAT WAY
which is here
Really?
then here!

BUNNICATOR
HERE
THERE

Nightwalking

Greg Girard

NO TAXI
PICK UPS
OR
DROP OFFS
USE TAXI ZONE AT
600 ROBSON
URBAN OUTFITTERS
OUTFITTERS
COMMODORE
OPEN
AUTOMATIC
SCORE KEEPING
SALE
20%

BEST BITE
DONAIR
OPEN
FATBURGER
KADOYA
FATBURGER
Sushi
IMPOSSIBLE
SERVED HERE

DAVIE

DAVIE

seaspan

North Vancouver Cemetery Masterplan and Buildings

CRYPT + COLUMBARIA EXPANSION

NORTH VANCOUVER CEMETERY, NORTH VANCOUVER, BC • 2005, 2013

In 2005, PWL and Pechet and Robb collaborated on a masterplan for the North Vancouver Cemetery. Located in the foothills of the heavily forested North Shore mountains, a new system of gates, pathways, wayfinding signage, and furniture were designed with the aim of linking disconnected parts of the cemetery together while enfolding adjacent hiking trails.

The masterplan provided up to 5,000 new burial sites on stepped terraces that followed the topography. As North Vancouver Cemetery is popular with the large local Persian community, careful attention was paid to aligning the new grave sites with Mecca. A series of columbaria and mausolea, punctuated by open spaces, would be nestled within the forest.

In addition, the designers proposed two new buildings. The first, a 2,700-square-foot administration centre and funeral hall was to be located on a ridge overlooking the existing cemetery. The program provided for offices and an archive as well as indoor and outdoor ceremonial gathering spaces. The filtered light of the surrounding fir and cedar trees would add warmth to the simple structure.

The second building, the Works Compound, would be located on a lower elevation at the entrance to the new burial terraces on the eastern side of the cemetery. As it would be seen from above, it was designed to have a large green roof. The large canopy would shelter the requisite machinery, bins of soil and gravel. The entire compound would be surrounded by a meandering landscaped wall to hide the machinery while allowing visitors to see the floating green roof above.

In 2013, a revised team of PECHETStudio and Daly Landscape Architecture was invited to design the expansion of crypts and columbaria.

Masterplan and Buildings
Pechet and Robb Art and Architecture
CLIENT: City and District of North Vancouver • **TEAM:** Bill Pechet with Chris Boldt, Tina Tajitsu / PWL Partnership Landscape Architects (coordinating firm) / Kerr Wood Leidal Associates / Kindred Construction / Hudema Consulting Group • **SKETCHES:** Bill Pechet • **DRAWINGS:** Bill Pechet (elevations), PWL and Bill Pechet (site plan) • **STATUS:** Masterplan in process, buildings unbuilt

Crypt + Columbaria Expansion
PECHETStudio
CLIENT: City and District of North Vancouver • **TEAM:** Bill Pechet with Gabe Daly • **STATUS:** Unbuilt

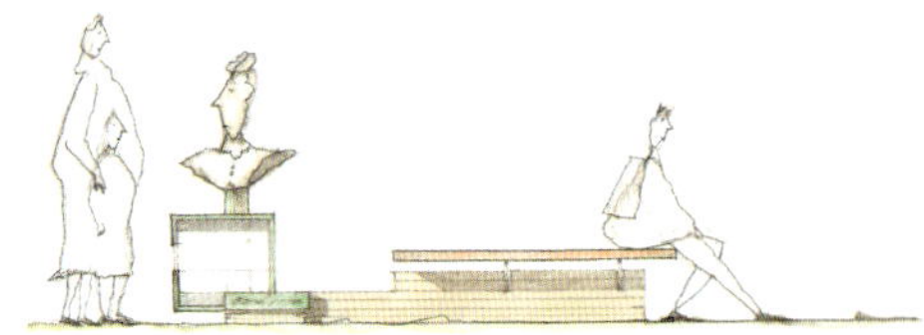

North Vancouver Shipyards I

NORTH VANCOUVER, BC • 1999–ONGOING

Seek and you will find Bill's fingerprints on three industrial zones that have undergone major transformations in recent decades. *Make West*, a public artwork in Coal Harbour, relays the history of the railroad and industrial waterfront in Vancouver, while *Ponte Bong*, a huge perforated steel pipe in False Creek, references the former City Work Yards. Here, at the *North Vancouver Shipyards*, Bill's prints are everywhere, and still multiplying.

Bill's earliest involvement with the site dates back to 1999, when he participated in workshops with Hotson Bakker, conducting early research and site studies. After Pinnacle bought the site, Durante Kreuk (now DK) became the coordinating firm and collaborated with Pechet and Robb on the 2005 rehabilitation of *The Pier* and the design of the new *Shipbuilders' Square* and *Punch Clock Plaza*. More recently, PECHET-Studio has been designing the infrastructure that dots the waterfront site. What follows is the story of an ongoing collaboration between a designer and an enlightened patron: the city of North Vancouver.

The conversion of the historic Burrard Shipyards from an industrial zone to a vibrant public space began with the rehabilitation of the derelict Burrard Dry Dock Pier. Extending 700 feet into the Burrard Inlet, offering spectacular views of downtown Vancouver, *The Pier* and part of the foreshore was the anchor attraction for the redevelopment of the area. In collaboration with Durante Kreuk, Pechet and Robb designed a new deck for the pier, under-lit benches that run its length, trash cans, and at the very end, a viewing platform with binoculars. All components were constructed from materials that preserved the original lexicon of shipbuilding fabrication.

From lower Lonsdale Avenue, today one can enter the Shipyards as thousands before, passing through *Punch Clock Plaza*, an homage to the workers employed in the Burrard Shipyards. On one side of the plaza, a giant sepia photo mural depicts the Shipyard workers in the 1920s; on the other side, rusting shoring steel retains the original topographic line of the shore before its industrial transformation. The public artwork, *x-long files* (a humorous pun on the hit TV show that was filmed in Vancouver), a gigantic file drawer cantilevered over a concrete foundation wall, contains files etched with timecards of workers who came from all over the world. "The piece speaks not only of those who came to Canada to build ships, but also of a nation built by immigrants and the bureaucracies that organized them." [BP]

The *Shipbuilders' Square*, a large, gently sloping event space loosely shaped by buildings on three sides, is marked by a bright yellow rolling crane that was original to the precinct. The crane not only makes a perfect meeting spot, it has become a North Vancouver landmark. The gridded paving of the plaza recalls the gridded floor of the shipbuilding hall where wooden planks were laid to trace components of the ships to full size. The steel canopy sheltering the stage was designed to evoke a peeled-back ship's hull. Both the crane and the weighty canopy shine light down onto the crowds.

Trashy Lights were designed to hang from the rebuilt skeleton structure of galvanized trusses that define the central road. "While reviewing countless photos of the Shipyards site taken during its heyday, we noticed that the clever designers, builders, and engineers of the industry often improvised to make things from scratch. Cars were made from old chassis and sheet metal, benches from buckets, and buckets from benches. We chose to do the same. To make lights, we used the trash cans we had originally designed for the pier, flipped them upside down, drilled some holes and put in lights." [BP] In addition to the trash cans and hanging lights, one can find Pechet and Robb's prints on the clamped wooden benches along the waterfront (made of recycled wood to harken back to the wood used on the gridded floor of the shipbuilding hall), lighting standards, and historical information boards. Like treasures on a hunt, these interventions (some hidden, some in plain sight) stitch together an unruly urban landscape, revealing the site's history in ways both serious and fun.

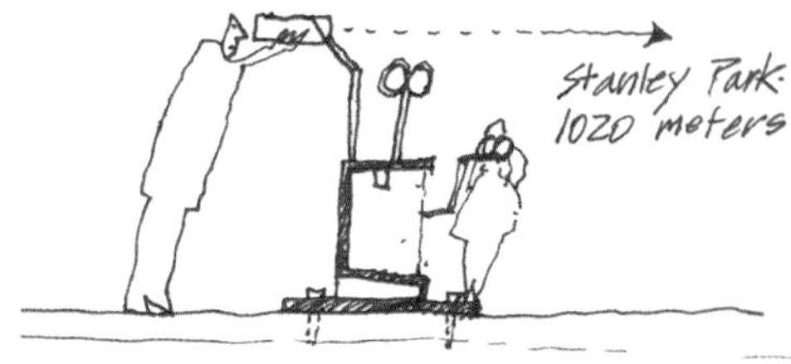

The Pier (2005–10) + Shipbuilders' Square (2010)
Pechet and Robb Art and Architecture
Pages 123–125

CLIENT: City of North Vancouver • **TEAM:** Bill Pechet (project coordinator) and Stephanie Robb with Chris Boldt, Gabe Daly, Heidi Nesbitt, Tina Tajitsu / Durante Kreuk (coordinating firm) / John Bryson and Partners Structural Engineers / Total Lighting Solutions • **FABRICATION:** Marcon Metalfab / Francis Andrew / Epic Metalwork / Mondiale Development • **PHOTOS:** Michael Perlmutter • **SKETCH:** Bill Pechet • **STATUS:** Built

x-long files + Punch Clock Plaza (2010)
Pechet and Robb Art and Architecture
Pages 126–127

CLIENT: City of North Vancouver • **TEAM:** Bill Pechet with Gabe Daly, Heidi Nesbitt / Durante Kruek (coordinating firm) • **FABRICATION:** Marcon Metal Fabrication / Mondiale Development • **PHOTOS:** Michael Perlmutter (left), Bill Pechet (right) • **SKETCH:** Bill Pechet • **STATUS:** Built

Trashy Lights (2010)
Pechet and Robb Art and Architecture
Page 129

CLIENT: City of North Vancouver • **TEAM:** Bill Pechet / Durante Kreuk (coordinating firm) / John Bryson and Partners Structural Engineers / Total Lighting Solutions • **FABRICATION:** Marcon Metal Fabrication / Mondiale Development • **SKETCHES:** Bill Pechet • **RENDERING:** Darren Swift • **STATUS:** Built

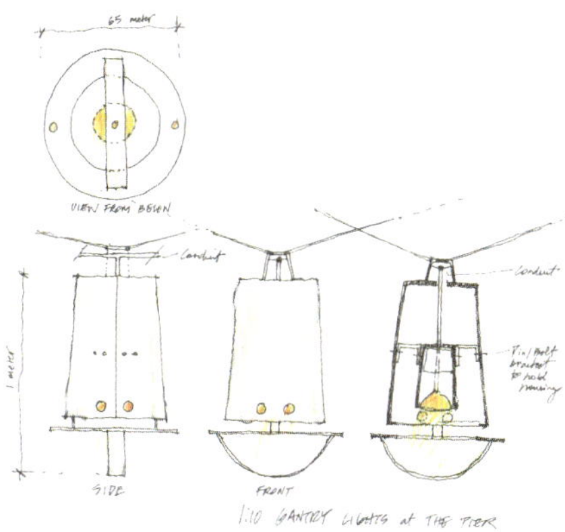
65 meter
VIEW FROM BELOW
Conduit
Conduit
1 meter
Pin/bolt bracket to hold housing
SIDE
FRONT
1:10 GANTRY LIGHTS at THE PIER

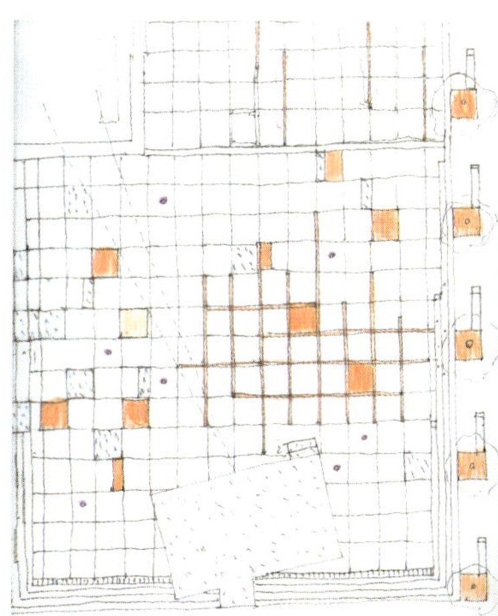

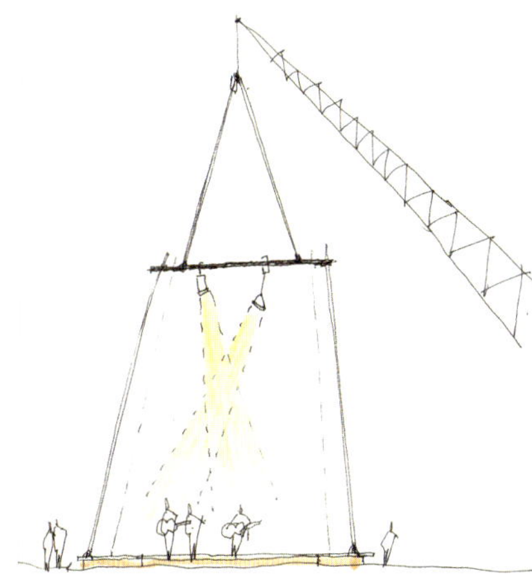

North Vancouver Shipyards II

NORTH VANCOUVER, BC • 2019–ONGOING

Nine years after the first phase of work on the *North Vancouver Shipyards* by Pechet and Robb, PECHETStudio was hired to design a series of infrastructural elements to improve communications, beautify a trip to the public restrooms, increase flexibility at events, offer new seating options, and institute a serious recycling program.

The first of these commissions was *infomoji*, a set of portable sign-stands for the posting of announcements. Inspired by emoji, with those big friendly eyes that beckon, the design picks up the forms, colours, and materials of the industrial elements of the Shipyards.

In *Yardifacts*, a collection of old pattern molds from the Shipyards are given a new life. As indices of the bronze, steel, and aluminum casting systems used in the shipbuilding industries of Western Canada, the molds, long freed from their original functions, are arranged in a variety of taxonomies based on their formal attributes. These arrangements are captivating as they invite an oscillation between wonder (curiosity) about the original function of the molds and wonder (awe) at the beauty of their forms.

Two new furnishing options, as yet unbuilt, were designed to be used in the covered plaza and surrounding public spaces. Easily moved, the *Multipede Tables* could be scattered individually or aligned in long rows for community dinners. In either case, their colourful legs would "create repeated patterns and shapes that are inspired by the patternmaking technologies and fabrication in the shipyards." [BP] *Loungers* would offer the public alternative ways of resting. Their yellow colour, a legacy of the shipbuilding traditions, picks up the yellow of the crane and the *infomoji*, drawing connecting threads through this busy landscape. The "odd-ball infinity shape" of the *Loungers* allows them to be flipped, one design, two different forms and ways of lounging.

The most recent addition to the Shipyards' built infrastructure is *Trash Talk*, recycling receptacles that allow visitors to sort their garbage into four separate waste streams. It is hard to describe the delight the studio had in designing personified trash bins that offer a friendly handshake to the staff that empty them daily. Kindness in a can.

infomoji (2020)
PECHETStudio
Page 130
CLIENT: City of North Vancouver • **TEAM:** Bill Pechet with Lőrinc Vass • **FABRICATOR:** Epic Metalworks • **PHOTOS:** PHOTOS: Michael Perlmutter (p. 130 top and bottom left) • **STATUS:** Built

Yardifacts (2019)
PECHETStudio
Pages 130-131
CLIENT: City of North Vancouver • **TEAM:** Bill Pechet with Lőrinc Vass • **FABRICATOR:** Gregory Ross • **PHOTOS:** Lőrinc Vass and Bill Pechet (p. 130 bottom right, p. 131)

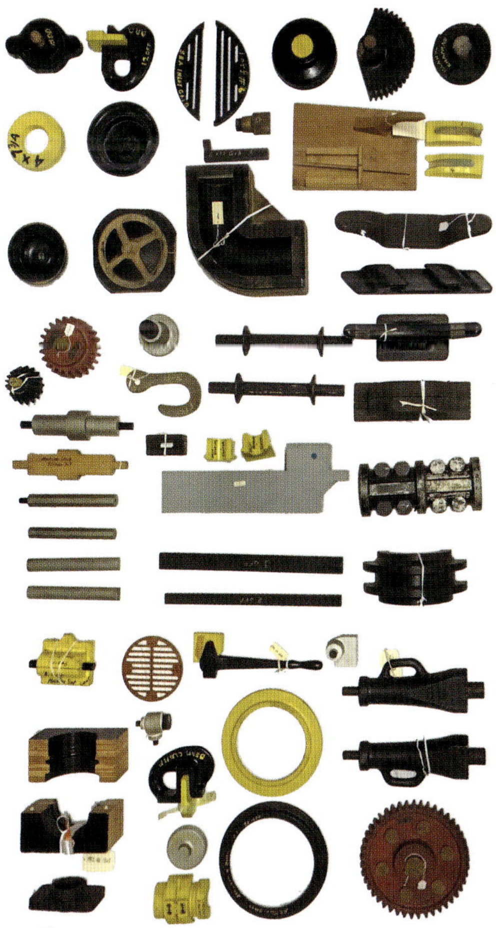

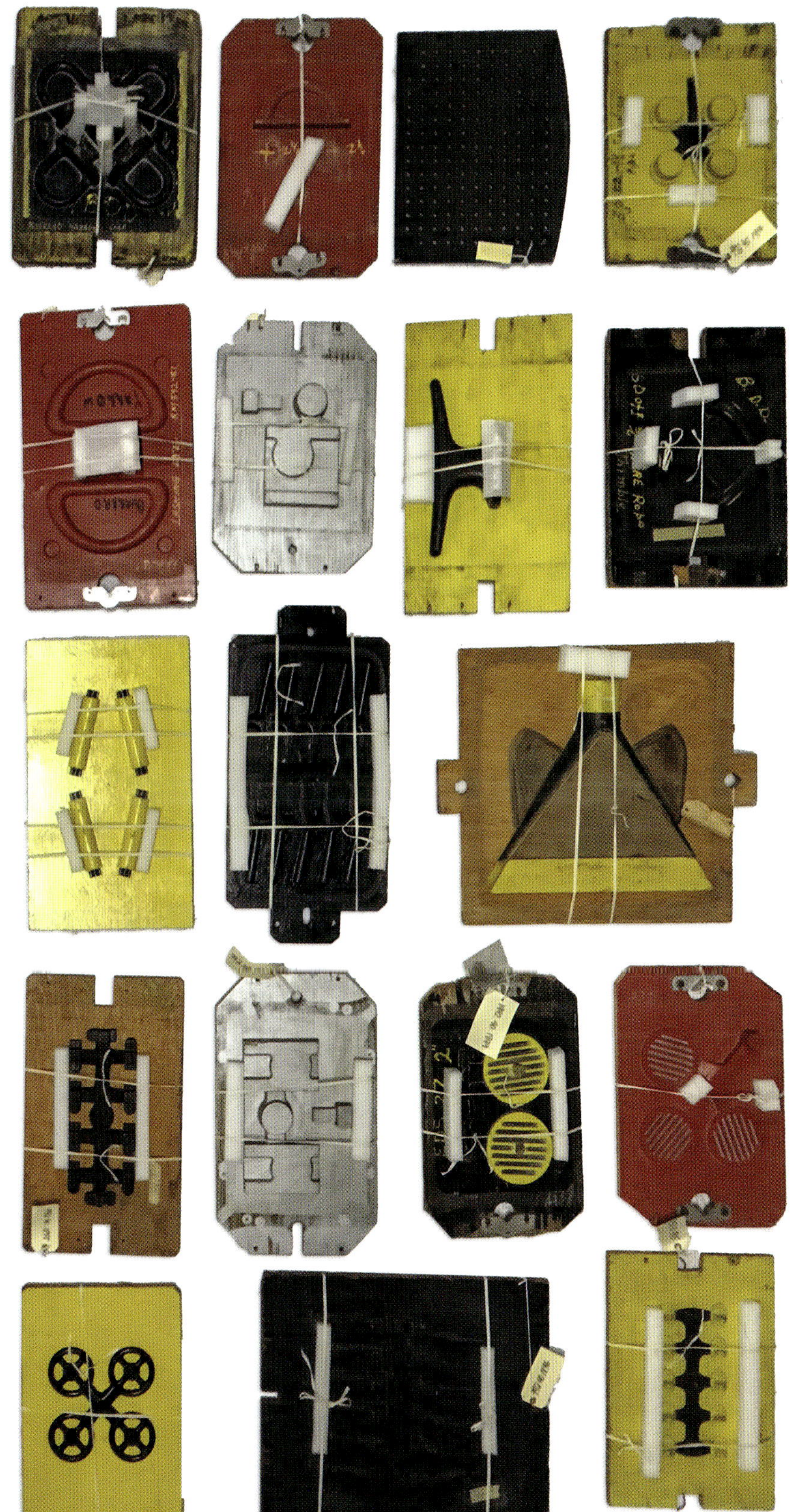

Loungers (2022-)
PECHETStudio
CLIENT: City of North Vancouver • TEAM: Bill Pechet with Lőrinc Vass • RENDERINGS: Lőrinc Vass • STATUS: ongoing

Multipede Table (2020-)
PECHETStudio
CLIENT: City of North Vancouver • TEAM: Bill Pechet with Vincent Perron, Lőrinc Vass • MODEL: Vincent Perron, Bill Pechet • RENDERINGS: Vincent Perron, Lőrinc Vass • STATUS: Ongoing

Trash Talk (2025)
PECHETStudio
CLIENT: City of North Vancouver • TEAM: Bill Pechet with Lőrinc Vass • FABRICATOR: Burrard Mechanical • DRAWINGS: Bill Pechet • PHOTOS: Bill Pechet • STATUS: Built and filling up

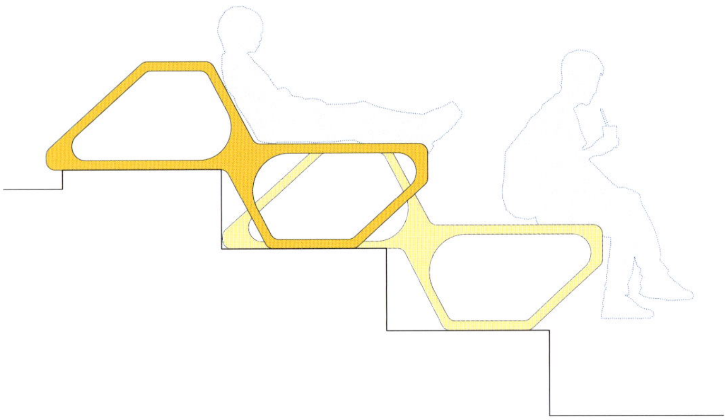

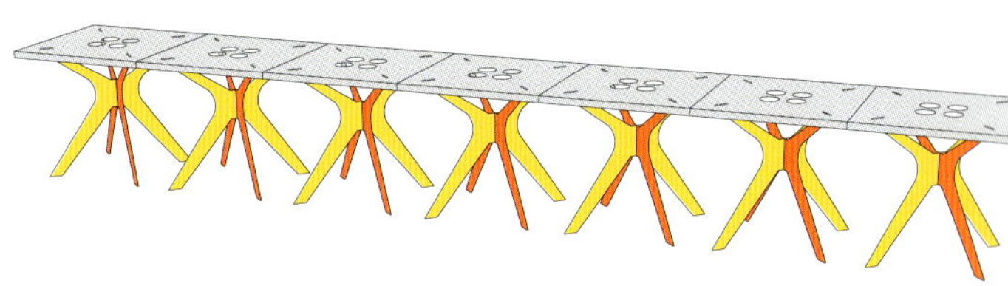

LANDFILL
FOOD WASTE
CONTAINERS
MIXED PAPER

LANDFILL
FOOD WASTE
CONTAINERS

Peeping Tom Thomson

PIER 27 DEVELOPMENT, TORONTO, ON • 2016

To fully appreciate the concept behind *Peeping Tom Thomson*, a giant freestanding keyhole, by definition a kind of threshold, it is helpful to know the history of its site. Pier 27 in Toronto is a story of constructed thresholds. Since the mid-1850s, the shoreline between the city and Lake Ontario has shifted roughly half a mile, from Front Street to just south of today's Queens Quay. The massive backfilling project provided new land for waste disposal and heavy industry close to the rails and waterways. Then, between 1955–66, transportation engineers built the Frederick G. Gardiner Expressway, a new threshold dividing the waterfront industrial zone from the city centre. Just as in San Francisco, Cincinnati, Detroit, Minneapolis, Portland, New Orleans, Tampa, and very nearly Vancouver, the expressway effectively blocked public access to the water.

In 1972, the federal government expropriated 100 acres of the south industrial lands for waterfront revitalization, jumping the expressway to build Harbourfront Centre. In 1986, the industrial property east of Yonge Street was sold to private developers. After a loud outcry from a public eager to maintain views to Lake Ontario, in 2007 Pier 27 was given the green light only after the developers made a major concession: the development would offer a porous threshold between the proposed private residences and a renewed public waterfront. West 8 and DTAH designated a space within the expansive landscape design for a public artwork, funded by the Percent for Public Art Program-Private Developer Program.

Peeping Tom Thomson proposed a porous threshold in the public/private space between the two twelve-storey residential buildings. The form of a giant keyhole speaks to the two-sided nature of the site, bridging between city and lake, public and private, framing views in both directions. The public was invited to walk through the keyhole as they would through an open door. At night, the two-sided nature of the keyhole would become apparent, with the lake-side illuminated in "shifting pulses and cascades of glowing lights," a beacon for sailors adrift, while on the reverse side, serving as a subtle, if not voyeuristic, nightlight for the residents.

Peeping Tom Thomson is a slightly cheeky reference to a Group of Seven painter who worked in the *en plein* air tradition, where the frame of the canvas delineated an idealized view. *Peeping Tom Thomson,* so specific to its site's history and locale, lost the competition to a work by artist Alice Aycock, *A Series of Whirlpool Field Manoeuvres for Pier 27*, three autonomous white swirls. Similar Aycock whirlpools have been spotted in the porte cochère at the casino MGM National Harbor in Maryland and on the NYU Abu Dhabi campus.

PECHETStudio

CLIENTS: Cityzen Development Group and City of Toronto • **TEAM:** Bill Pechet with Gabe Daly, Thomas Gaudin, Sam McFaul • **RENDERINGS:** Gabe Daly, Thomas Gaudin, Sam McFaul • **STATUS:** Competition finalist, unbuilt

Poetry and Apocalypse

VANCOUVER EAST CULTURAL CENTRE + VARIOUS INTERNATIONAL VENUES • 1992–95

Known for a style of modern dance that has been described as "gruelling" and "ferocious," Noam Gagnon and Dana Gingras, co-artistic directors and choreographers of The Holy Body Tattoo Dance Company, set *Poetry and Apocalypse* in the context of a dance marathon, a ruthless scenario of human endurance. They envisioned suspended bags of sand as literal and metaphoric vessels, or bodies, that dripped their contents into conical piles, slowly deflating until finally giving up and expiring along with the dancers.

Years earlier, Noam Gagnon was in *Savage Parade* and performed a breathtaking solo in the sandbox Bill designed as part of the set. It is likely because Bill was working with sand at the time that Noam approached him to design the sandbags. They made several prototypes, adjusting the bag size and hole opening until the time it took for the sand to drop and the length of the dance coincided. In addition, Bill also designed the ground plane for their performance in Vancouver, a "cracked world" surface of heaving plaster. Unfortunately, only the sandbags could travel, but a film version of the piece, created in collaboration with Vancouver filmmakers William Morrison and Valerie Nelson, was released two years later.

CHOREOGRAPHY: Noam Gagnon, Dana Gingras of Holy Body Tattoo Dance Company • **FABRICATION:** Pearl Bellesen, Holy Body Tattoo Dance Co. • **PHOTO:** Courtesy of Holy Body Tattoo • **SKETCHES:** Bill Pechet

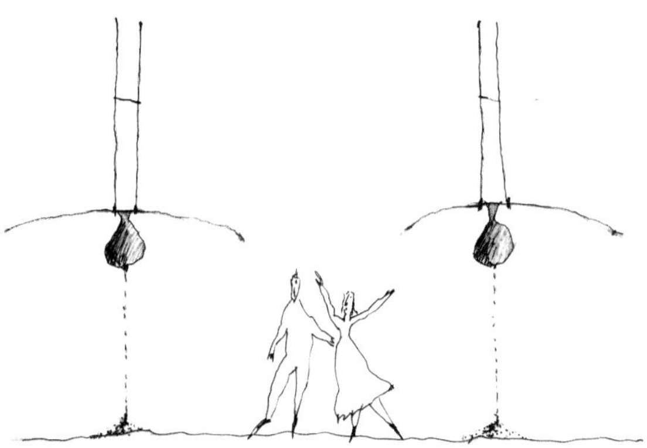

Ponte Bong

HINGE PARK, VANCOUVER, BC • 2010

The Winter Olympics were coming to Vancouver and the athletes needed somewhere to stay. Ambitious plans were drawn up for the southeastern shore of False Creek, converting the industrial lands into Vancouver's first sustainable neighbourhood. PWL was hired to design the landscape for the nearly eighty-acre site. There were to be passive park spaces and spaces for active play and exercise. In keeping with the city's goals of creating an enduring and vibrant, ecologically and socially sustainable neighbourhood, the industrial site was transformed through the creation of a shoreline habitat, rewilding and storm management, as well as the introduction of a village square and other public gathering spaces.

Hinge Park, one of two parks embedded in the landscape plan, was designed in collaboration with PECHETStudio. Designed by PWL, this wetland park, home to a variety of plant and animal species, controls the runoff from the surrounding neighbourhoods. A small hill offers children a sense of agency in the park as they control the flow of water down a channel and into the naturalized wetland environment. On any given day, you will find kids running up and down the mound, tracing the water's path.

To facilitate crossing the wetland, Bill designed *Ponte Bong*, a perforated bridge of Corten steel with historical references to the City Works Yard. It is a great delight to watch the munchkins rolling around inside the giant pipe, trying to climb its curved walls, sticking their heads and arms through the openings. "In its name and form, there is something in *Ponte Bong* for the amusement of kids of all ages, just like with my illustrations for children's books." BP

PECHETStudio

CLIENT: City of Vancouver • TEAM: Bill Pechet, PWL Partnership Landscape Architects (coordinating firm) • FABRICATION: TYBO Contracting • SKETCH: Bill Pechet • PHOTOS: Michael Perlmutter (p. 136 left, p. 137), Rachel Oye (p. 136 right) • STATUS: Built

PWL Office Interiors

WEST PENDER, VANCOUVER, BC • 2000

As longtime collaborators on numerous projects, this was not the first occasion PWL reached out to the studio for help designing an office space in Coal Harbour. A magnificent view of the North Shore served as inspiration for the interiors of the new PWL West Pender office. Blue and green partitions, floating and movable, reflected the transmutable landscape of the Burrard Inlet. Orange-red columns beckoned to the cranes in the distant Port of Vancouver. Perforated stainless steel and woodgrain laminate gave shape to the reception desk as historically steel and wood had to the waterfront. A rotating message tree, fabricated by bicycle manufacturer Toby's Cycle Works, held pink message slips, like so many dangling petals on a cherry tree. Outside in, inside out.

Pechet + Robb Studio
CLIENT: PWL Partnership Landscape Architects Inc. • **TEAM:** Bill Pechet • **FABRICATION:** Toby's Cycle Works, Granville Island Woodworks • **PHOTO:** Emma Chorostecki • **SKETCHES:** Bill Pechet • **STATUS:** Dismantled (2000)

Qingdao Cemetery Masterplan

QINGDAO CEMETERY, SHANDONG PROVINCE, CHINA • 1999

In the twenty years preceding this masterplan, the population of the Qingdao tripled from approximately one million to three million inhabitants, and since 1999, the population has doubled to over six million. With such rapid growth, the need to aggressively expand the number of available interment spaces was evident and a masterplan was commissioned. The new cemetery would at least make a dent in the shortfall, providing space for 300,000.

As China was becoming a market economy, the design team was explicitly instructed to create interment options reflecting choice and social standing, something that had been suppressed for decades. Like North American cemeteries, wealth and status should be apparent in the scale and footprint of the funerary monuments, just as they are in the living city.

The forty-two-acre sloping site selected for the cemetery is located next to, and downstream from, the heavily forested Laoshan National Park. The designers' ambitions were to allow the park's waters to flow through the cemetery in canals and streams, to keep forty percent of the site in its natural state of pine forest and grasses, and to terrace the site formally and informally. Unfortunately, there was no mention in the brief of any of the old stone buildings on the site belonging to an abandoned village quite literally wiped off the map, nor any site visits before the masterplan was designed. Had there been, the team would have recommended rehabilitating the structures as resting pavilions or ceremonial sites.

The diagram of the cemetery design is crystal clear, but as with all good diagrams, it is tweaked and softened as the concept adjusts to the particularities of the site and program requirements. A north-south axis, roughly following a topographic line, divides the lower, more formal entry sequence and terraces, from the upper, more informal, wooded terraces and interment sites. An east-west axis leads one from the parking lot, through an administrative centre and tower columbaria, common in Asia, and a bamboo-and-water-garden court for funerals and gatherings, past terraced interment sites, and onwards up the hill. This axis suggests a bilateral symmetry, but the plan is far more subtle, with the east and west sides of the axis balanced in what might be called a contingent symmetry. Near the crossing of the two axes, a public monument marks the centre of the cemetery.

Pechet and Robb Art and Architecture
TEAM: Bill Pechet with Nicolas Osenton / PWL Partnership Landscape Architects (project coordinator) • **DRAWINGS:** Bill Pechet • **STATUS:** Masterplan completed

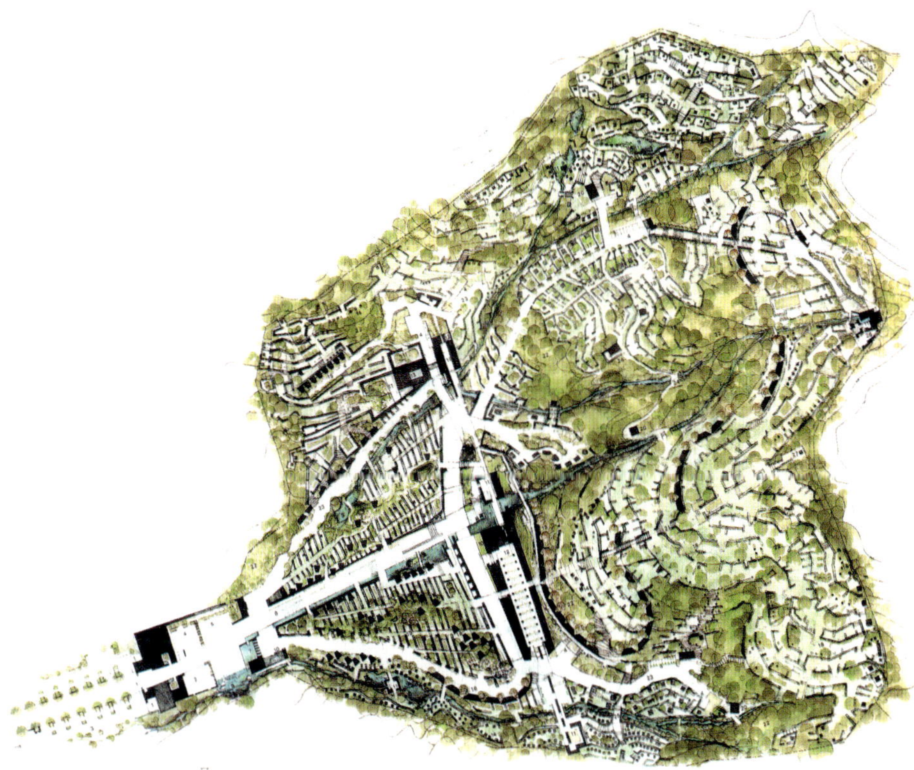

Rec Room

MULTIPLE THEATRES ACROSS CANADA • 1992

"One of my favourites!" BP

It was the early Nineties and the dance scene in Britsh Columbia was in full swing. Flush with funding, companies could afford to hire designers to experiment with their choreographers and dancers. It was during this period of abundance that Bill formed productive collaborations with several companies.

As the story of *Rec Room* goes... one night while looking out his office window, lawyer-choreographer Harvey Mellor became mesmerized by the sight of a lone worker slowly polishing a newly poured slab of concrete. The sighting conjured a vision of a dance based on a person caught in a repetitive, hypnotic task. Originally Mellor wanted a set with a concrete floor, but as the production was to travel extensively, the weighty material was ruled out of the question. He agreed to a floor made of lighter materials, but insisted on a polisher being a part of the performance.

The dance floor, as seen from above, appeared like an array of agricultural fields, each square plot comprised of layers of plywood on insulation foam frosted with faux finishes of brick and stone. The name *Rec Room* was a direct reference to the simulacrums of real materials often used in basements to elicit feelings of charm and history. Suburban rec rooms are also typically a site of play.

Each square field was outfitted with tabs allowing the dancers to easily arrange and rearrange the pattern. They spent a good half of the performance pushing the panels out of upright, space-defining boxes and laying and relaying the floor, requiring cross-cables holding the perimeter frame in tension to be tuned and retuned throughout the performance. The dancers' seemingly arbitrary and repetitive motions did indeed achieve the desired mesmerizing effect of a Sisyphean exercise.

CHOREOGRAPHY: Harvey Mellor, Dancecorps • **TEAM:** Bill Pechet • **FABRICATION:** Dancecorps • **PHOTOS:** Bill Pechet

Rings on Alberni

ALBERNI STREET, VANCOUVER, BC • 2014

The Downtown Vancouver Business Improvement Association and the city of Vancouver sought "proposals to conceptualize and design both functional and decorative lighting schemes for the two-block commercial section of Alberni Street" between Bute and Burrard, one of four commercial districts in the West End Community Plan, as the initial stage of a more complete masterplan for the district.

Rings on Alberni proposed for this "luxury zone"—home to Tiffany's, Prada, De Beers, Hublot—floating lights that evoke expensive jewelry and cigar smoke rings on one hand, while on the other hand, "humorously suggest a visiting colony of extraterrestrials coming down to shop." BP

The proposal builds on the studio's long track record of successful collaborations with Eos Lightmedia: in Vancouver, the *False Creek Energy Utility Stacks*, *Dichroic Vancouver*, the decorative lighting vision for the West End Business Improvement Association; *emptyful* and *heaven between* in Winnipeg; and the *Waving* proposal for Houston. When you find a reliable collaborator to help further your work, why mix it up? Why, indeed.

PECHETStudio

CLIENT: Downtown Vancouver Business Improvement Association (DVBIA) and City of Vancouver • **TEAM:** Bill Pechet with Gabe Daly, Margarita Krivolutskaya / Eos Lightmedia • **RENDERINGS:** Margarita Krivolutskaya • **STATUS:** Still a possibility

Robson Public

ROBSON STREET, VANCOUVER, BC • 2014–15

Robson Public, a proposal commissioned by the Robson Business Association with support from the city of Vancouver, demonstrated the possibility of transforming streets and sidewalks from pure circulation corridors to great public spaces. To accomplish such a makeover, several design strategies were proposed for three blocks of Robson Street, between Jervis and Burrard.

The proposed changes were minimal, but impactful. Widening sidewalks created small plazas with rest stops for weary shoppers or people watchers. A parking space surrendered became a parklet. New mid-block crosswalks allowed for easy flow across impossibly long blocks, no doubt a benefit to the businesses. By converting passages between Robson Street and the alleys into plazas with stepped seating for people and performances, and by closing one block of Bute Street, adding street furniture and small rain shelters, new lighting, paving and other furnishings, the nature of Vancouver's public space could be radically altered. We have seen how transformative such ideas can be in test cases.

As an advocacy document, *Robson Public* was the catalyst for the city's decision to proceed with constructing a version of this study, albeit designed by their staff. While Vancouver, still stuck in the pop-up phase, has been slow to pedestrianize, the city-led construction project currently underway (2024–25) is one of several initiatives that could see the city evolve.

PECHETStudio

CLIENT: Robson Business Association and City of Vancouver • **TEAM:** Bill Pechet with Gabe Daly, Thomas Gaudin, Margarita Krivolutskaya • **DRAWINGS:** Thomas Gaudin, updated by Lőrinc Vass

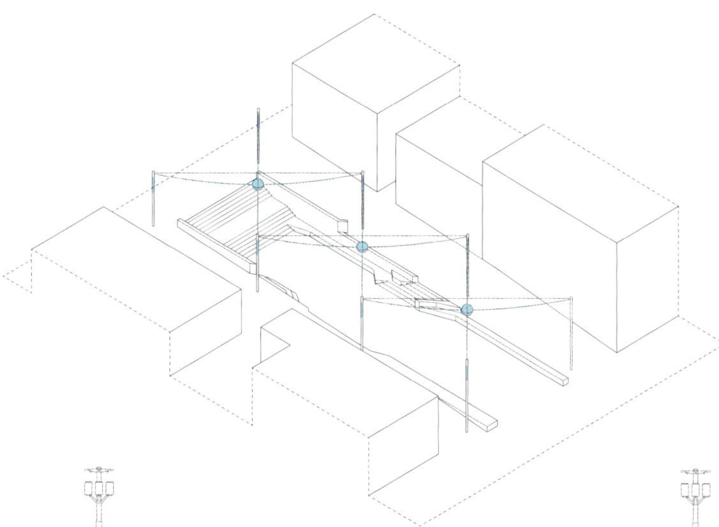

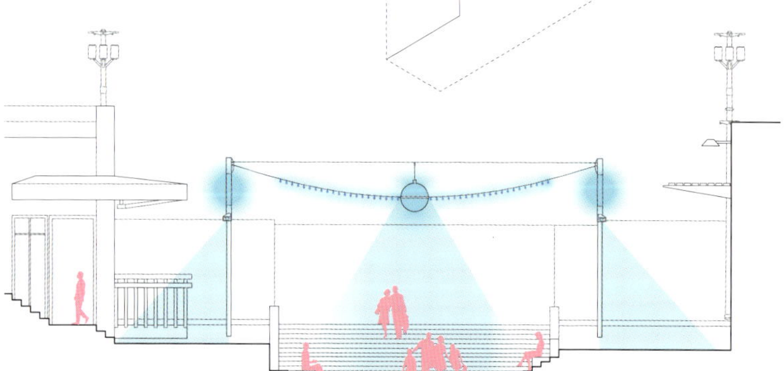

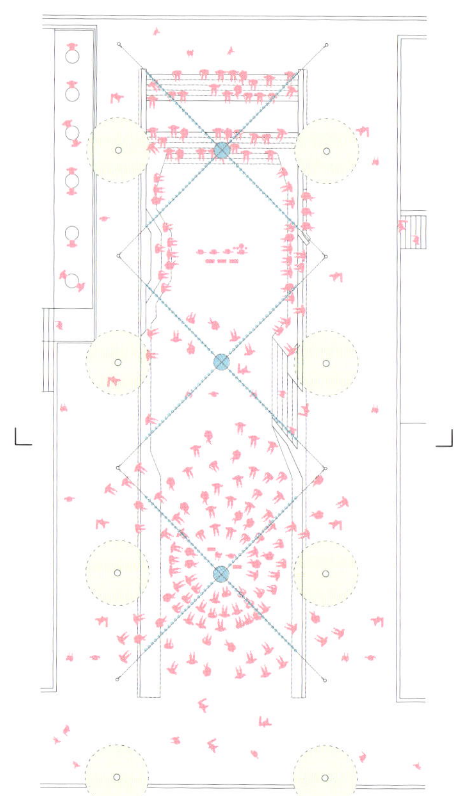

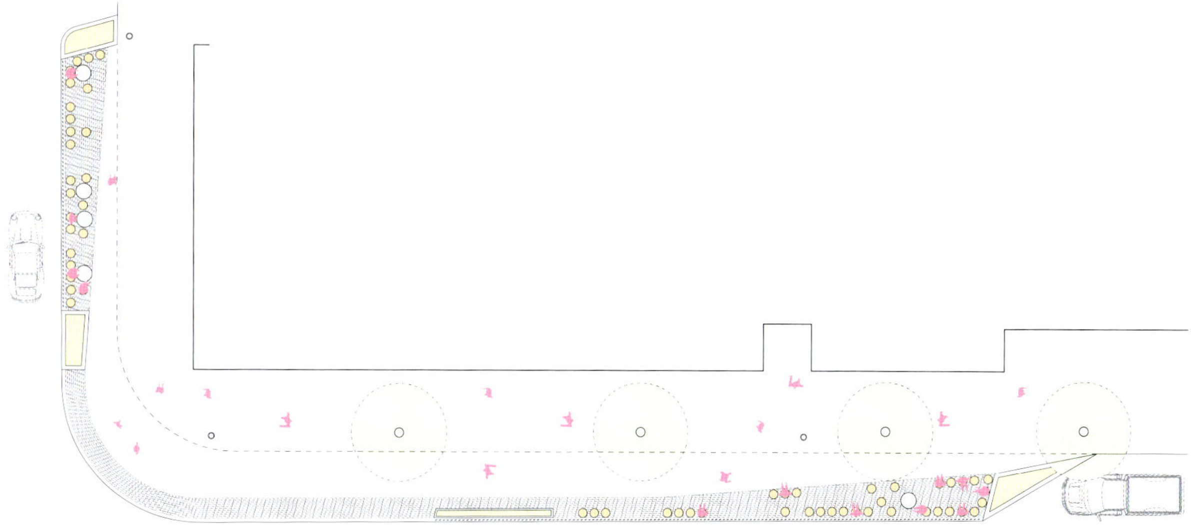

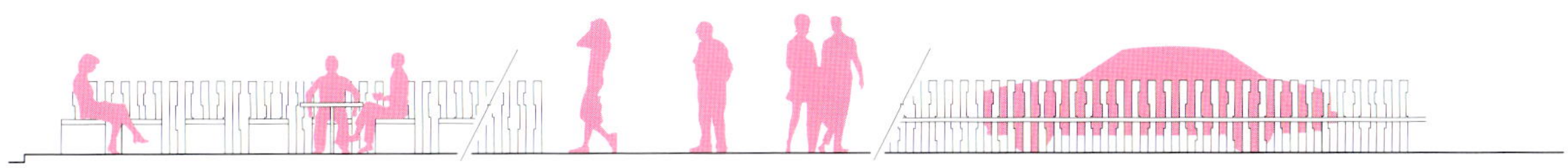

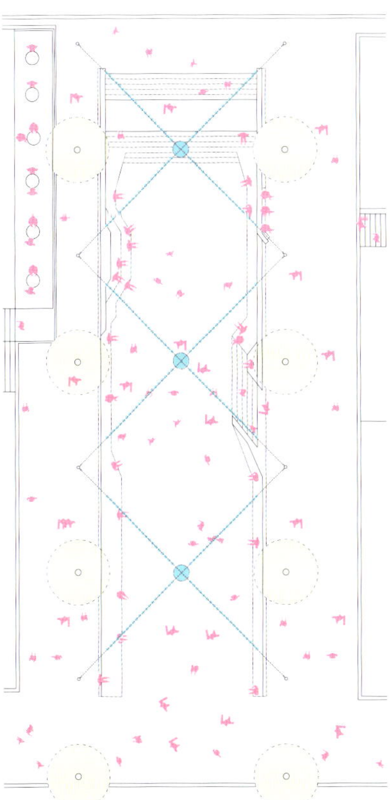

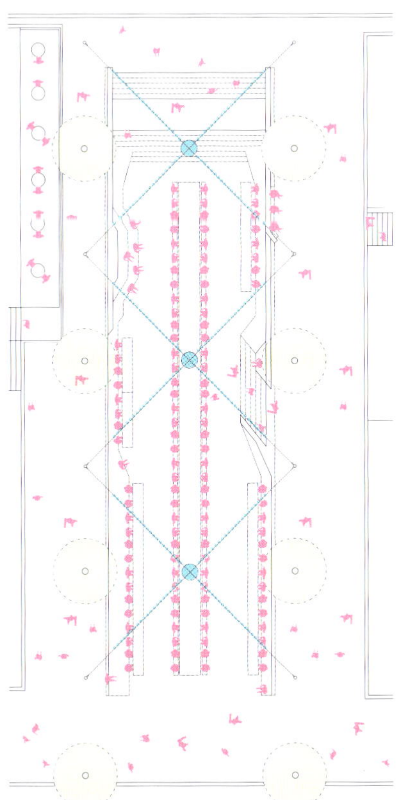

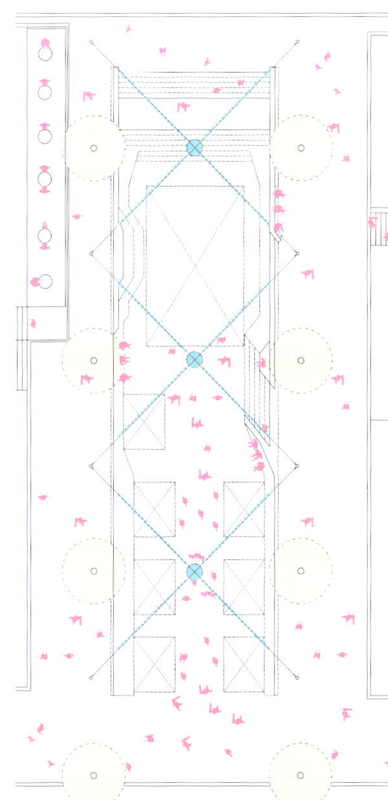

roger that

TUSCANY LRT STATION, CALGARY, AB • 2015

The northern Calgary neighbourhoods of Tuscany and Rocky Ridge/Royal Oak had long been divided by Crowchild Trail. With the new LRT station bridging the highway, the communities were finally connected. *roger that* celebrates this conjoining with a shared public artwork. "Like two neighbours chatting over a fence, the elements of the artwork create a cross-highway dialogue—inviting each other over to experience the artwork from all sides, and through all seasons and time of day." [BP]

In deference to the site as a transit hub, *roger that* is composed of repurposed, readymade, roadside elements. 221 amber coloured safety lights positioned on four-stories tall galvanized poles stand directly across from one another on either side of the highway. From some angles, the poles appear like a "random grove of trees, festooned with buds or birds." [BP] But from the sweet spots within each grove, suddenly what appeared random becomes a perfectly round and radiant constellation. The effect is especially powerful at night when the solar-powered lights radiate the sun's energy back to earth, a reminder of the larger orders of the universe.

The name *roger that* refers to the physicist and philosopher Roger Penrose, whose tile geometry of repeated parallelograms was used to determine the positioning of the lights on the poles, "creating both discernible patterns and random ones, much like the stars above us, and our own movements below." [BP] In communications, *roger that* also means "message received." "It is so important for public art to have 'AHA' moments, where a feeling of belonging or understanding is manifest." [BP]

PECHETStudio

CLIENT: City of Calgary, Transportation Department • **TEAM:** Bill Pechet with Gabe Daly, Sara Zonouzi / RJC Consulting Engineers / Aurian Consulting / Tetra Tech • **FABRICATION:** Valmont West Coast Engineering / Highline Electrical Constructors / SolarMarkers • **PHOTOS:** Stock (p. 144 top), Bill Pechet (p. 144 middle), Michael Perlmutter (p. 144 bottom, p. 146-147), Kristopher Grunert (p. 145) • **SKETCH:** Bill Pechet • **DRAWINGS:** Lőrinc Vass • **STATUS:** Competition winner, built

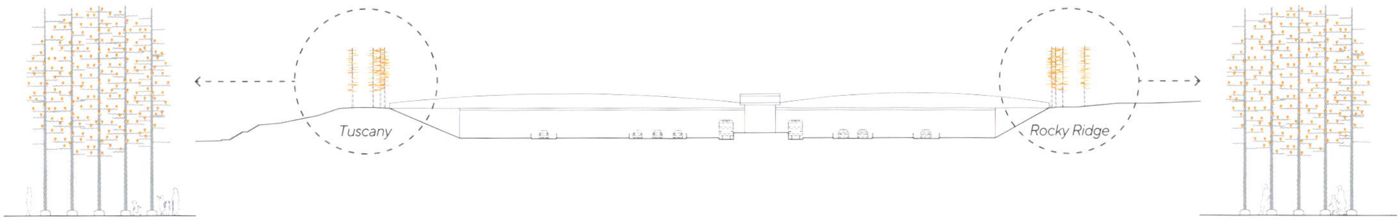
Tuscany
Rocky Ridge

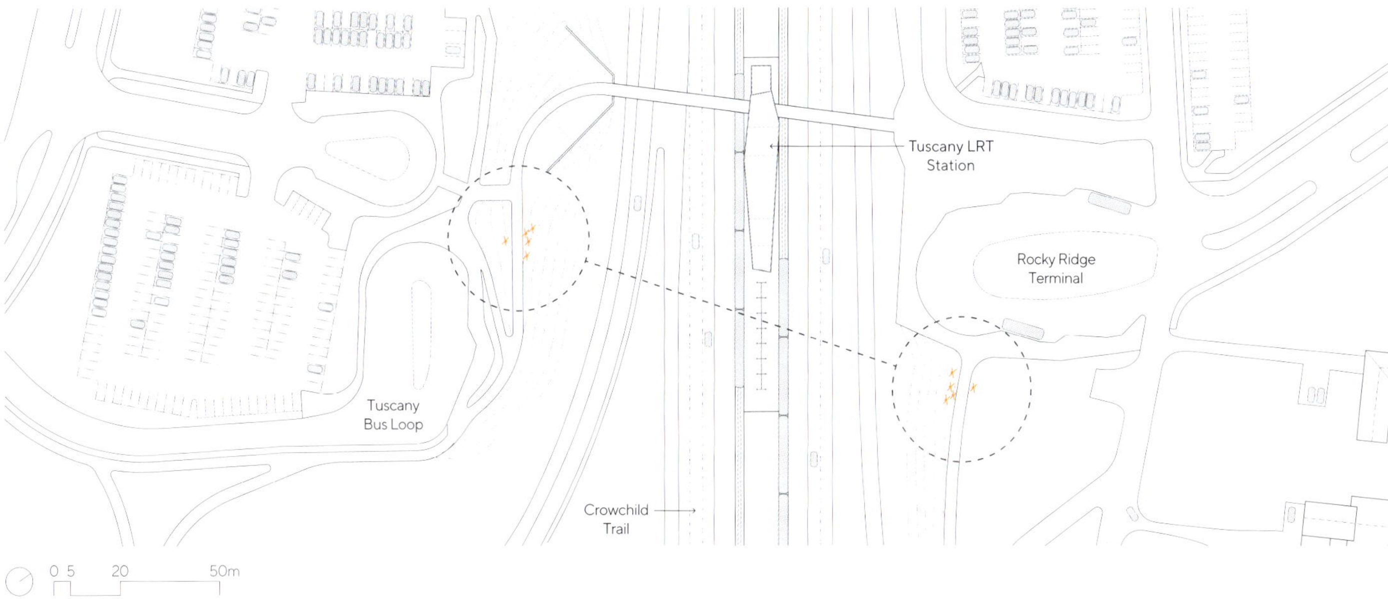
Tuscany LRT
Station
Rocky Ridge
Terminal
Tuscany
Bus Loop
Crowchild
Trail
0 5 20 50m

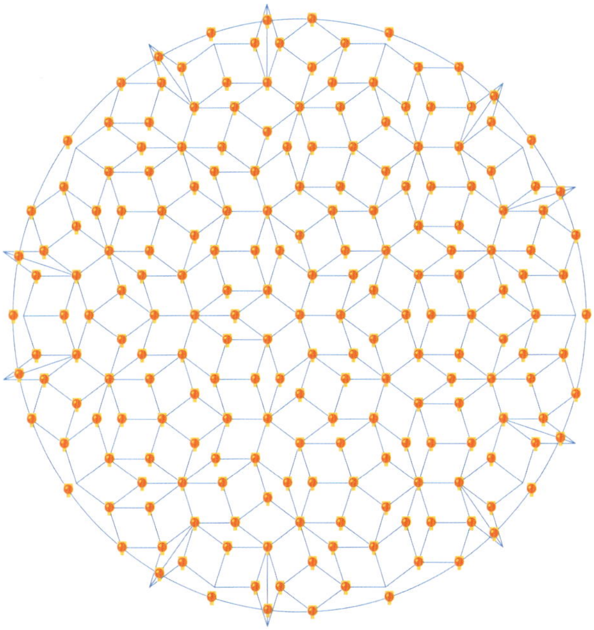

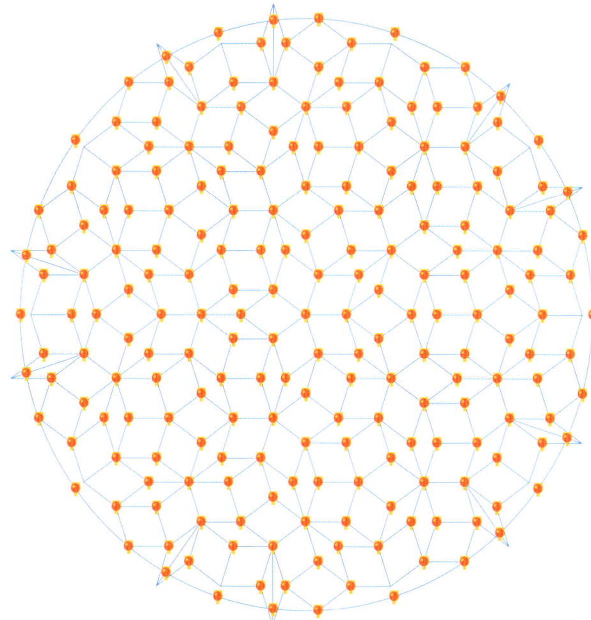

Ross Bay Cemetery Masterplan

VICTORIA, BC • 2004–07

Established in 1872 overlooking the Strait of Juan de Fuca, the Victorian-era Ross Bay Cemetery is one of the most beautiful in Canada and the final resting place of such Canadian luminaries as Emily Carr and Billy Barker, a legendary character of the gold rush. Although initially the site was quite barren, by the 1930s the cemetery was fast becoming an arboretum, filling with pines, ornamental cherries and plums, holly and yew, laurel, boxwood and lilac. It became so rich in flora, the city of Victoria snipped clippings to grow trees elsewhere.

The perimeter of the historic cemetery has always been quite porous, the edges defined alternately by a low concrete wall here, and trees, hedges, an embankment there. After a period of severe and recurring vandalism between 1988 and 2002, the city of Victoria solicited a plan to better secure the cemetery. *Ross Bay Cemetery Masterplan* proposed an edge over a half mile long, bent at the southwest corner of the site. It addressed three of the most problematic edge conditions: Memorial Crescent to the west, the prominent corner at Memorial Crescent and Dallas, and along Dallas Road.

The masterplan proposed the addition of a new holly hedge and fence south of May Street, along Memorial, low enough to preserve views into the cemetery, its fenceposts designed to be slowly modified into columbaria in the decades to come. A new vehicular entry and two pedestrian entries would be added and the pines along Memorial Crescent and at the corner of Memorial and Dallas would be replaced. New waterfront columbaria terraces and memorial walls were designed and prototyped to add thousands of new interment sites, significantly improve security and enhance the beauty of the cemetery's waterfront edge.

Pechet and Robb Art and Architecture

CLIENT: City of Victoria • **TEAM:** Bill Pechet (project coordinator) with Chris Boldt, Mark Dennis, Heidi Nesbitt, Tina Tajitsu / Mortimer's Monumental Works / Island Columbaria • **DRAWINGS:** Bill Pechet • **STATUS:** Completed masterplan, unbuilt

Savage Council

LANGARA COLLEGE, VANCOUVER, BC • 1996

"... we can stand in a room full of dear friends, knowing that nine-tenths of them, if the pack demands it, will become your enemies."
— Doris Lessing
Prisons We Choose to Live Inside

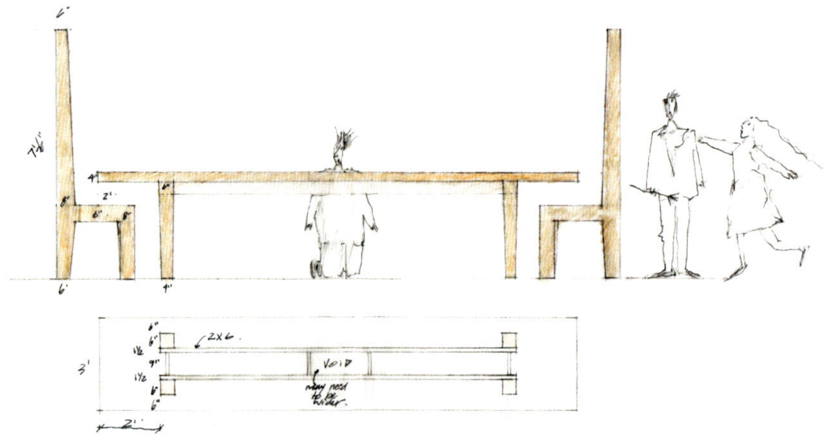

Choreographed by David Bloom and Chick Snipper and performed by Studio 58 Langara College students exploring the common ground between theatre and dance, *Savage Council* was the story of a savage meeting.

The set design, consisting of two big chairs and a long table, is a sequel to *Big Chairs* (1994) and a prelude to *GRANtable* (1998). But unlike those two public artworks, both cast in concrete, the furniture for the set of *Savage Council* was constructed of plywood to allow for its rearrangement during the performance. As the chairs moved about the stage, the props. took on different roles. Positioned at opposite ends of the table, they suggested a tribunal. Laid flat on their backs atop the table, feet to feet, they defined a prison cell. A horizontal ladder on the underside of the table allowed two performers to hang horizontally, as if imprisoned in a jungle gym, while a group of accusers encircled the table. *The Ubyssey* (February 16, 1996) concurred with Studio 58's promise that *Savage Council* would be "one of the most visually unusual productions in Studio 58's history."

We are happy to report that the furniture for this solemn performance had a cheerier after-life. The chairs were relocated to the backyard of *Exeter House* (2004) in Victoria and the long table has been serving UBC architecture students at Friday Good Times in Lasserre for over a decade. As an aside, recently two additional *Big Chairs* from the PWL interiors have been added to the student space. It's a party, even before the party.

CLIENT: Studio 58, Langara College • **TEAM:** Bill Pechet and Stephanie Robb with Nicolas Osenton • **FABRICATION:** Studio 58 • **PHOTOS:** Bill Pechet

Savage Parade

FIREHALL ARTS CENTRE, VANCOUVER, BC • 1992

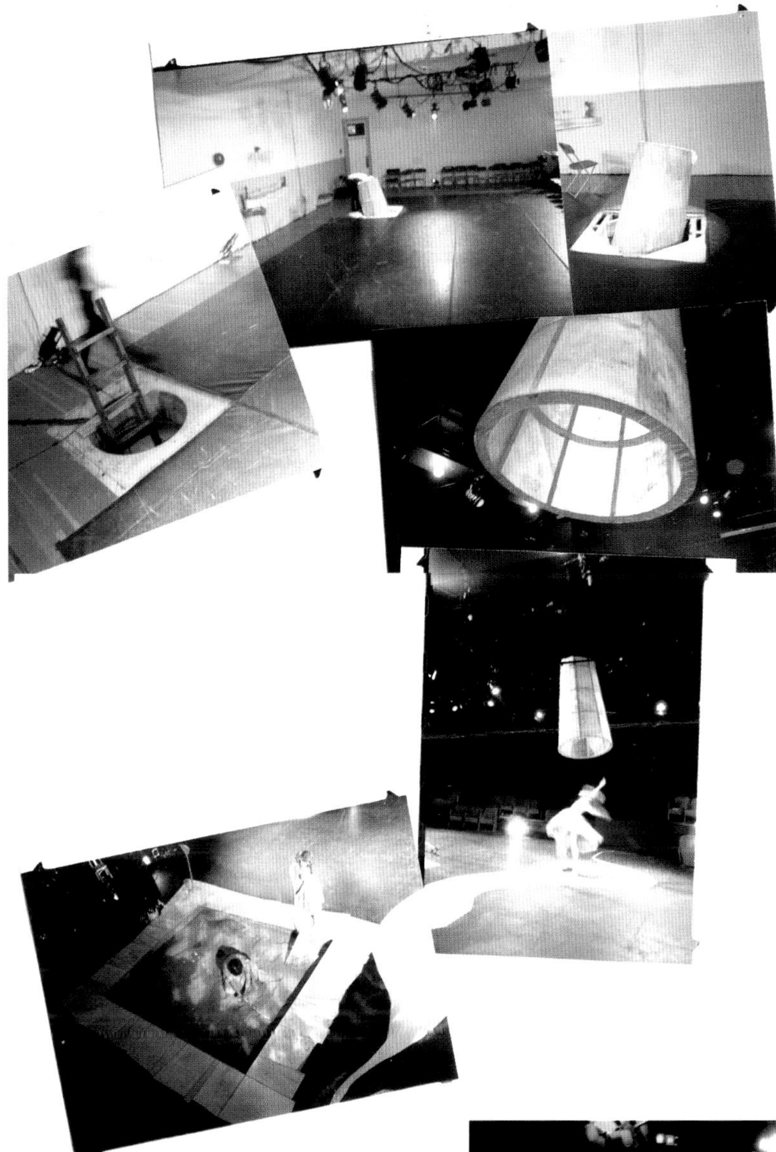

Choreographer Cornelius Fischer-Credo, collaborator of Harvey Mellor (*Rec Room*), needed designers who could "think different," as the old Apple commercial goes. The theatre for the performance of *Savage Parade* was anything but a neutral black box or tabula rasa. The dance was to be performed in the Firehall Theatre (a converted firehall, now known as the Firehall Arts Centre), not on one stage, but on two, not on one level, but on one over another, the two connected by old firepole holes.

Savage Parade was conceived as two contrasting, interconnected sets: the lower level, a dark space, a mysterious underworld, the upper level, a brightly lit setting for a silly Karaoke performance of Seventies pop songs. A ladder in one hole and a translucent parchment chute in the other physically connected the two scenes, while a large sandbox downstairs and a smaller one upstairs created a memory connection.

The performers moved between the two levels, carrying objects from one world to the other. Occasionally a shoe or some glitter or a ray of light would fall through a hole as well. At intermission, it was the audience's turn to switch spaces and watch the dance for a second time from a new perspective.

CHOREOGRAPHY: Cornelius Fischer-Credo, Dancecorps • FABRICATION: Bill Pechet with Charlie Gardiner, Jay Gower-Taylor / Dancecorps • PHOTOS: Bill Pechet

Schara Tzedeck Cemetery Addition

NEW WESTMINSTER, BC • 2016

This commission grew out of an ongoing relationship with the Schara Tzedeck Cemetery Board, a not-for-profit organization operating Jewish cemeteries in New Westminster, Surrey and Vancouver. The surgical interventions at the New Westminster cemetery were modest, as the primary task was to create space for new grave sites to increase revenue. By narrowing an existing road and converting it from two-way to one-way, a hundred new grave sites could be accommodated. In the process of solving that shortage, other opportunities to add public amenities emerged. Adjacent to the narrowed road, a small plaza was created with a 360-degree bench surrounding a cherry tree. A new memorial wall with the names of loved ones buried elsewhere was tucked into a stand of first-growth fir trees. The addition of retaining walls with woodgrain texture defined the edge of the newly cobbled road with planting added under the supervision of landscape architect, Joe Daly.

"There is really no planning for a Jewish funeral," Howard Jampolsky, executive director of the Schara Tzedeck Cemetery Board described in the *Jewish Independent* (August 18, 2023). "A Jewish funeral, as we provide one, is pretty much the same for everybody." Unlike in other traditions, there is no music to choose, no flowers to select. The caskets Schara Tzedeck offers are simple pine boxes intended for speedy decomposition per Jewish tradition. "We believe that everybody comes into the world equal, they should go out of the world equal and, to the best of our ability, that's what we try to do."

PECHETStudio

CLIENT: Schara Tzedeck Cemetery Board • **TEAM:** Bill Pechet with Gabe Daly, Sam McFaul / TOD Contracting (project management) / DALY Landscape Architecture / Glotman Simpson / Creus Engineering / GeoPacific Consultants / Radix Tree & Landscape Consulting • **CONSTRUCTION:** Four Brothers Masonry & Cement • **PHOTOS:** Michael Perlmutter • **DRAWINGS:** Lőrinc Vass • **STATUS:** Built

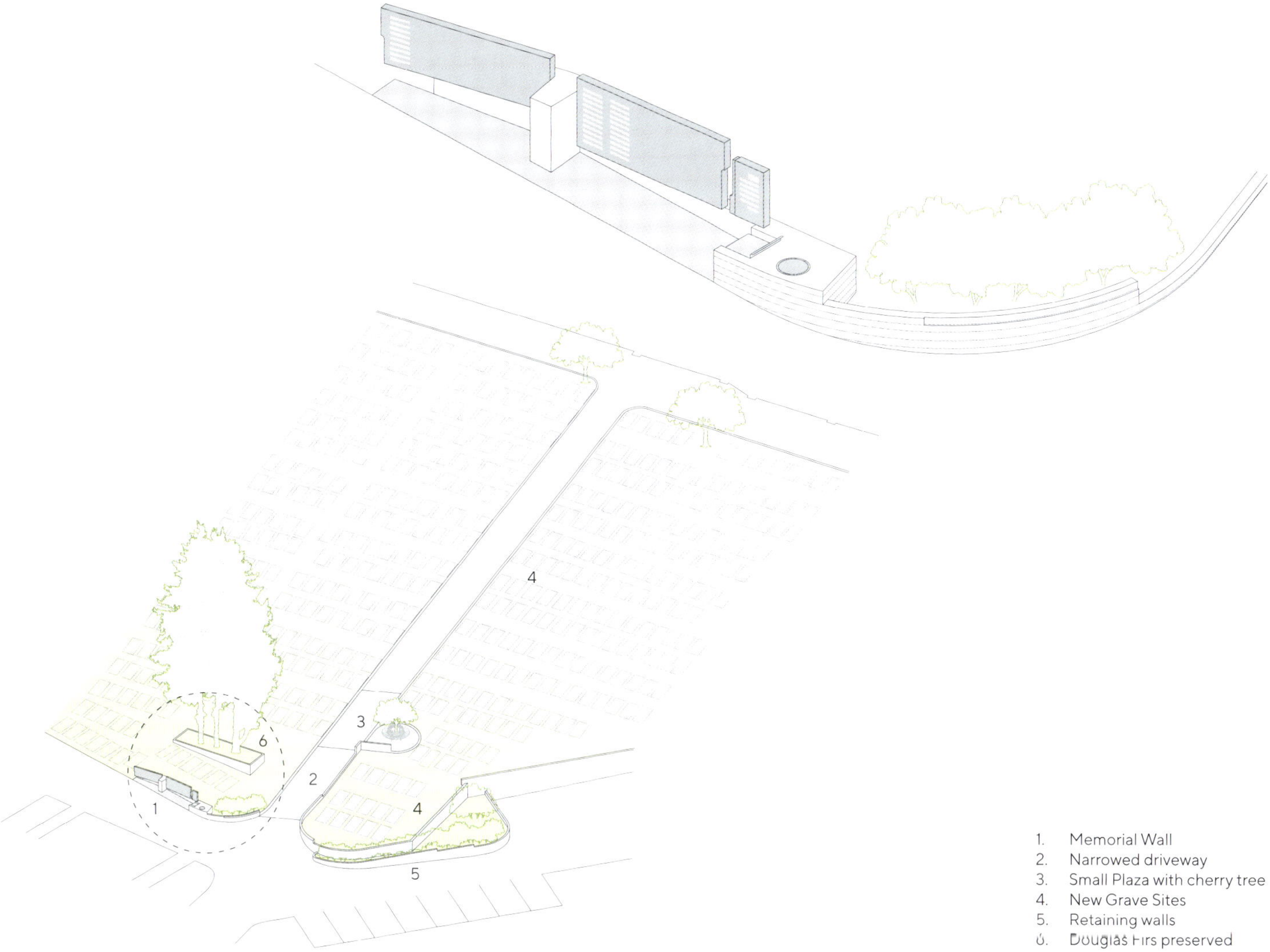

1. Memorial Wall
2. Narrowed driveway
3. Small Plaza with cherry tree
4. New Grave Sites
5. Retaining walls
6. Douglas Firs preserved

Seaview Cemetery Masterplan

ROBERTS CREEK, SUNSHINE COAST, BC • 2011

In response to the population growth on the Sunshine Coast, the new Seaview Cemetery was established in Roberts Creek in 1937, replacing the oldest cemetery for European settlers on the Sunshine Coast, Mount Elphinstone Pioneer Cemetery in Gibsons, considered too steep, too remote, and too small for expansion. Seaview occupies a triangular, south-facing sloped site, buffered by trees from the adjacent Sunshine Coast Highway and the Lower Road.

By 2011, Seaview was in need of a masterplan to insure its growth and financial future. PECHETStudio and DALY Landscape Architecture prepared a proposal to expand the "active life" of the cemetery by identifying additional casket and in-ground cremation lots, the only two burial options then offered. They also proposed new interment possibilities—columbaria, green burial, a scattering area, small-scale mausoleum and a commemorative wall—as well as other improvements and amenities such as roads to the new interment sites, a pavilion for shelter and funeral ceremonies, a service compound for equipment storage, and the restoration of the creek. As so often happens with masterplans, a new one, prepared by LEES + Associates in 2022, replaced the older one before it could be implemented.

Should you find your way to the Sunshine Coast, a visit to the charming Seaview Cemetery is well worth the detour. Like other active small town cemeteries, Seaview allows for highly personalized memorials that collectively convey a rich local culture. A hike to the old Mount Elphinstone Pioneer Cemetery is also worth the climb, but don't forget the bear spray!

PECHETStudio

CLIENT: Sunshine Coast Regional District • TEAM: Bill Pechet with Gabe Daly / DALY Landscape Architecture • SKETCHES: Bill Pechet • DRAWING: Gabe Daly • STATUS: Masterplan completed

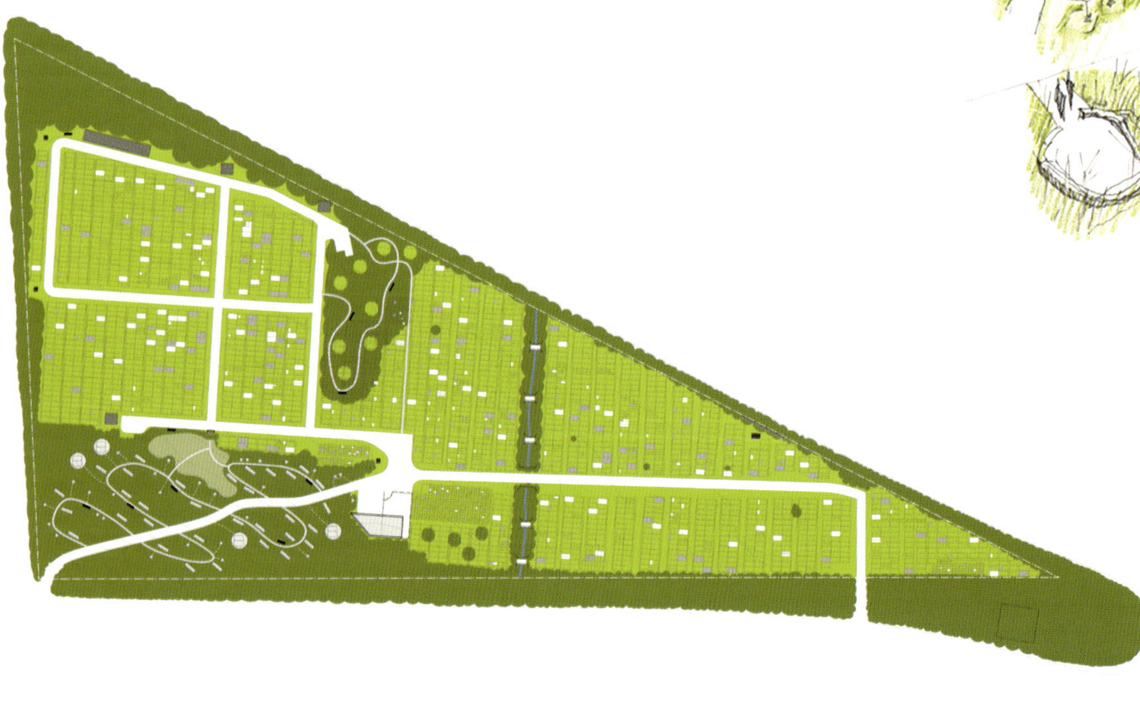

Semiahmoo Ancestor Repatriation Chambers

SEMIAHMOO FIRST NATION CEMETERY, SEMIAHMOO PARK • 2023

For decades, the Semiahmoo band has been engaged in the slow process of repatriating the ancestral remains of the Semiahmoo First Nation that have been unearthed through disruptive public and private land development practices. When the sacred relics of 200 ancestors, stored in seventy-eight bankers boxes and held by the Department of Archaeology at Simon Fraser University, were at last returned, the band sought assistance for the design of a worthy burial site.

The Semiahmoo traditional territory spanned what is now the province of British Columbia and Washington State. The imposition of the border divided the nation, but the Semiahmoo remain in close and cooperative contact with the Lummi, as the Washington State band is known. The remaining hundred or so Semiahmoo live almost entirely in what is now known as South Surrey / White Rock, many on the Semiahmoo reserve which contains both Semiahmoo Park and the Semiahmoo First Nation Cemetery.

With the cemetery's lowest point at sea level, a train track berm is its only protection from ocean waters. Unfortunately, trains pass twenty-eight times a day. Due to the danger of sea level rise and storm surges, it was determined that the burial site would be located on the upper portion of the cemetery, tucked in among the trees.

Traditional Semiahmoo burial practices have included burials under cairns of rocks or shell middens on the beach; sometimes burials were underground and sometimes on platforms in trees. Given the site's second challenge, many unmarked graves, digging was not a good option.

It was determined that the remains would be placed in ceremonial cedar boxes, made by band members, and the boxes would be placed in sealed, stainless steel vault chambers in the shape of traditional reefnet canoes. These "canoes," adorned with traditional iconography, are raised on concrete bars, allowing the impression of souls floating off into the afterlife as in Semiahmoo beliefs.

The Nootka rose is a traditional plant used by the Semiahmoo for a variety of purposes and a native plant traditionally grown along this part of their land. The community had been taking cuttings from these plants and were nurturing over sixty pots on the reserve. The designers proposed the wild pink roses could be planted around the periphery of the cemetery to mask the chain link enclosure and further protect the sacred grounds as its impenetrable thicket and prickly stems grew as high as the fence.
A few would also be planted behind the canoes to create a more beautiful backdrop by hiding the view to the road. In this seaside habitat, the Nootka rose also wafts a beautiful fragrance.

The repatriation of the ancestral remains to the Semiahmoo, an extremely significant and meaningful event, was celebrated in a private ceremony at the cemetery on November 3, 2023.

PECHETStudio

CLIENT: Semiahmoo First Nation • **TEAM:** Bill Pechet with Lőrinc Vass / Alpin Martin / Urban Grove Tree Care and Consulting / Terrane Geotechnical Group • **FABRICATION / CONSTRUCTION:** Marcon Metalfab, Pebble Creek Contracting, Semiahmoo First Nation **MODELS:** Lőrinc Vass • **ARTWORK:** Leonard Wells • **DRAWING:** Lőrinc Vass • **PHOTOS:** Lőrinc Vass • **STATUS:** Built. Restricted access.

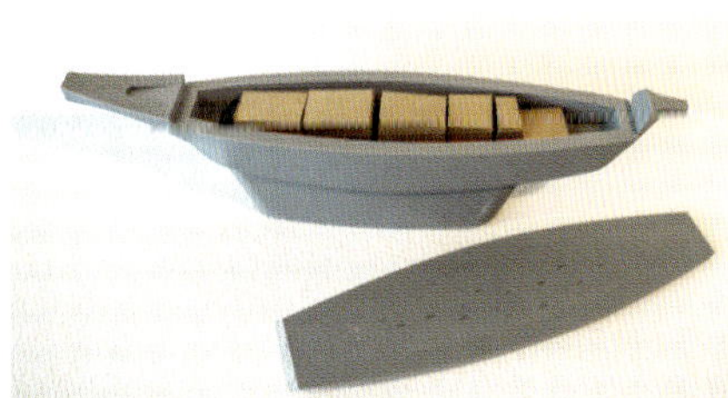

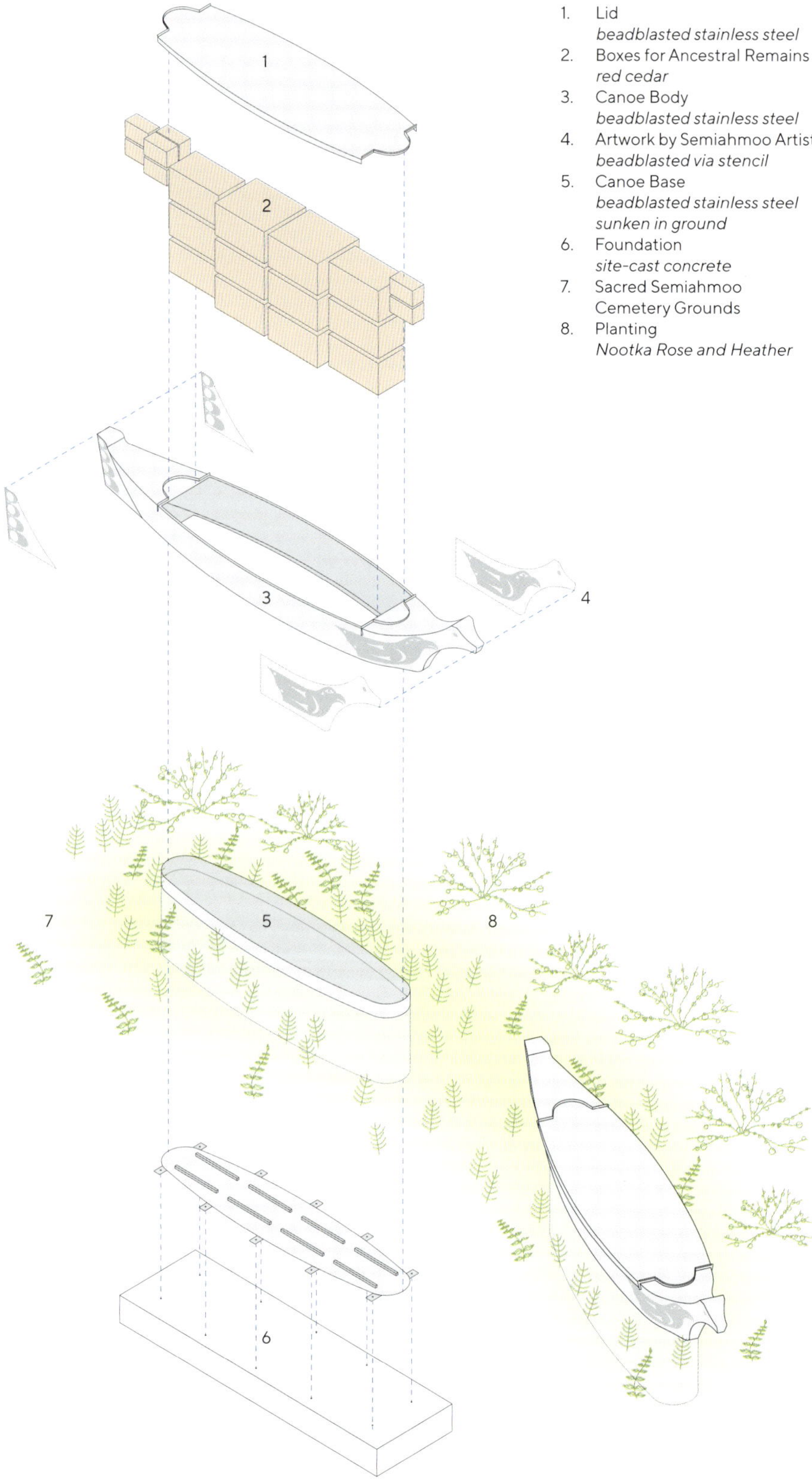

1. Lid
   beadblasted stainless steel
2. Boxes for Ancestral Remains
   red cedar
3. Canoe Body
   beadblasted stainless steel
4. Artwork by Semiahmoo Artist
   beadblasted via stencil
5. Canoe Base
   beadblasted stainless steel
   sunken in ground
6. Foundation
   site-cast concrete
7. Sacred Semiahmoo
   Cemetery Grounds
8. Planting
   Nootka Rose and Heather

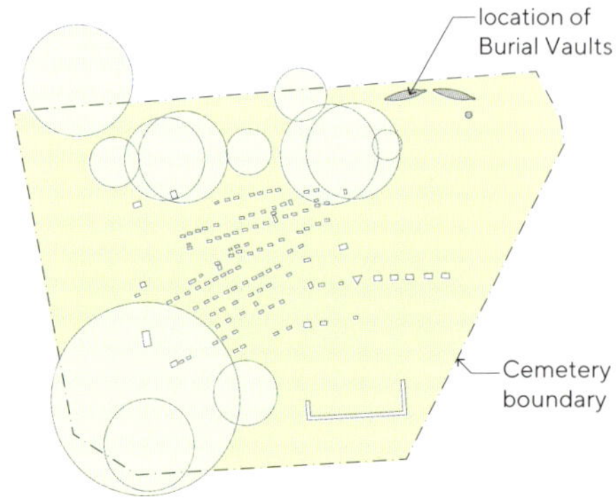

Southlands House

VANCOUVER, BC • 1997

Located in Southlands, an enclave on the southwest edge of Vancouver, in a neighbourhood of large estates, hobby farms, and equestrians, the *Southlands House* draws its inspiration from the vernacular agrarian architecture of the Fraser Valley and the clients' aspirations to live a life of gentility, surrounded by animals and gardens. For nearly thirty years, the family of five has coexisted with a succession of creatures: dogs and cats, chickens and bees, koi and ducks, a rabbit, a groundhog, and in earlier times, a stable of horses. Home as farm is an apt description.

The *Southlands House*, comprised of three discrete buildings—a two-story house, a carport, and a barn with stables and a painting studio and apartment above—hugs the northern edge of the long and narrow site, allowing the house and stables to open onto a generous south-facing lawn. Lush landscaping masks the neighbouring property, and at the low end of the site, a retention pond addresses site drainage while serving as a visual focus for the house.

There are two long, almost parallel promenades that link the three buildings, one for more formal arrivals and departures, one for insiders. Along the north side of the complex, a long driveway and gracious trail leads visitors to the front door; on the south side, an inside-outside path leads from the kitchen service corridor, out under a covered walkway (gloriously covered in vines) and into an open-air workspace, through the stables, and back out to the garden with the most magnificent of willow trees. These two promenades converge in the entry foyer with its garden view, a circular hinge space that sorts the visitors and inhabitants centrifugally into adjacent spaces: the library, the grand open stair to the bedroom level, the steps down into the living and dining rooms with their shared fireplace, and the service corridor leading to the kitchen. "The effect of the convergences of corridors, sliced geometries, views and levels produces an almost cubist dismantling of space that creates delicious ambiguities of inside and outside, up and down, near and far." BP

Compounding the dizzying effect of this spatial complexity, the house upends expectations. From the north, the house appears opaque and designed to maximize privacy, but from the south, it gapes open, a long, continuous curtain wall revealing its interior. The result is a front-back dichotomy of opacity and transparency seen again many years later in *Exeter House*. It would be reasonable to expect a tall, hollow space inside a silo, but in the *Southlands House* the silo is divided in two, between the entry hall below and a child's fantasy bedroom above. The shifted roof structure and planes sheltering the house, if righted, would reform in the image of a traditional barn roof. Exposed wood roof joists have different lengths, zinc siding morphs into roofing, vertical concrete walls are embossed with ghosts of stone paving. Here a wink, there a wink, everywhere a wink wink.

TEAM: Bill Pechet with Andrew Power, Shauna Giles-Smith • **CONSTRUCTION:** Schueck Construction • **PHOTOS:** ALP Studio (p. 158), Martin Tessler (p. 160, p. 161 top, bottom left), Bill Pechet (p. 161 bottom right) • **DRAWINGS:** Lőrinc Vass • **STATUS:** Built, lovingly cared for

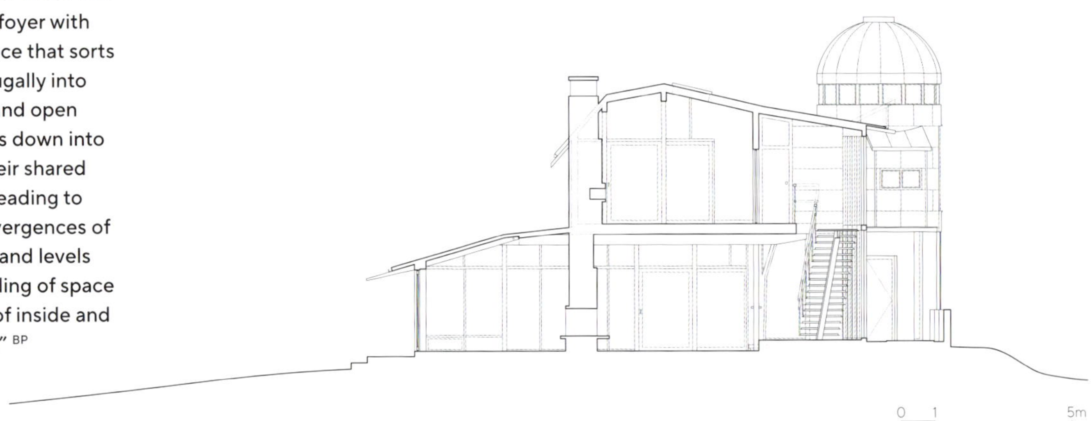

1. Entry
2. Main hallway
3. Study
4. Living Room
5. Dining Room
6. Kitchen
7. Pantry
8. Family Room
9. Laundry
10. Mechanical
11. Master Bedroom
12. Bedroom
13. Terrace
14. Carport
15. Stable
16. Storage
17. Multipurpose Space
18. Office

Souvenirs from the Museum of Sand

UNIVERSITY OF BRITISH COLUMBIA, VANCOUVER, BC • 1986–

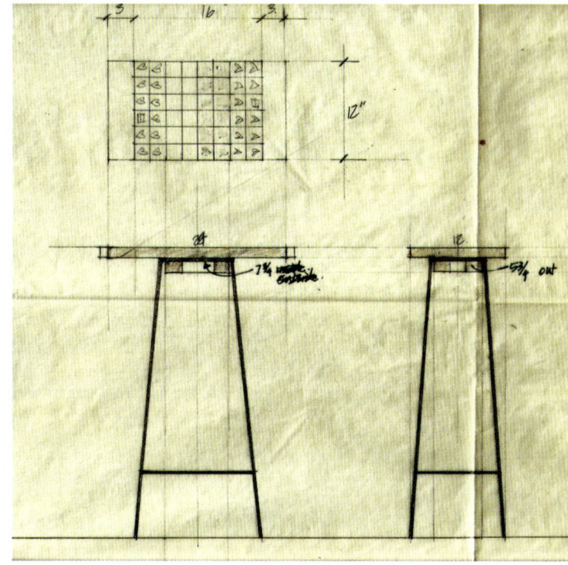

The story of Bill's practice begins on the cusp of his graduation from architecture school in 1986, when he presented his thesis to a design jury before flying the coop. It was on this occasion that he introduced *The Museum of Sand*, its fictional "touristic and therapeutic spaces" sited in the heart of his beloved Tokyo. And like every enterprising museum, this one had a gift shop/souvenir store. *Souvenirs from the Museum of Sand* began with a collection of concrete boxes filled with sand, rakes and other small objects that were presented alongside the drawings of the museum.

Following his graduation, Bill continued to produce the sandboxes in a variety of scales and added quirky new souvenirs to the collection: cast concrete miniature chairs, small platters, a water jug, "wet de la tête." The collection grew to include concrete mountains blanketed with a snowfall of candle wax (*Montagnes Flottantes*) and oversized spoon-planters, votive honey bears in concrete and resin, chessboards, lamps, and small, balcony-sized barbecue entitled *Wibachi*. Bill continues playing in his sandbox to this day.

Souvenirs from the Museum of Sand might just have been another architecture student thesis, albeit a particularly delightful one, if we did not later learn that these charms have served as seeds for four decades of professional practice. *Souvenirs from the Museum of Sand* recalls Marcel Duchamp's *Box in a Valise*, only in reverse. Here, the miniatures came first.

SKETCHES, OBJECTS, PHOTOS: Bill Pechet

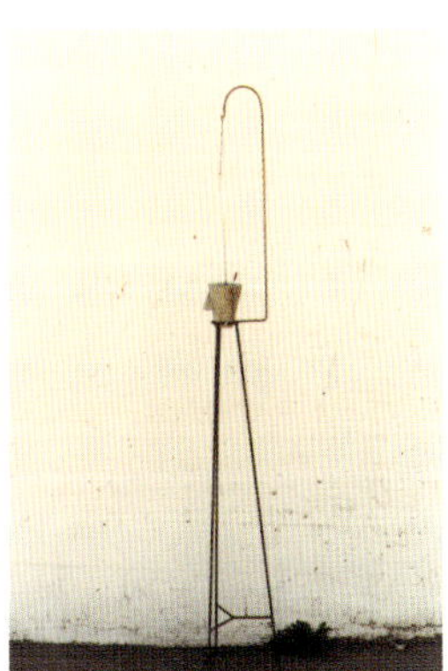

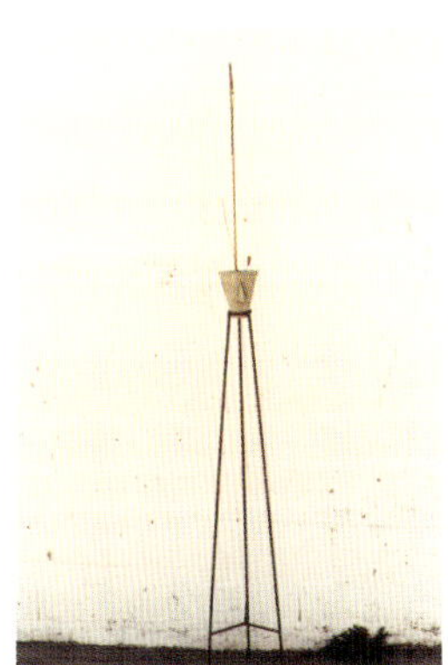

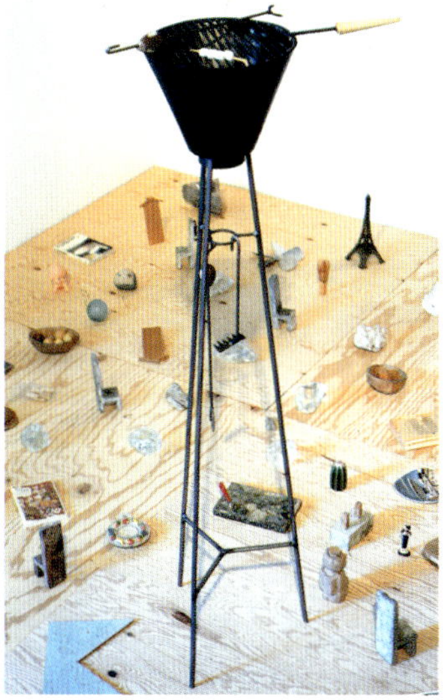

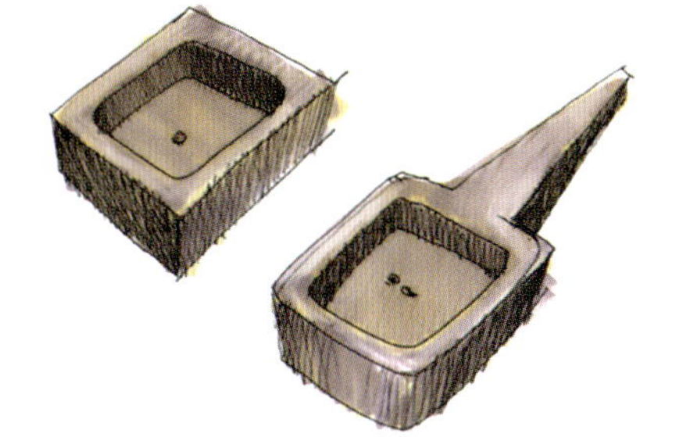

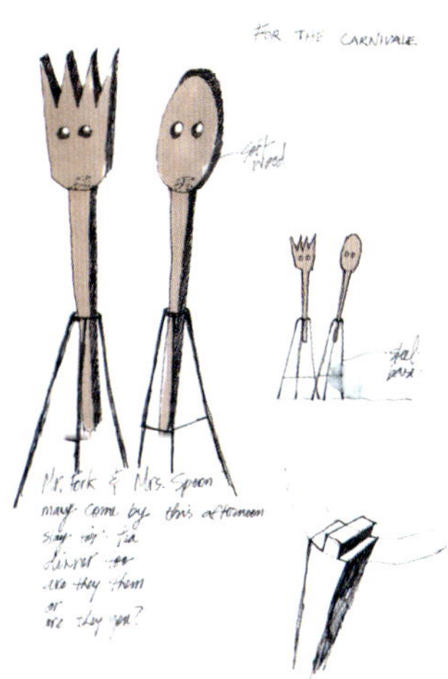
FOR THE CARNIVALE
Mr. Fork & Mrs. Spoon
may come by this afternoon

Spirit Square Renovation

CENTENNIAL SQUARE, VICTORIA, BC • 2009

As with so much of what was built in the 1960s, an era of misguided and poorly designed infrastructure—infamous oversized, wind-swept plazas, parking structures the length of city blocks, waterfront freeways—Centennial Square was by almost any measure a failed public space. Built in the mid-sixties as part of a larger initiative to revitalize the downtown in celebration of the 100th anniversary of the incorporation of the city of Victoria, its ongoing failure to serve as a vibrant and welcoming public space was baked into the original design.

Consider the givens. The ill-shaped plaza is formed by the mismatched buildings surrounding it. Not only does the architecture not provide a strong backdrop associated with more successful squares, the buildings do not spill life generously onto the plaza. The centrally-located Centennial Fountain divides the space, making it challenging to host major events, and the unwelcoming Douglas Street access means passersby, well, just pass on by.

This is the story of one effort to right the wrong. Fifty years after the construction of the plaza, the city of Victoria was awarded a $500,000 CAD grant as part of the BC Spirit Squares Program for the planning, design, and construction of improvements to Centennial Square. Consistent with the Spirit Squares Program guidelines, the city matched the financial contribution of the province, and as required, included a First Nations element in the revitalization plan.

The process kicked off in spring 2008, when the City Council held a design charette. There it was decided that only the western portion of the plaza would be addressed. A "natural" setting should be created for two new works of First Nations art, the old Knot Garden replaced by something more useful, and a stage added between the Knot Garden site and the northeast corner of the McPherson Theatre. New infrastructure to support vendors and markets should also be included. Things moved fast, and by July 2008, the city of Victoria awarded a contract to a team led by DALY Landscape Architecture and Pechet and Robb Art and Architecture.

Sometimes the most significant design moves are invisible, subtractions, or underground infrastructure. The design team removed the ring of lights surrounding the fountain, opening up more space for concert seating with unobstructed views. They removed the knot garden of boxed hedges, making room for additional seating, including new egg-shaped benches with misters. They removed a big box on the rear of the theatre and replaced it with a steel cabinet to store sound equipment, risers and chairs, adding a large canopy to define a stage. Accessibility barriers were also removed making the plaza more welcoming. Electrical upgrades costing 100s of 1000s of dollars included integrating systems into walls and adding accessible plug-ins in the plaza surface for market stalls. Collectively, these moves, many subtractive and invisible, helped activate the square quite successfully, at least during special events.

To address the concerns about the western edge of the plaza, and to meet the Spirit Square mandate for the inclusion of First Nations art, the *Big Dipper,* a giant spoon-as-drinking- fountain, runs off into an "island landscape" which provides the setting for two carved totems by the Songhees artist Clarence "Butch" Dick.

Efforts to further improve the square are ongoing. In 2024, the City of Victoria engaged the design firm DIALOG to continue the repair.

Pechet and Robb Art and Architecture

CLIENT: City of Victoria • TEAM: Bill Pechet with Gabe Daly / DALY Landscape Architecture (project coordinator) / Genivar • FABRICATION: Accent Stainless Steel Manufacturing / Farmer Construction • PHOTOS: Bill Pechet (p. 164), Michael Perlmutter (p. 166–167) • SKETCHES: Bill Pechet • DRAWINGS: Lőrinc Vass • STATUS: Built

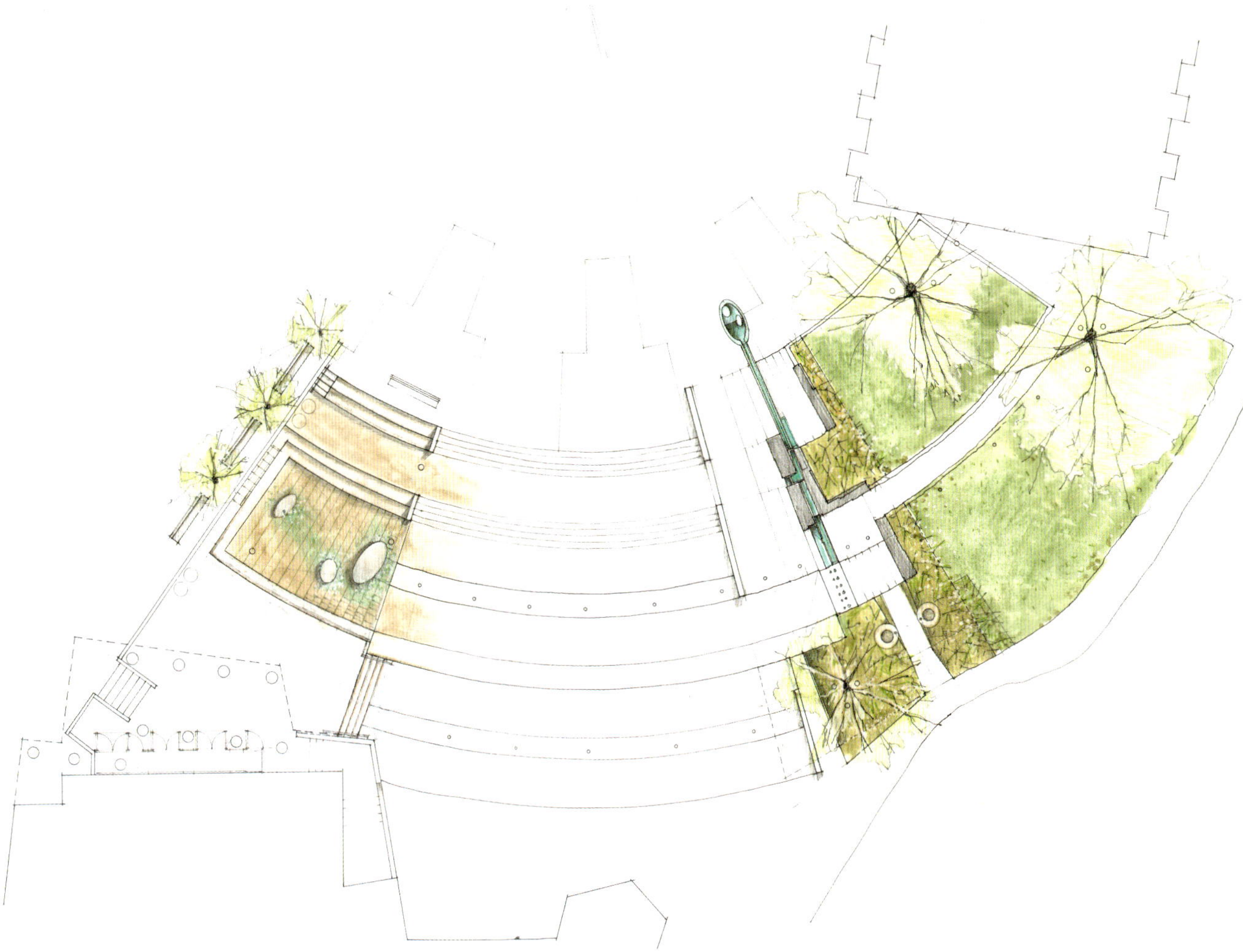

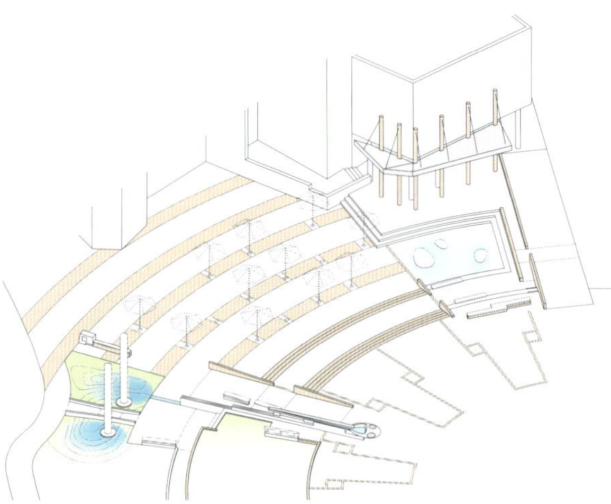

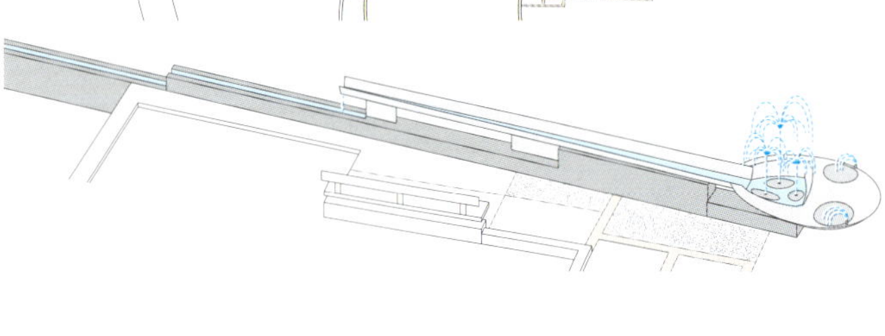

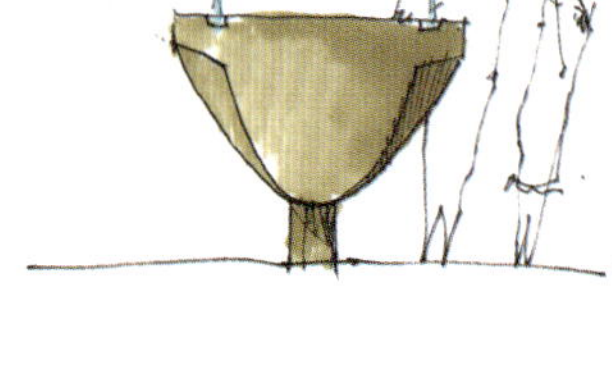

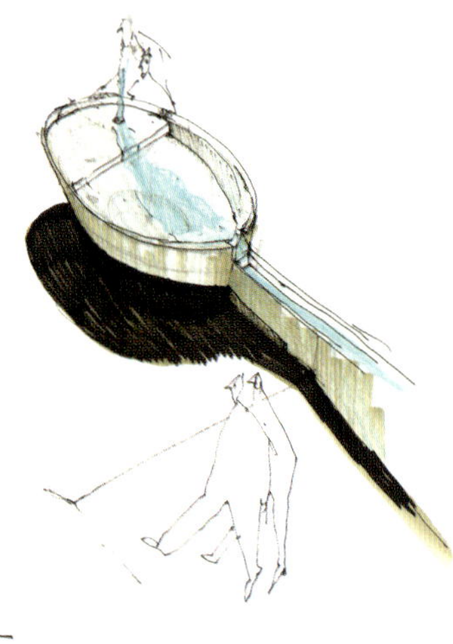

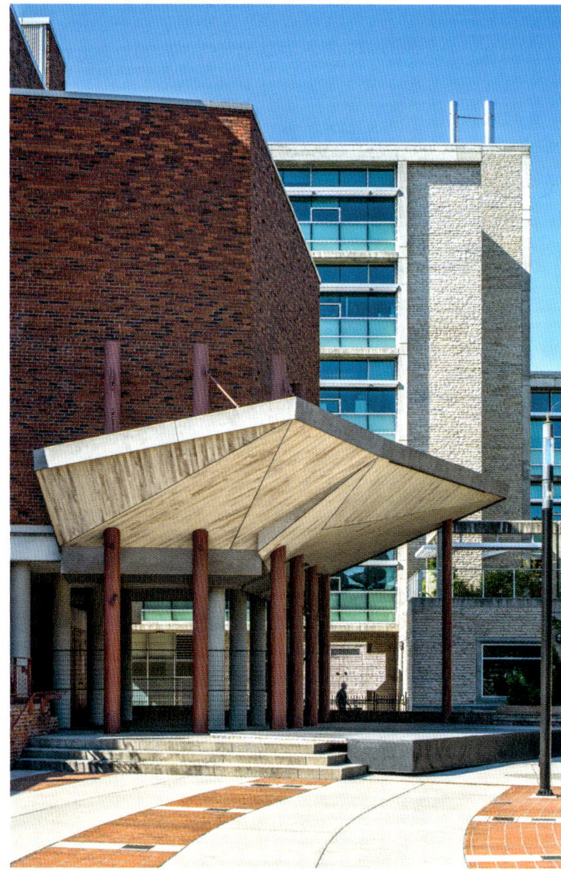

St. Andrew's Park

NORTH VANCOUVER, BC • 2002

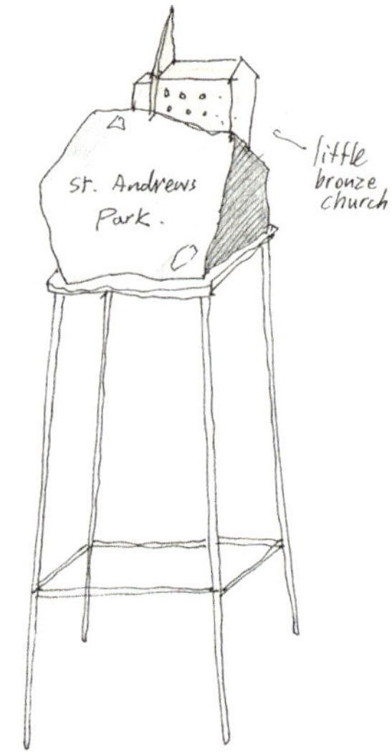

Imagine a charm bracelet at the scale of a public park. The chain, or in the scaled-up version, the path that rings the park, curves this way and that, climbs up and down over gentle topography, changes materials from concrete to wood, bridges here to cross a water channel and widens there to form a plaza. The concept for the circular path was conceptualized in concert with the North Vancouver Parks and Recreation Department which assumed responsibility for drawing up the park plan.

Pechet and Robb introduced the primary charms: integrated public artworks attached to the path. *The Gateway*, the 11th Street entrance, with a welcome sign on one side and on the other, a granite boulder topped with a cast bronze miniature of the park's namesake, St. Andrew, inspired by *The Castle of the Pyrenees* by René Magritte. *The Living Ruin* is an outdoor living room with stone chairs and sofas, tables, and a buffet decorated with stone portraits of family members drawn by local children. *The Rain Garden*, a concrete plaza with fixed boulders—a nod to the rock gardens of Isamu Noguchi—washes with water and wets a sandbox at the push of a button.

Between these three charms, others are added: a circle of boulders for storytelling, a stone chessboard for matches and rematches. From time to time, charms are moved from one location to another, making room for new charms: a playground, a new seating area, who knows what's next? Park-as-charm-bracelet (author's reading) is the perfect concept for a play park that continues to change as generations of children come and grow.

Pechet + Robb Studio /
North Vancouver Parks and Recreation
CLIENT: City of North Vancouver • **TEAM:** Bill Pechet and Stephanie Robb (coordinating partner), with Tina Tajitsu, North Vancouver Parks and Recreation • **FABRICATION:** Burrard Mechanical / JB Newall Memorials • **PHOTOS:** Michael Perlmutter (p. 168, p. 169 top), Bill Pechet (p. 169 bottom) • **SKETCHES:** Bill Pechet • **STATUS:** Built, rearranged

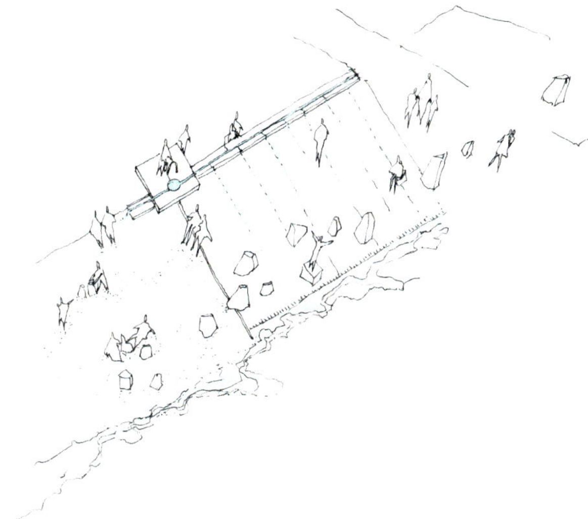

SweaterLodge

VENICE BIENNALE IN ARCHITECTURE, VENICE, ITALY • 2004-06

Every two years, the Venice Biennale of Architecture selects a prominent curator who sets the theme for the international exhibition. For the 2006 event, Ricky Burnett, then director of LSE Cities, chose "Cities, Architecture and Society." Pechet and Robb won the opportunity to represent Canada with their commentary on Vancouver's culture of mass consumption and love of the great outdoors.

Their installation, *SweaterLodge*, an allusion to the textile origins of architecture, featured a bright orange, supersized (by eighteen times), sweater suspended within the Canadian Pavilion in Venice. Made from recycled polar fleece, *de rigueur* for sporty Vancouverites, it was itself made from recycled plastic bottles, "the installation had fun with the notion of recycling as an act of absolution in a film fantasy of a city overrun by plastic water bottles." [BP/SR]

Within the giant sweater, visitors pedalled three side-by-side stationary bicycles to project a film, its speed and direction determined by energy and whims of the "cyclists." The film, shot from the revolving restaurant atop Vancouver's Empire Landmark Hotel (since demolished), depicted a panoramic view of the city with giant sweaters and plastic bottles superimposed, further playing with shifting scales.

To ship the sweater from Vancouver to Venice was no small feat; wasting nothing, the packaging was recycled as seating. *SweaterLodge* offered a welcome respite from the Biennale's exhausting 100,000+ square feet of exhibitions.

Pechet and Robb Art and Architecture

CLIENT: Canada Council for the Arts, Foreign Affairs, Canada • **TEAM:** Bill Pechet and Stephanie Robb with Hanako Amaya, Gabe Daly, Mitch Gelber, Andrew Maclean, Heidi Nesbitt / Chris Macdonald (curator) / Greg Bellerby (curator/commissioner) / Jeremy Gruman (bicycle/projectors) / Miriam Blume (fund-raising) / Elia Kirby (rigging) / Global Mechanic (film production) / Robin Mitchell and Judith Steedman Graphics / Toby's Cycles (bicycle modification) / Blue Imprint Books • **FABRICATION:** Linda Chow (seamstress) and team • **PHOTOS:** Bill Pechet (p. 170, p. 171 bottom left, p. 173 upper, bottom middle, p. 176-177 various), Scott Massey (p. 171 bottom middle, right, 172 top), Allyson Clay (p. 172 bottom left, right, p. 173 bottom left, right), MOV and UBC Outdoors Club (p. 176-177 various) • **SKETCHES:** Bill Pechet

Recycled bottles become polar fleece

Polar fleece becomes sweaters

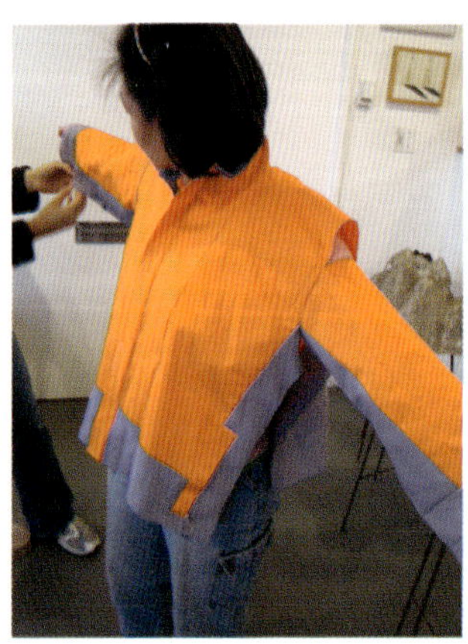

Sweater becomes SWEATERLODGE,
Canada's official representation at
the 2006 Venice Biennale in Architeture
by Pechet and Robb Studio

SWEATERLODGE becomes Pavilion

Pavilion becomes a community legacy

SweaterLodge

SweaterLodge

SweaterLodge

CANADA

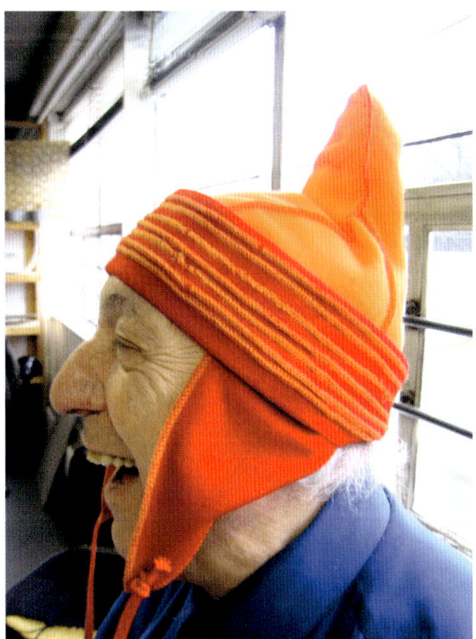

SweaterLodge Unlatched

MUSEUM OF VANCOUVER, VANCOUVER, BC • 2011

SweaterLodge came home from Venice, and five years later, was "unlatched" and installed in a new exhibition at the Museum of Vancouver. In the largest gallery dedicated to the exhibition, the giant sweater was suspended, seemingly levitated, creating a space within the space. Visitors, having removed their shoes, could dwell inside its warm and fuzzy interior.

In a second gallery, the museum goers were invited to take a piece of spare polar fleece home to create something new: a hat, a purse, leg warmers, maybe a human-scaled sweater. By sending photos to the MOV Flicker site, the public's recycled creations became part of the dynamic exhibition.

Upon the closing of *SweaterLodge Unlatched*, the giant orange sweater was gifted to the UBC Outdoor Club. In exchange, their members agreed to recycle the material (for a fourth time!) into outdoor wear.

Pechet and Robb Art and Architecture

CLIENT: Museum of Vancouver • **TEAM:** Bill Pechet and Stephanie Robb with Gabe Daly / Museum of Vancouver / Elia Kirby • **FABRICATION:** Linda Chow (seamstress) and team, Museum of Vancouver staff • **PHOTOS:** Gabe Daly (p. 175), Bill Pechet, Chad Manley, Chris Macdonald, Mac Perry, UBC Outdoors Club, Museum of Vancouver (p. 176-177) • **RENDERING:** James Eidse (p. 174 top) • **GRAPHIC:** Courtesy of Museum of Vancouver (p. 174 bottom) • **STATUS:** Gifted to UBC Outdoor Club for recycling into outdoor wear

SweaterLodge
XL

SweaterLodge
unlatched

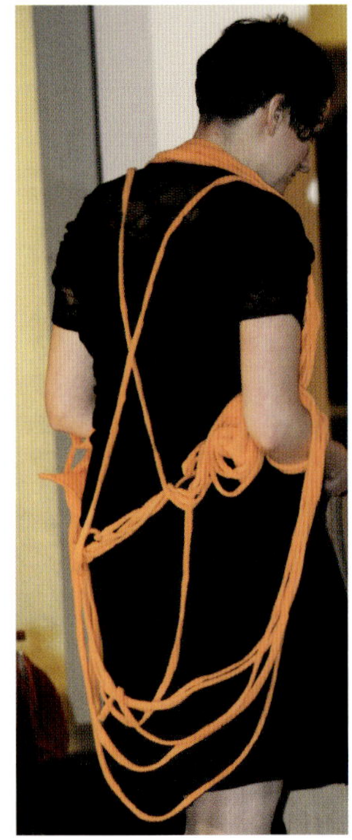

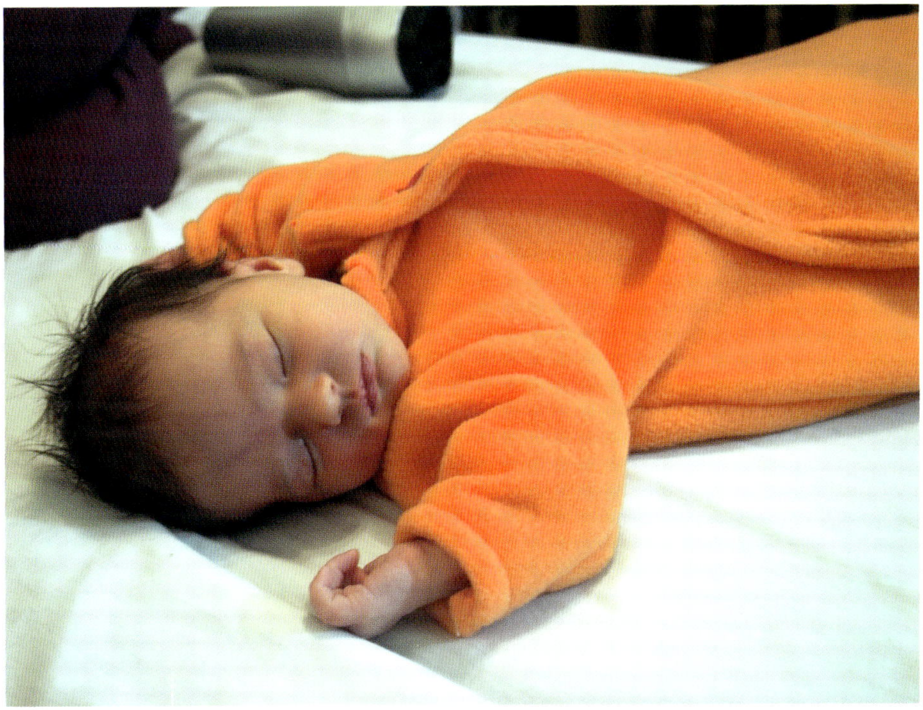

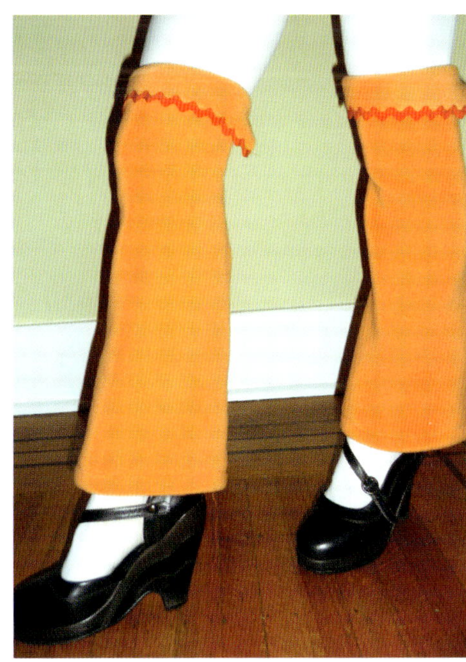

Thanks

From Leslie

For your early and enduring trust, thank you, Bill. When I first came to you with the idea of writing a monograph on your life and work, you probably did not realize just how many hours you would have to spend scouring your archives, discussing your projects, reviewing texts, but obviously, without your generosity, this book would never have been possible. I am so grateful to have had the experience of working with one so adept at collaboration. You taught me a great deal, without even trying. It is my hope that this volume is worthy of all that is you.

To all those who helped create such a rich picture of this artist, designer, teacher, playmate, colleague, friend, goofball, and so much more, thank you for your invaluable contributions. To Thena Jean-hee Tak, thank you for revealing what makes Bill such a beloved teacher. Your conversation about his pedagogy is revelatory and will no doubt inspire his colleagues and students, past and present. To Lőrinc Vass, I so appreciate you delicately mining Bill's personal sense of otherness in a way no one else could, revealing how his sexual identity and time spent in Japan have shaped him and his work. And, Lőrinc, for your contribution of so many meticulous drawings and for your eagle eyes, a million thanks. To Robin Laurence, only a firsthand account would do, so thank you for allowing us to republish your excellent review of *finding sudoku*. And Bill Richardson, I am extremely grateful you agreed to write Bill's life story. Your biography is the dessert that anchors this 88-course feast. Thank you also for your gentle and thorough copyediting. I pinch myself daily. Truly.

To Michael Perlmutter, longtime friend and collaborator, thank you for foregoing precious summer weeks in Sweden to come and capture Bill's work in Canada. Your elegant photographs provide a critical backbone for the book. And to Greg Girard, thank you dear friend for photographing Bill's public works as they live in the night.

To the photographers who allowed me to publish their images gratis—Jonathan Carter, Kristopher Grunert, Gerry Kopelow, Maurice Li, Martin Tessler—your appreciation of Bill shines through in your generosity. To others who find their photos within, thank you for helping me tell this story: Allyson Clay, Emma Chorostecki, Gabe Daly, Jose Gonzales, Jingyi (Xiamen) Works of Art Co. Ltd., Scott Massey, Chris Macdonald, Chad Manley, Museum of Vancouver, Rachel Oye, Mac Perry, and UBC Outdoors Club.

Thank you to all who came out to adorn the sites: Shirley Barnett, Ben Bialek, Daniella Givon, Josh Kalef and daughter Marilyn, Gayle Nesbit, Bernard Pinsky, Stepen Quigley, Bill Richardson, Jay Starnino, Lőrinc Vass and Sharyn Yuen. To Mira Locher and Kuma Murakami, actors par excellence, who also generously hosted us in Winnipeg, thank you for your many contributions and enduring friendship. Finally, Sydney and Jerome Robert Kalef, your warm hospitality in Victoria made this project all the more fun!

Early and generous funding from the Canada Council for the Arts was the requisite foundation for all that was to come. The book was further honoured with a grant from the Yosef Wosk Publication Fund at Vancouver Heritage Foundation, garnered in recognition of Bill's deep engagement with the history of his sites. On the occasion of my tenth collaboration with you, Pablo Mandel, many thanks for once again assembling a wide variety of material into a handsome volume. It is, as always, a pleasure collaborating with you. To Gordon Goff of ORO Editions, a debt of thanks for your continuing trust and an essential publication subvention. And to Jake Anderson of ORO, thank you again for your precision vision. You help keep things tidy.

Finally, to Ross Caddell, your ongoing engagement with this project has been so meaningful to me. I am grateful to you for your bright insights and your unwavering love and support.

From Bill

The multi-year process of working on this book has floated, and, at times, submerged me into an ocean of introspection. For you, the reader, I wish to illuminate that, save for a few autonomous art projects, everything else presented herein was born through a process of collaboration, and yes, *negotiation* with others. For me, the *idea* was easy to come by, whereas the building of a team to bring the work into fruition was the *deepest* part of the experience. I don't think that many people realize that a project, while often presented as *genius brainus emergis*, does not happen without the gift of other people providing lifeboats (I know, let's lose the water analogy) of support. A few deserve to be distinguished with special thanks.

Dear Gabe Daly, Nicolas Osenton, and Lőrinc Vass, you brought immeasurable layers of support to the works within which you are cited. Without your tremendous intelligence, creativity, organizational prowess, and technical skills, these projects would not have become what they became. I will forever be in your debt and want the reader to understand that, although my name is officially associated with the works, they are also yours.

Dear Margot Long, Peter Kreuk, and Joe Daly, all of you Landscape Architects! Your inclusion of my studio to collaborate on projects of significant scale and import gave me the chance to illuminate and hallucinate in public.

Dear Stephnie Robb, we shared decades of ideas and experiences together. And while we went our separate ways eventually, I traverse mountains of memories of our collective adventures. And for what it's worth, you have the best sense of humour a partner could have ever wanted. Heart Emoji. And let's never speak of that noodle thing that happened with Marlene, or that giggle-fest trip to Campbell River with Fernando.

William J. Richardson, for feeding me risotto and books-full of beautiful images to illustrate.

Finally, galaxies of thanks to Leslie Van Duzer for initiating this book; devoting years of research and listening. You miraculously found a way to synthesize all the ups and downs of almost forty years of experiments into this precious compendium. Arigato, Toda Raba, Gracias, Ankyouthay, and all the other ways to say it in the universe.

Listed below, are those who came along with me in this journey and I am deeply grateful to all of them:

Hanako Amaya
Jill Anholt
Rochelle Bacigalupo
Bryan Beca
Pearl Bellesen
Eric Boelling
Chris Boldt
Nancy Bryant
Andrew Carnochan
Linda Chow
Judith Cowan
Clinton Cuddington
Gabe Daly
Mark Dennis
Sandra Eng
Michael Fugeta
Charles Gardner
Thomas Gaudin
Mitch Gelber
Shauna Gillies-Smith
José González
Jeff Gravenstein
Jeremy Gruman
Zahra Henderson-Peal
Matt Hessey
Scotty Keck
Cameron Koroluk
Margarita Krivolutskaya
Hiroshi Kurosaka
Herman Kao
Maureen Kwong
Cindy Lee
Ian Lowrie
Samuel McFaul
Esteban Matheus
Andrew Mclean
Matt McLeod
Heidi Nesbitt
Nicolas Osenton
Vincent Perron
Andrew Power
Stephanie Robb
Warren Scheske
Jeremy Schipper
Steve Suchy
Tina Tajitsu
Shizuka Sasaki
Jay Gower-Taylor
Brian Wakelin
Ricky Ting
Lőrinc Vass
Sara Zonouzi

The Three-Cornered Hat

CHAPEL ARTS + SCOTIABANK DANCE CENTRE, VANCOUVER, BC • 2015

The Three-Cornered Hat was a collaboration between the choreographer, the dancers and the designer from the start. The project began with a simple question: What happens if you distribute hundreds of spiral-bound sketchbooks to dancers and set them free on a runway in a retired funeral parlour? Early sketches showed great potential. The possibilities were endless: books as lampshades, books as headphones, books as masks, stacked books as platform shoes or opened books as seats on a Ferris wheel. With pages aflutter, a book could appear as a bird in flight.

During the performance, the dancers balanced open books on their wobbling heads and strapped piles of books to their feet. Single books became stepping stones in a perpetual chain crossing an imaginary pond. A tall stack of books became a wall, a shorter stack, a stool. A book formed a container for a story told, became a flying fish on the end of a line, served as a pair of binoculars with pages rolled. You can't do all that with a tablet!

CHOREOGRAPHY: Jennifer Mascall, Mascall Dance • **SKETCHES:** Bill Pechet

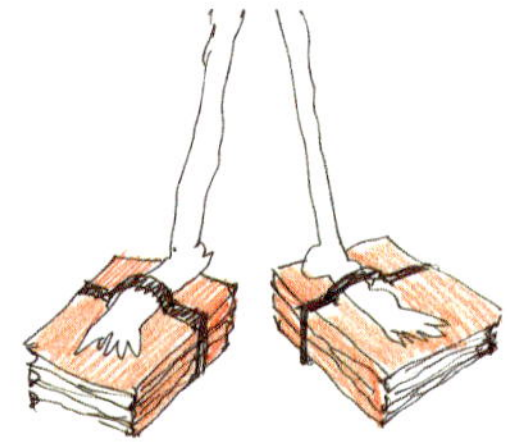

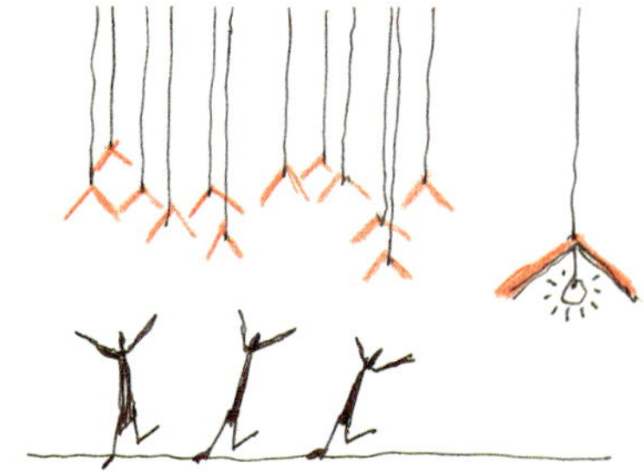

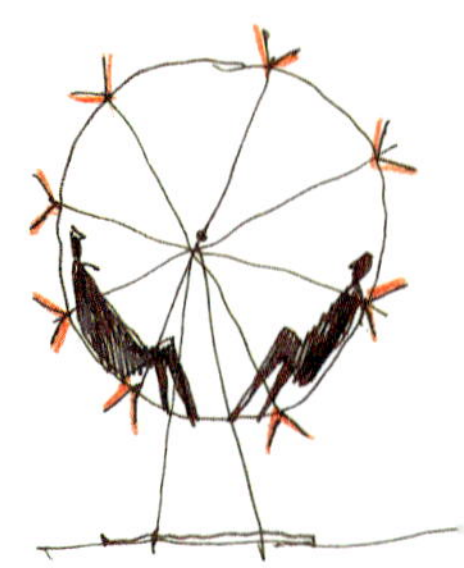

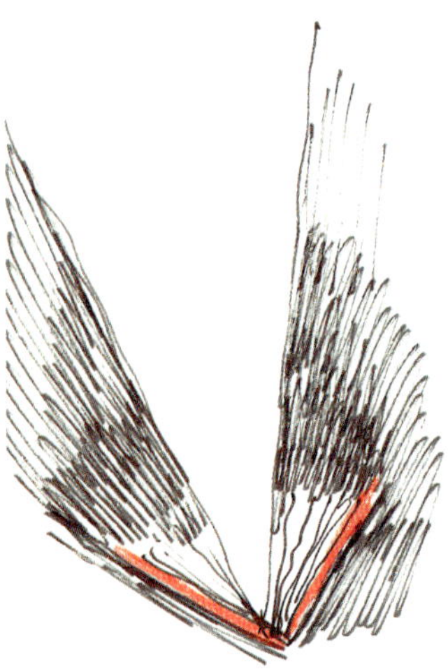

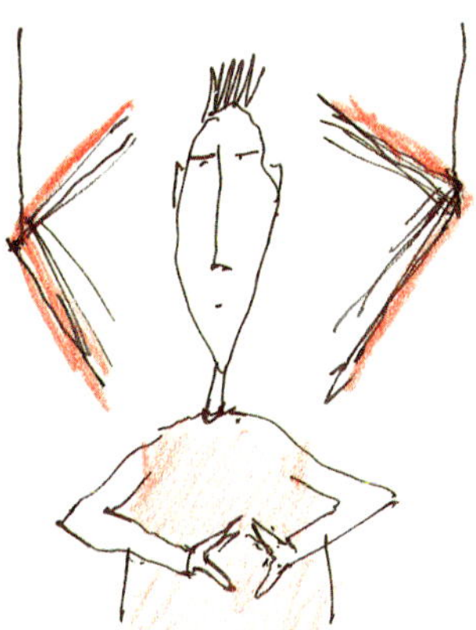

The Athinian Restaurant

DENMAN STREET, VANCOUVER, BC • 1991

The Athinian was the first of many collaborations between Bill Pechet and Stephanie Robb. The ambition for the design of the restaurant interior was to evoke the atmosphere of the Mediterranean while avoiding tired cliches commonly found in Greek restaurants. You know, photo murals of villages draped with fishing nets, faux stone walls, rows of emptied ouzo bottles filled with water, plaster busts of Socrates.

The team took on the challenge of a design-build project with the innocence and enthusiasm of recent college graduates. Working within a tight budget, they established surfaces of plywood and MDF for counters and "rescued" tiles for the floor. Wooden sticks appeared here and there as inexpensive, decorative elements on the ceiling, as a delicate partition, as an armature for ledges covered with trinkets. Around the top of the fireplace chimney, wooden cooking spoons created a "sculptural crown." [BP] The colourful globes, reconfigured from found fixtures, are an early instance of Bill's ongoing interest in lighting.

CLIENT: Marlene Nikolopoulous • **TEAM:** Bill Pechet and Stephanie Robb • **FABRICATION:** Granville Island Woodworks • **PHOTOS:** Martin Tessler • **STATUS:** Dismantled

The Brutal Telling

MASCALL DANCE, VANCOUVER, USA, EUROPE • 1997

One year after the production of *In the Course of Sleeping,* the storybook ballet set in a fairy airport with translucent suitcases in a giant walnut luggage cart, the set of *The Brutal Telling* puts luggage centerstage again.

The Brutal Telling is the story of the life of Emily Carr, the British Columbian painter and writer. The empty, dimly lit stage was brought to life with live music and vocals (in the words of Emily Carr) by Veda Hille and large sepia toned projections from her life. A steel cart referencing Carr's mobile home, or the "Elephant" as she called it, was stacked high with wooden suitcases of diminishing size that transformed into furniture, lights and other props, including a folding table with shoe trees for feet. The steel structure is a luggage cart when full, but when emptied, a climbable prop. The cart also served double duty as a way to transport the set on its long journey to international performances.

Pechet + Robb Studio
CHOREOGRAPHY: Jennifer Mascall, Mascall Dance • TEAM: Bill Pechet and Stephanie Robb / Veda Hille • FABRICATION: Mascall Dance • PHOTOS: Bill Pechet (lower left), courtesy of Mascall Dance (right)

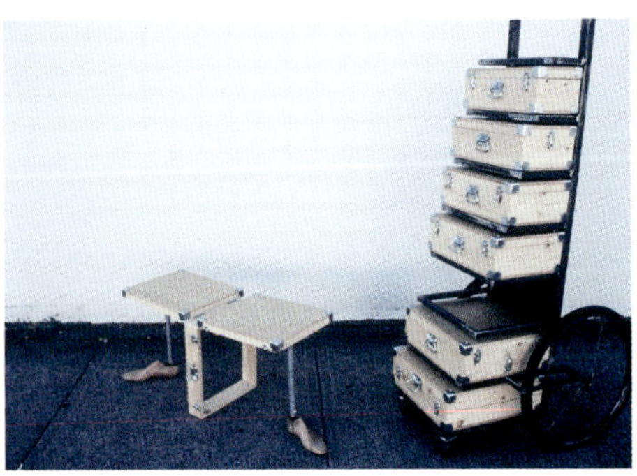

The Encyclopediette

1994

What does one do with their old encyclopedias, those shelf-eating volumes that were once upon a time indispensable for grade school reports and settling family arguments?

The Encyclopediette offers one solution: a miniature encyclopedia remix. Pages from discarded encyclopedias were recycled and bound into 500 small books. Arranged alphabetically, like any good encyclopedia, fragments of information and images were randomly juxtaposed, creating fresh, liberating relationships.

"Ignorance is a treasure of infinite price that most men squander, when they should cherish its least fragments. ... Leaf through a dictionary or try to make one, and you will find that every word covers and masks a well so bottomless that the questions you toss into it arouse no more than an echo." - Paul Valéry, *Sea Shells* (original 1937, translation by Ralph Manheim 1998)

FABRICATION: Bill Pechet • PHOTOS: Bill Pechet • STATUS: Distributed

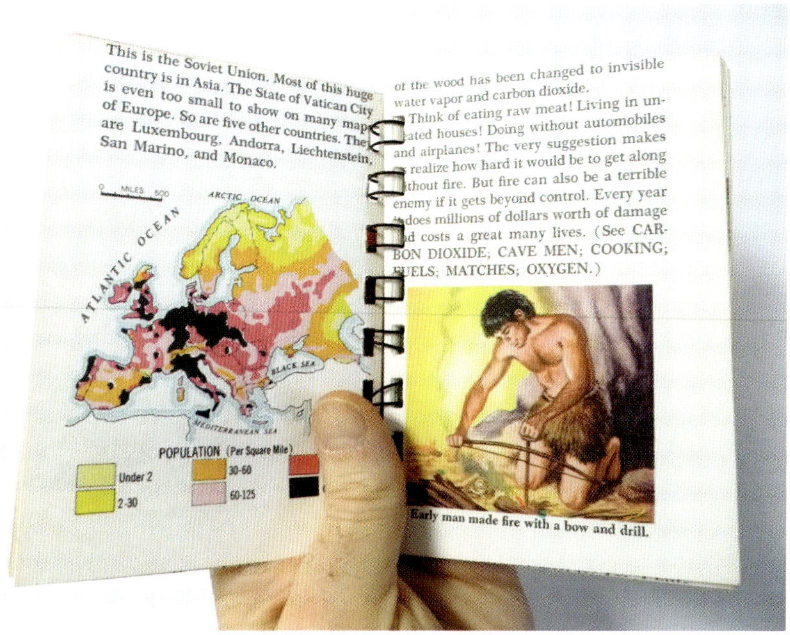

The Gathering

UNIVERCITY, BURNABY, BC • 2013

Already in 1963, when Arthur Erickson and Geoff Massey designed the new campus for Simon Fraser University, they envisioned an adjoining residential community atop Burnaby Mountain. More than thirty years later, SFU and the city of Burnaby signed an agreement to allow the development of a new neighbourhood, later named UniverCity. By 1996, all the approvals needed were in place to move forward with the construction of a dense, mixed-use community that could eventually house as many as 10,000 residents.

Given that Simon Fraser University's Art Collection holds over 5,800 public works, many of them installed in academic buildings and public spaces on the Burnaby and Vancouver campuses, it is not surprising that their public art program, launched with the installation of two mosaics by Gordon Smith in 1965, would be extended from the academic campus to the new, adjacent residential neighbourhood.

ARTWalk, UniverCity's public art program, installed its first work in 2007, *Yellow Fence* by artist Erica Stocking. As new buildings were erected, new artworks were commissioned. In 2013, *The Gathering* was proposed in a public right of way, just off University High Street between the then new Nest and Lift Buildings.

The Gathering was similar in intent but different in design from an earlier work, *GRANtable* (1998). In both cases, a long table was proposed, but this time as a "cross-cultural symbol of collectivity," offering the possibility for group dinners, parties, game nights, and deliberations. Distinct from the table in Vancouver in program and also material, this 23′-long table was designed as a composite structure, not poured concrete, but rather a tabletop of basalt strips and full-length benches of fir, both supported on a steel structure, both locally sourced.

Three native dogwood trees would grow up through the table, marking the change of seasons: sprouting flowers in the spring, turning autumnal colours in the fall, and bearing red berries in the winter. The trees suggest both humans and nature should be invited.

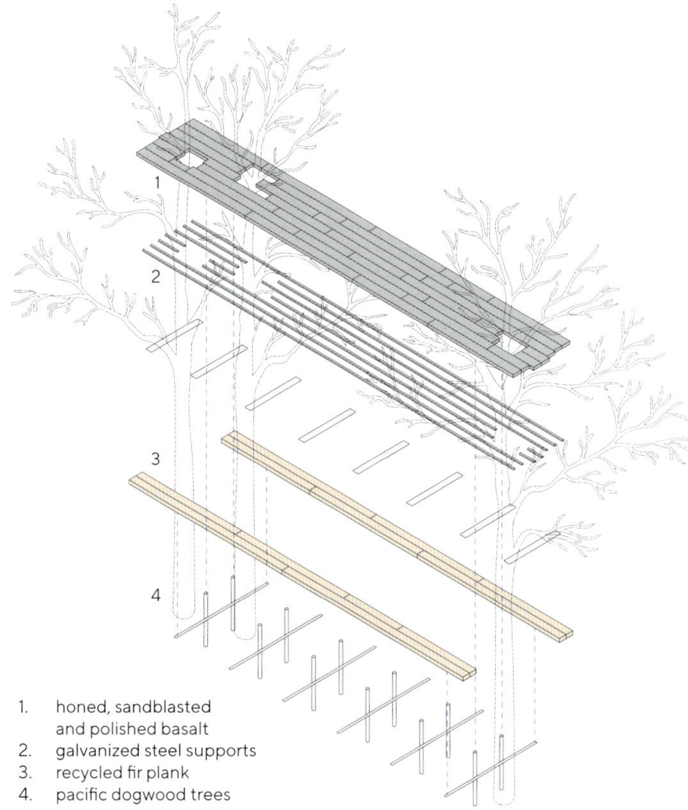

PECHETStudio
CLIENT: UniverCity • **TEAM:** Bill Pechet with Gabe Daly, Esteban Matheus • **DRAWING:** Gabe Daly, updated by Lőrinc Vass • **MODEL:** Esteban Matheus • **PHOTO:** Gabe Daly • **STATUS:** Competition finalist

The Goldberg

BALLET BC, VANCOUVER, BC • 1998

Two years after collaborating with John Alleyne on *In the Course of Sleeping*, Alleyne again approached Bill to design the scenery and props for *The Goldberg*, a ballet performed to J. S. Bach's *Goldberg Variations*. Since 1938 when William Dollar, a George Balanchine protégé and innovative American dancer and choreographer, premiered *Air and Variations* with the Caravan Ballet Company, there have been at a minimum twenty choreographed versions of J. S. Bach's *Goldberg Variations* performed around the world. In her book, *Johann Sebastian Bach's Goldberg Variations Reimagined*, author Erinn E. Knyt dedicates an entire chapter to the history of dances set to the piece. Unlike some previous versions accompanied by a live pianist, the Ballet BC full-length production was set to Glenn Gould's recording.

The dancers and the set played with gravity and its absence, with earthbound people and levitated props, with scale shifts playing tricks. The set for the Vancouver production included some familiar and some prescient objects. There were the familiar chairs—plywood versions on rolling carts, chairs defying gravity, profiles of chairs cut in polycarbonate projected on the scrim—and mobiles with translucent planets, telescopes small and 30′ net sieves on long sticks, Little Dippers foreshadowing the *Big Dipper*.

CHOREOGRAPHY: John Alleyne • **TEAM:** Bill Pechet • **FABRICATION:** Main Sheet Metal / Ballet Caravan • **SKETCHES:** Bill Pechet

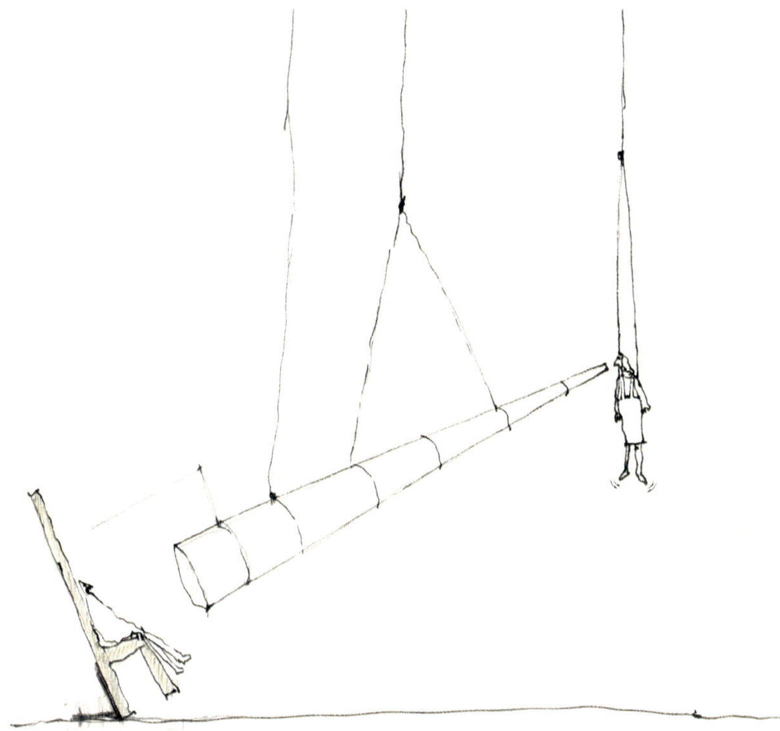

The Lady from Kent: A Story for Girls, Boys and Bees Dressed Up as Fleas

2018

Each section of the narrative is a funny poem that traces the story of two characters, a lady and her sidekick, a raccoon, as they traverse through decades of fantastical adventures together. To bring gestalt to the illustrations, I kept their outfits consistent throughout, with a limited colour palette for every scenario. Is she delusional or not? One of the final drawings shows the raccoon tenderly helping (or preventing) the lady from putting both her feet in one shoe (this wasn't in the poem). This was something I directly observed when a friend of mine, who had early onset dementia, tried to do the same thing. I wanted to hint that the stories we tell ourselves and others float in a sea of ambiguity. — Bill Pechet

STORY: Barbara Nichol • **ILLUSTRATIONS:** Bill Pechet • **BOOK DESIGN AND TYPOGRAPHY:** Zab Design • **PUBLISHER:** Pedlar Press

The Last Great Naïve Acts of the 20th c.

FIREHALL ARTS CENTRE, VANCOUVER, BC • 1993

The context for this dance was a gallery filled with portable and fragile objects at the turn of the twentieth to the twenty-first century. Here, a vessel shaped like a head that crumbled when hugged; there, a skirted velvet chair that emitted music when strummed. For the choreographer, a hundred cast concrete shoes appeared as shifting piles of rubble with echoes of the Holocaust. Throughout the performance, a translucent parchment screen was rolled around the stage to act as both space divider and projection surface. In addition to creating the props, Bill designed the layered and distended costumes that were slowly stripped away to reveal the dancers' vulnerabilities and essential natures.

CHOREOGRAPHY: Chick Snipper, Danstabat • TEAM: Bill Pechet • PHOTOS: Bill Pechet • SKETCHES: Bill Pechet

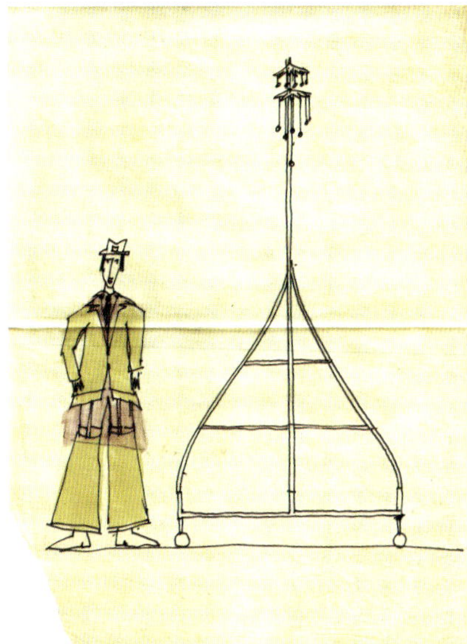

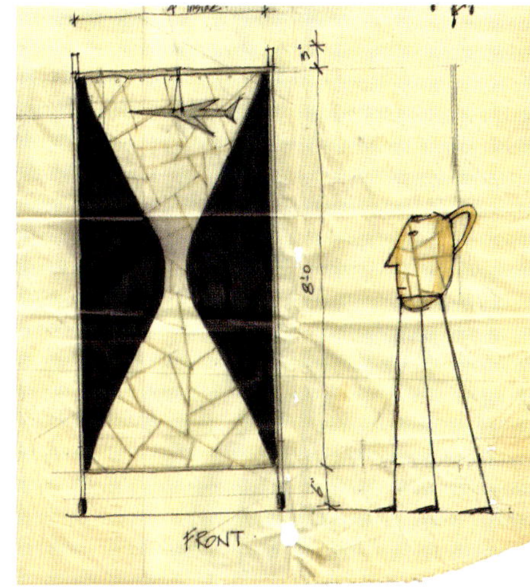

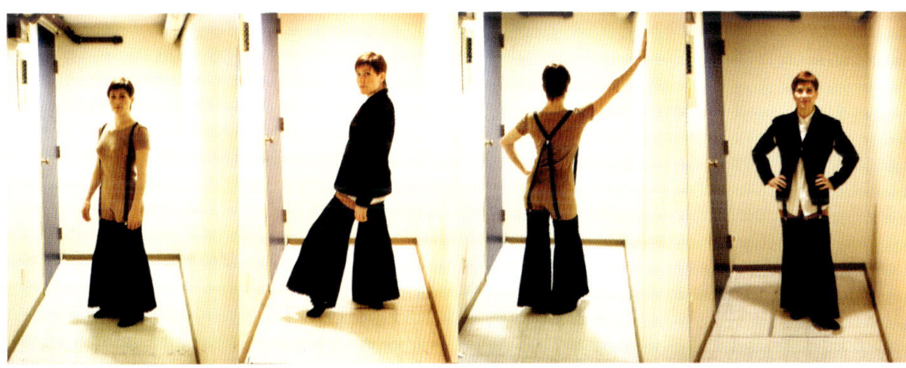

The Woods I and II

CAPILANO VIEW CEMETERY, WEST VANCOUVER • 1993–2013

Upon entering Capilano View Cemetery, an isolated stand of conifers enclosed by a stone wall beckons from across a great expanse of lawn. As one approaches the enclave, the entrance is marked by a weighty stone sign, *The Woods*, itself a kind of tombstone from honed verde primavera granite. An informal arrival space bridges the two distinct phases of this twenty-year project: *Woods I* (1993), a tangle of labyrinthine ruins, and *Woods II* (2013), orderly rows of contemporary columbaria.

Woods I harkens back to the eighteenth and nineteenth centuries when artificial ruins and the aestheticizing of entropy were popular in English romantic landscapes. Thomas Whately described the emotive power of ruins in *Observations on Modern Gardening, and Laying out Pleasure-grounds, Parks, Farms, Ridings etc.* (1770), "At the sight of ruins, thoughts of variability, destruction and devastation naturally come to mind, and behind them stretches a long string of other images, slightly tinged with melancholy, which the ruins inspire."

Multiple pathways into *Woods I* offer a meander without prescription. One is easily lost in time and space, wandering past and lingering in the many open-air rooms for columbaria and contemplation. As one's attention drifts from one detail, an ornate grate, to another, an upside-down ziggurat pool, any sense of the whole is elusive. The experience is episodic, suspenseful, bewitching, with a bittersweetness all its own.

Small openings in the stone walls provide periodic views to a fallen, old-growth tree at the centre of the ruins, mother of the second growth offspring that encircle the site. What is not readily apparent is the central role played by this ancestor and the hole in the sky created by her absence. Her death opened an aperture to the heavens and brought light to earth.

"...Think of the refuge,
The point of sky,
The certain castle,
The certain presence..."
— John Glassco, "A Point of Sky," inscribed on the entry sign

It is difficult to reconcile the deeply moving experience of inhabiting *Woods I* with its crisp plan of walls radiating from this centre. It is remarkable how such a clear formal logic and a limited material palette—stone walls, water pools and concrete roofs like "funerary beds, little houses or the tilting gestures of birds' wings"—can create such complexity. [BP] Rich variation within the repetition of elements is given by the context in any given moment, when pools fill after a rainfall and reflect the sky, when the moss thickens and obscures, when the sun finds its way through an oculus and a memento fills a niche. The experience is fleeting, never twice the same. "The ideas ruins evoke in me are grand. Everything comes to nothing, everything perishes, everything passes, only the world remains, only time endures." (Denis Diderot, 1767)

Over the years, private columbaria have been commissioned within *Woods I*, adding new interment space to the 500 initial niches. *8-Person Columbaria* (1994), a tower of concrete and granite, stands as a sentry on the perimeter, a feng shui expert having ensured the measurements and orientation were appropriate. *Family Columbaria Courtyard* (2003) for three generations evokes Carlos Scarpa's Brion-Vega Cemetery with its suspended granite gate, floating concrete roofs, bronze font, and basalt benches. The *2-Person Columbaria* (2004), designed for a couple with many stories, is etched with their own words.

The adjacent *Woods II* (2013) offers an entirely different experience. Without the protection of the tree canopy, the space is open to the sky, sun-soaked, standing in strong contrast to the dark and moody *Woods I*. Here, rows of columbaria with niches clad with honed Virginia Mist granite for the accommodation of 768 urns, are sheltered by floating concrete roofs that recall forms in the ruins. Defying gravity, the sloped roofs guide our view up towards the sky.

While the rows of prefabricated columbaria lack the intimacy and patina of the first phase, the stone walls surrounding *Woods II* are embedded with charming and unexpected details: a framed opening, small brass memorial plaques, a rear window overlooking the rest of the cemetery. A large stainless steel urn, an ancient form fabricated from a contemporary material, bridges the two halves of *The Woods* and provides access to an underground ossuary for the interment of 300 remains. Positioned near the common entry, the sheltered urn serves as a "central figure" during funeral services.

PECHETStudio

CLIENT: District of West Vancouver • **TEAM:** Bill Pechet with Pearl Bellesen, Gabe Daly / JM Engineering / CY Loh Associates / Wilco Civil • **CONSTRUCTION:** District of West Vancouver / Brunato Rock Work / Jay Gower-Taylor / Island Columbaria / Sunset Memorial and Stone / Epic Welding and Fabrication / Merletti Construction / Lang Structural Engineering/ AMS Industries / O-Bronze / James Koester • **PHOTOS:** Michael Perlmutter • **DRAWING:** Lőrinc Vass • **STATUS:** Built

THE WOODS

11
12
13
8
9
10

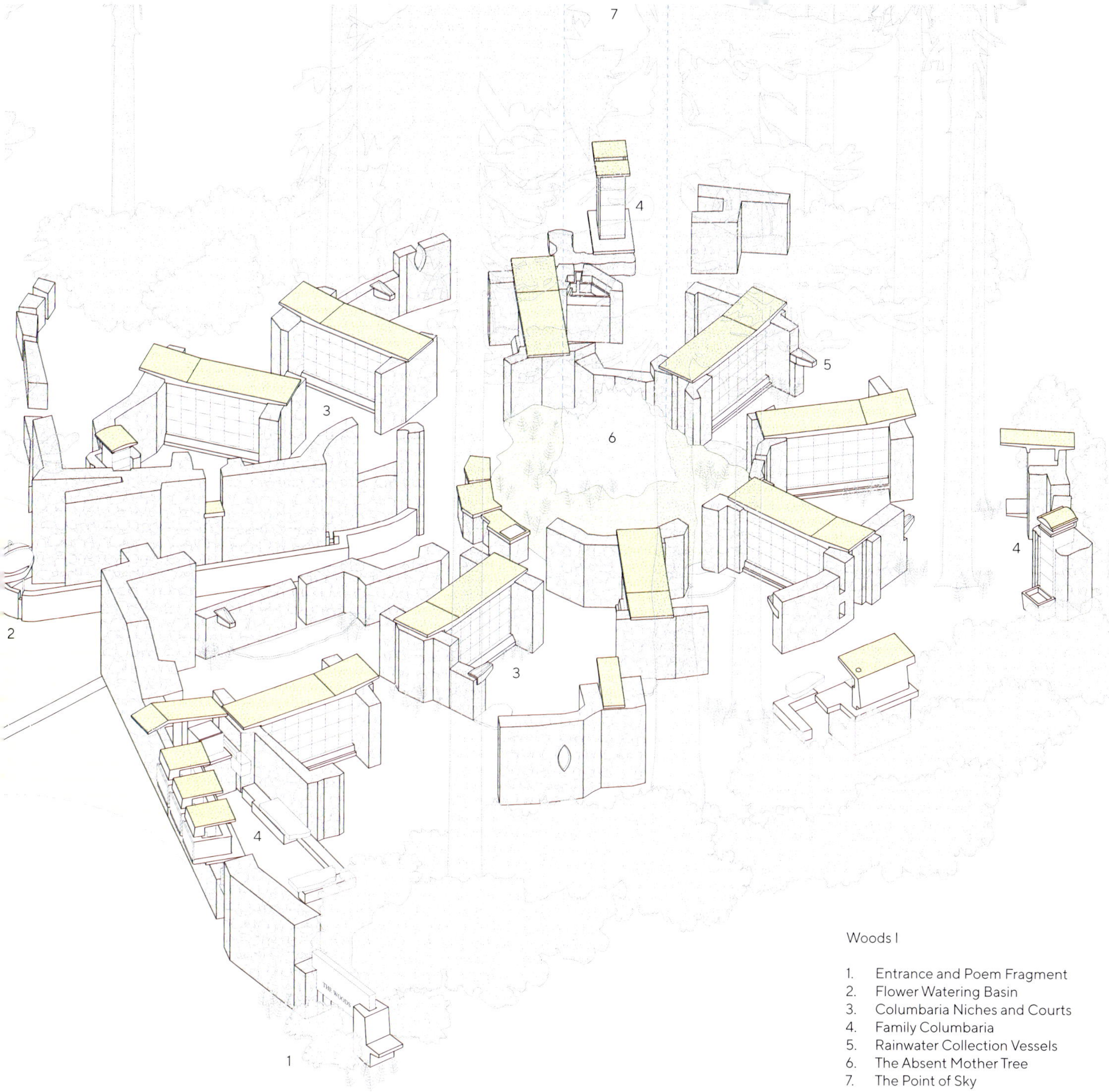

Woods I

1. Entrance and Poem Fragment
2. Flower Watering Basin
3. Columbaria Niches and Courts
4. Family Columbaria
5. Rainwater Collection Vessels
6. The Absent Mother Tree
7. The Point of Sky

Woods II

8. Altar
9. Ash Vessel and Subterranean Ossuary
10. Memorial Wall
11. Columbaria Niches
12. Sunset Window
13. Future Niche Walls

YEH

ANDREW VEE SAY SHAW
NELLIE LING CHIEN SUI SHAW

Velvet Bent

WEST PENDER PLACE, VANCOUVER, BC • 2009

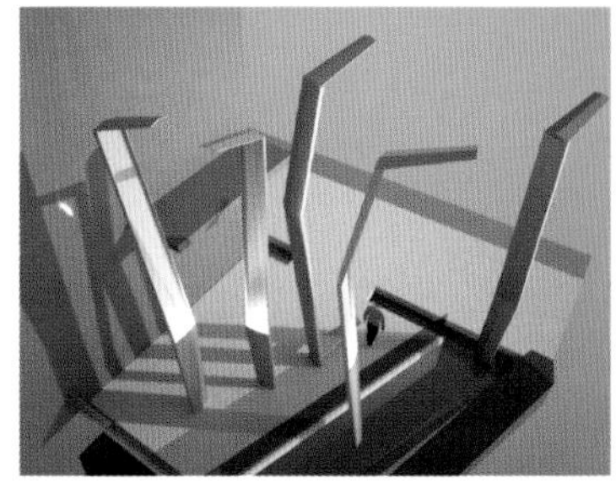

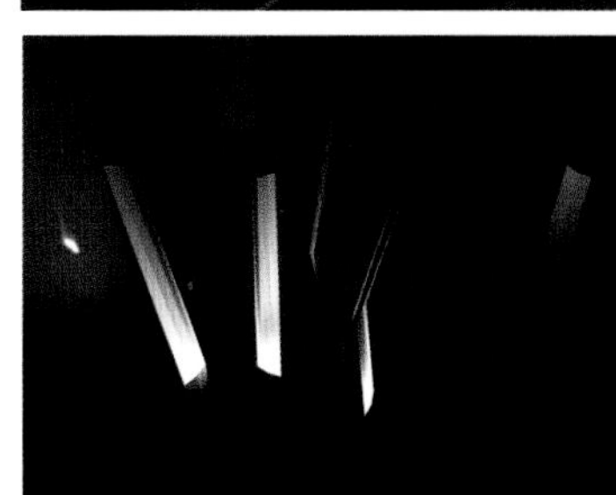

Drawing on extensive experience designing sets and working with lighting designers, Pechet and Robb answered the call for a light artwork, for a new residential development, West Pender Place. Located at the western entry to downtown in the pedestrian-friendly neighbourhood of Coal Harbour, *Velvet Bent* aimed to prominently mark the site in the larger urban context while enhancing the pedestrian's experience.

Velvet Bent (otherwise known as *Agrostis canina*, a common grass species) resembles giant blades of grass, or alternately, flocking birds or even bendy straws, if your imagination allows. Three lights would be clustered at the east entrance at Broughton and five at the west entry court at Nicola, some growing out of water and plantings, some from the paving. While there were actually only two different lighting fixtures, the varying height, position, and orientation of the eight "blades" created the impression of sprays of grasses. The fixtures would be coated with a luxurious, bead-blasted, stainless-steel finish that would bounce light, sunlight during the day and LED lighting changing hue and intensity at night. Sprays of water would bead up on their surface like on blades of grass after a rainfall.

Pechet + Robb Studio

CLIENT: Reliance Holdings • TEAM: Bill Pechet and Stephanie Robb with Bryan Beca, Gabe Daly / Eos Lightmedia • SKETCH: Bill Pechet • RENDERINGS: Bryan Beça • STATUS: Competition finalist, unbuilt

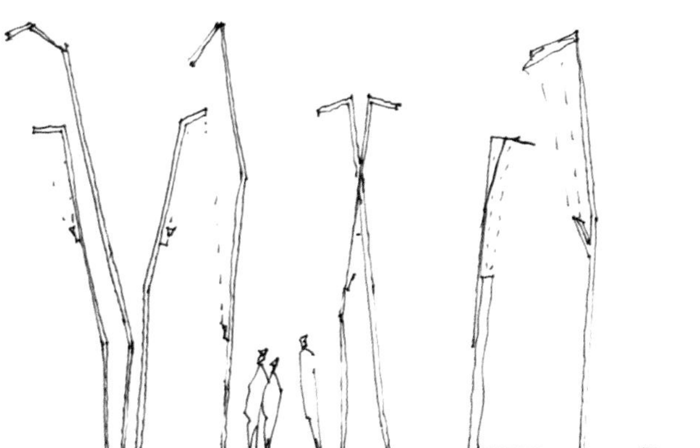

Viskers on Kittens

Bill Pechet

An Ode to Fabricators

To be sung to the tune of "My Favorite Things"
from The Sound of Music

Welders and elders and clip-boarded holders
Molders and toolers with substantial shoulders
Bringers of wisdom with piping and hose
Thank you so much from my heads to my toes

Blasters and casters and honers and etchers
Wrenchers and hammers and lots of you betchers
Alchemy really is your me-oh-my
You did the work so that I could say I

When the lights start
And the kids run
And the ribbon's cut
I simply remember your transforming benders
Your treating of seams with a host of new menders
Your questions of "what?" when I showed you some renders
Your belted suspenders and waterjet enders
Your sanders and banders and question of genders
Your dreamers and schemers and gloss-covered fenders
Your wise-cracking comments when we went for tenders
Your look of "come on" when I quoted Wim Wenders

You made it all beeeeeeee alright!

With love and thanks from BP

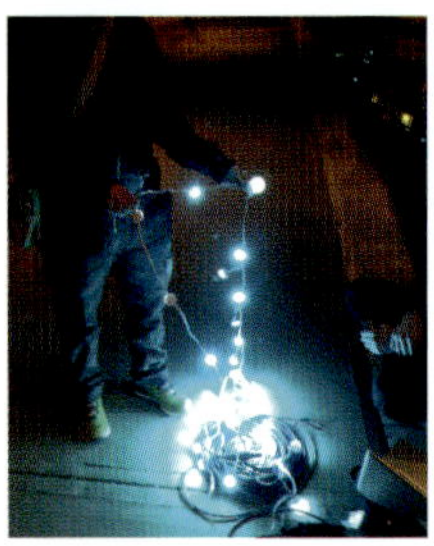

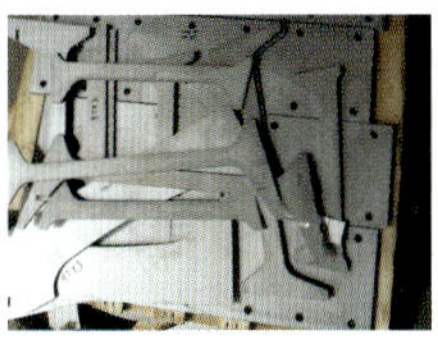
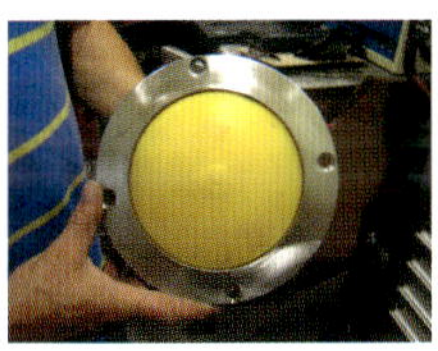

BLENZ
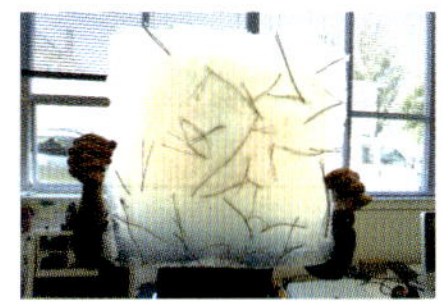

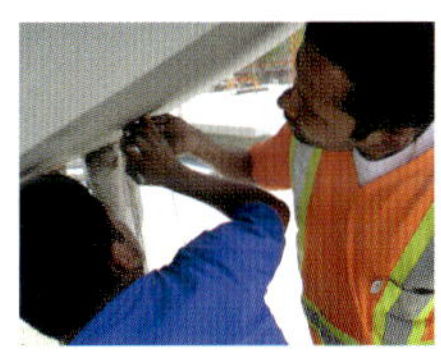
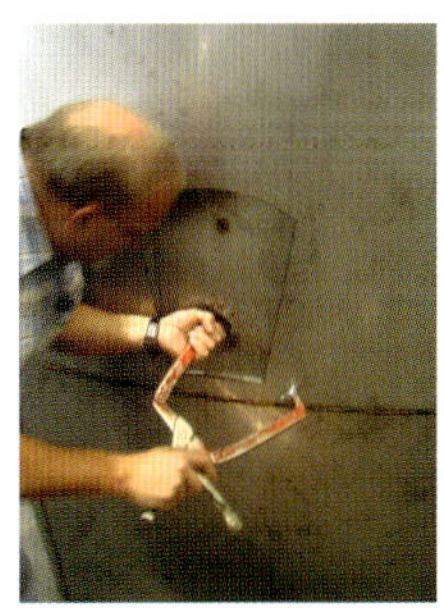

LANDFILL

Victory Square Memorial Lights

VICTORY SQUARE, VANCOUVER, BC • 2002

What is now Victory Square was once Government Square, the historic centre and "hinge pin" of Vancouver, where the western edge of the Old Granville Townsite Survey met later CPR surveys, creating the irregular, trapezoidal site. It was a hive of activity in its day and the site of Vancouver's first provincial courthouse, an anchor in the city's financial and legal district. When Francis Rattenbury's new courthouse was built on Georgia Street (1911-13), the original structure on Government Square was demolished. A muster station for enlisting soldiers during WWI replaced the vanquished courthouse, and in 1924, the Victory Square Cenotaph assumed the spot.

Victory Square had good bones from the start. It was surrounded by late Victorian and Edwardian buildings, had views to the North Shore, was built with fine stone walls and was lined with specimen maples, reputedly the oldest trees in the city. But by the late 1980s, the area was in decline. When Woodward's department store closed in 1993, the City Council initiated a Concept Plan, presenting it to the public in 1997. In 2005, an updated plan for the revitalization of the derelict square, the Victory Square Policy Plan, supported by a local community group, The Friends of Victory Square, was completed. This advocacy group included members from Veterans Affairs Canada, and as Bill had previously worked with the organization on a smaller veterans' memorial in West Vancouver, Pechet and Robb were commissioned to illuminate the cenotaph environs and to propose a larger strategy for illuminating the buildings surrounding the square.

Victory Square Memorial Lighting was part of the overall park refurbishment. The new light fixtures serve as memorials themselves by co-opting the helmet form to honour the fallen. The design stems from a military tradition known as "Battlefield Cross" where a helmet perched atop a rifle symbolizes the final farewell to a fallen soldier. The same symbol can be found carved into the base on the cenotaph. The soldier lights stand "at attention" in the parade circle, lighting the amphitheatre steps and a path around the cenotaph. The rest of the lights stand "at ease," positioned informally on the grassy slope.

Pechet and Robb Art and Architecture
CLIENT: Vancouver Park Board, Veterans Affairs Canada • TEAM: Bill Pechet and Stephanie Robb (project coordinator) / Michael Graham • FABRICATION: Rebelle Architectural Lighting • PHOTOS: Bill Pechet (p. 200 top) / Michael Perlmutter (p. 200 bottom, p. 201) • STATUS: Built

Wake

VANCOUVER EAST CULTURAL CENTRE,
VANCOUVER, BC • 1999

Wake was an interdisciplinary theatre and dance production by Battery Opera. The sets and costumes in this eulogy turned the world upside down, at times placing the audience on the ceiling. An upended couch periodically transformed into a coffin, and a refrigerator, as needed.

The costumes were created from remnants of men's formal wear, the cummerbunds silkscreened with wood grain, a humourous material transformation referencing coffins and other furniture. Lambswool bows and patches allowed the dancers to transform into animals. In this production, everything had two or three meanings.

Pechet + Robb Studio
CHOREOGRAPHY: Lee Su-Feh and David McIntosh, Battery Opera • **TEAM:** Bill Pechet and Stephanie Robb • **FABRICATION:** Battery Opera • **SKETCHES, PHOTOS:** Bill Pechet

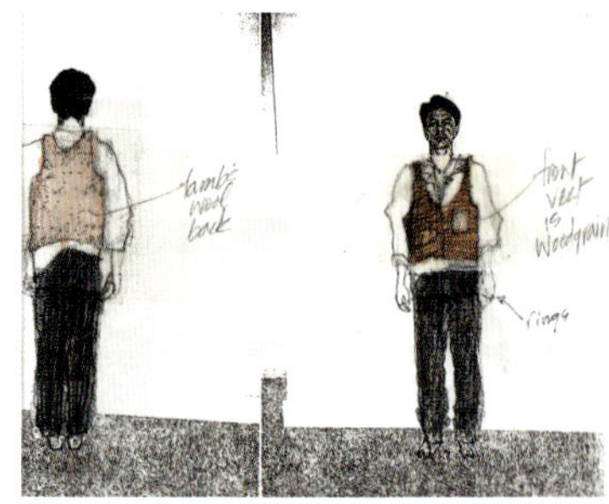

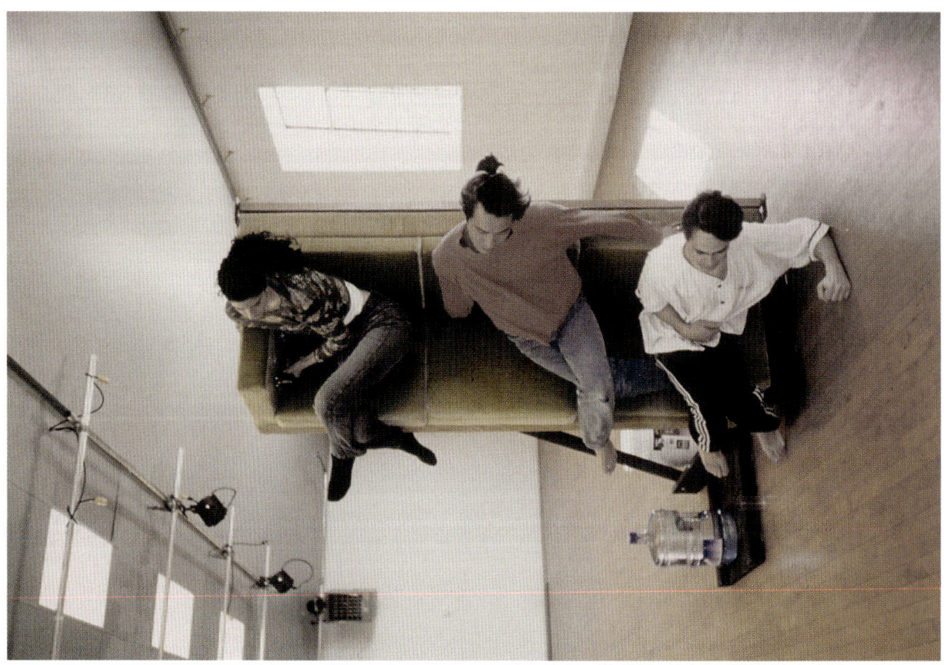

Wassup?

In conversation with Thena Jean-hee Tak

TT: For many, it is difficult to imagine the School of Architecture and Landscape Architecture without your presence. You've spanned many generations over thirty years and are now a keeper of the school's institutional memory. Can you share how you first began teaching and what those initial experiences were like?

BP: Yes, sometimes when I ascend the terrazzo steps of Lasserre, I imagine that I am inhabiting the Roger Penrose drawing of an endless stair in a continuous cycle of up and down that traverses time. It's not a creepy feeling; it's more like a haptic internalization of thirty years of teaching and many more before that as a student. I am the stairs and they are me.

My first teaching experiences were being invited to graduate project committees and then being asked to join Bud Wood to co-teach his last studio. Bud structured it as a series of short two-week exercises that condensed "everything I ever wanted to teach" into one semester. It was a carnival of weird exercises, which included pumpkin carving at Halloween. He asked the students to find a space inside the pumpkins and then everyone brought them to his house for a party. I was about six years out of school at that time, disenchanted by a series of not-so-happy office jobs, and I found the experience of working with Bud and the students, for lack of a better word, "natural." The energies flowed easily and I felt like I had found a kind of home.

I was also in awe of some of the senior professors at the time and marveled at their intelligence and commitment. Patricia Patkau held a deity status in my thirty-something mind. I could listen to Pat's and Chris Macdonald's reviews forever, doing butterflies in their insights and discourse. And then there was George Wagner, the smartest and funniest guy ever. His superpower of reading people and spaces was astounding. Our trips to Italy, Japan, China, Brazil, and even Metrotown remain highlights of my life. There was so much giggling, but with *meaning.* And then there are subsequent generations of marvelous people who still serve as teachers for me, like you Thena.

That's really generous of you to say Bill, especially since I hold your teaching in such high regard. As educators and designers, we tend to pull inspiration from many dimensions: places, people, memories, senses, etc. I'm curious what kinds of experiences have influenced your ways of thinking and being both in your teaching and beyond?

Gosh, such a big question. How much time do you have? Well, I guess it goes to my childhood of living in a family where design, art, music, and physicality all mattered, not in an academic sense, but as a living practice. It seemed natural to talk about the house going up across the street, or the new tallest building being built downtown, or my sister's dance performances, my dad's hockey career, my Mom's lipstick and her amazing cooking that always looked beautiful too, my brother's band, our house being renovated in a radical way ("OMG they are turning their garage into a living room"), art lessons, tons of arguments about this and that, continuous discourse with our expanded family about the state of the world. We were a postwar, difficult, engaged, passionate Jewish family swimming in the wake of WWII, confronting everything from marital discord to the cultural revolutions of the Sixties. The house was never stable, and while that may not be the ideal condition for a pudgy little fellow, it did teach me that multiple viewpoints are a given in life, that people don't always see eye to eye. But when they do, when they find that the sense of connectedness that makes two or more people feel as one, it is a beautiful thing. This helped me with students and professionally. Our large family was split amongst those in the prairies of Canada and New York so there was always an awareness that lives in different places *are* different. The expanded family dinners were forty people yelling at each other while eating amazing food.

In terms of other influences, I had a photography teacher in art school, Freddy Douglas, who was part of the conceptual photography movement fomenting on the West Coast, and I was his studio assistant. He had a way of looking at you and responding to one's ideas as if they were important and really mattered. He'd raise his eyebrows and say "no way!" or "jeez, you're right" or "I've never thought of it that way before." He made me feel heard, as if my juvenile ideas were worth discussing, which is so important for a student.

Another point is that humour had a way of connecting everyone. My family were laughers, all my best friends are too. And my syllabi are too, if one looks deeply enough. I think that humour is the best tonic for all the crappy crap that's out there. It is the apogee of intellect.

I love this notion of humour as the apogee of intellect and I think it's palpable in your teaching. Many of your studios have a sense of levity. What do you feel is the role of play in your teaching and learning? What does it mean to teach through both rigour and playfulness?

Honestly, I don't know if even half of the students get some of the goofy puns and visual shenanigans that pepper my syllabi. For example, right now I am teaching a cemetery studio called *The Planes Between,* which is a syntactic scramble of their first-year exercise, one that everyone hates, then loves, called *Between the Planes.* No one has even mentioned it, so either they are just humoring me or they aren't getting it. My public art project titles are mostly puns and word-play: *Ponte Bong, Peeping Tom Thomson, "roger that," Closer Than, emptyful,* ... but no one ever asks me about the titles. I feel so lonely (not).

But back to your question, I feel that in all the drudgery of their super-tough and serious coursework, they need a playground to play in that opens up their imagination, and yes, *enjoyment* of the creative process. It works for some but not for others, depending on wavelength. It's not that the actual subject matter of the studios is funny. It's just that irony, criticality, satire, they are all useful tools in repositioning one's place relative to the problem. The best form of investigation is humour because it is initially disarming. Then, like a cheetah, I go in for the kill.

I often got into trouble in art and architecture school for producing work that was a bit on the cheeky side, poking fun at tropes and genres. But honestly, behind the veneer of comedy, the work was founded in at least what I thought were truths and foibles of culture. My mom subscribed to *The New Yorker* my whole life, and as a kid, I couldn't wait to look at all the cartoons because: a) they were visually fabulous, and b) they taught me about positionality.

We all know the world is crappy, unjust, complicated, unresolved, but having the ability to stand slightly outside of all the maudlin is so liberating. I could never date anyone who isn't funny. It's the sexiest thing.

Very much so, and as you're suggesting, humour increasingly holds such an important space in the context of our present-day conditions. Given this shift over generational time, how might you say your teaching has evolved? Have there been changes in what you teach or how your teaching methods have developed?

I think this needs to be answered first from the point of view of the students. In some regards, they have stayed the same, being wonderfully idealistic, which is the best kind of naivety. I have to admit that this naivety is still alive in me. So, I try to reinforce their good intentions while slowly introducing the tools they'll need to argue their points as they confront the future.

Students of today are encumbered with so many worries related to the challenges of climate change, social justice, economic struggles, that there is generally more anxiety free-floating around the studio that definitely gets in the way of them just getting down to creative invention. They have more reasons *not* to try something than they have to try, so I attempt to create a safe space for them to simply start making.

I've had similar observations, as I think many educators have. Can you speak more about this? What is it about that initial making that is so important? Do you feel it emancipates encumbered minds?

When you start the creative part of your brain moving, I think there is a kind of dopamine moment where the act of taking hold of a problem or condition and *working* with it produces a frisson condition, a "brain tingle," that releases you from the bounds of reality, jettisoning you into a magic world of possibilities. The initial making opens up ways of speaking with the students that allow new kinds of conversations about the design problem that they initiate. I think their way of listening in that conversation is much deeper than if we just give them answers because they generated it. From there you can start them on the road of a universe of relationships. Sometimes students are afraid of being highly judged, and in those cases I just say: "try a sketch, it's only a drawing, and we'll find seeds of moving forward through that."

Related to this is the extreme distraction of social media and the general attention-span issues that come as a result. I find that their current mode of conducting research often just interrogates the first three hits of a Google search and so the depth of some of their ideas is unsurprisingly superficial. Of course, this is not all students, but increasingly more students. It's part of the challenge of living in our world today, so I find that I am always trying to get them to think at least one level deeper. I don't know if this is just because I am an old guy who has lived a bit of life, but because "I see dead people," I am seeing things in a more complex way than they are. Does this sound paternalistic? I try to muster patience to open up, through discussion, other ways of tackling a situation so they can see a bit further than their current line of sight. I use levity, again, to disarm and catalyze their imaginations; again, like a cheetah, I am scanning the field for the potentiality of each student's ideas and then striking when the time is right. Predation with the best of intentions.

Knowing when to "strike" and understanding when a student is ready to enter a space of experimentation and risk requires real patience and insight. What are your thoughts on this space within an architectural education and what does it mean for you to have this responsibility?

Yupsters, you are right, that space is critically important. Each student has their own method of generating ideas that is filtered through their own life experiences, sense of ethics, cultural frameworks, preconceptions, sense of aesthetics and a host of other contributing factors. So I tend to give out preliminary assignments that allow me to get to know them through a project and then the cheetah emerges. Just kidding! Well, not entirely. It really is a lot of mental effort, but you need to figure out where students are before you can effectively guide them into creating something, anything. They need to see you as an ally on one hand, but also accept you as a devil's advocate for the flipside of their preconceptions. It takes a lot of energy to establish this kind of trust. Occasionally there will be a student who, for one reason or another, continues to delude themselves.

And yes, the responsibility is *huge*. I was educated through an architectural pedagogy that harbored a lot of unhelpful and even abusive critiques, so I try very hard to demonstrate respect for the student while still pointing out other ways of thinking and making. Lately my mantra goes something like, "I appreciate ambitious failures as much as I appreciate safe success." I like the look on their faces when I say this as they try to process what it means, particularly when they are trying so hard to tick off all the boxes in a not-so-interesting way. Another thing is, at least in our school, the students come from such disparate backgrounds educationally, so I encourage those from non-design backgrounds to really harness their other interests in life. I find this gives them a stronger conceptual foundation for their ideas.

It's quite clear that the circumstances of our present-day conditions are actively informing the studio floor and its energies. With so much conflict, polarization, environmental unraveling, and global uncertainty, where do you hold the relevancy and importance of architectural education? How do you articulate the value of our training?

I guess that one of the many outfalls of all this noise is that an individual can feel powerless against the largeness of the issues. At least with all the dreaming that goes on in an architectural education, the students can look at some of the systems that need fixing and postulate how design can help. Hopefully this gives the students a feeling of agency to help address something, at least at an embraceable, visualizable scale.

Additionally, the training in seeing problems as multilayered, requiring technical, aesthetic and other solutions, can help shape architecture graduates into generalists capable of collaborating with specialists. But sometimes I wonder if we are still teaching anachronistically, giving preference to the sole thinker, the auteur, when actually, learning to operate in teams is better preparation for practice.

I've often thought about this too, and increasingly so. Collaboration is an art form that should be cultivated. But as you said, design studio typically privileges the singular designer even though real-world frictions necessitate working for and with others. Have you noticed a marked difference in studio projects when they are structured individually vs. in groups?

I am not sure that group work necessarily creates different types of projects because there is usually someone in the group who takes the role of prime vision-maker as that's their strength. And depending on their personality, they may or may not be the best group leader, so it's always a bit of a crap shoot. However, students in teams do learn how to work with others in the process and some come out of it with a positive experience that serves them well later in their post-school lives. Something I'd like to try is to give different team members surrogate "roles" so that they can become avatars of different interest groups. Like, for example, Josie, you're a neighbouring NIMBY, Petunia, you're an idealistic designer with a background in Marxism, Andy, you're a hardline developer with a fondness for Blobitecture, Harriet, you work for the planning department and always have a bowl of caramels for visitors. Maybe the scenario process would release the students from being themselves and allow them to channel and understand the problem through the eyes of others.

I truly think it's a challenging time to be young with the relentless barrage of horrible things that endlessly fill our feeds. It breaks my heart that our youth are inheriting such a twisted set of conditions, but I guess that trying to develop ways to repair *something* is a better way to spend time than just swimming in the muck.

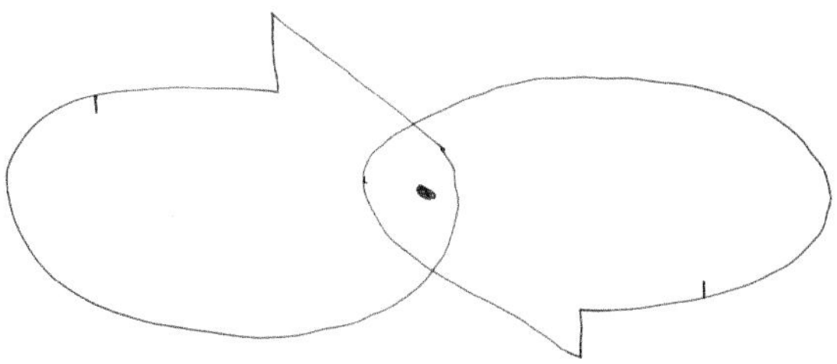

SKETCH: Bill Pechet

1995-2025
PECHET DESIGN STUDIOS and
STUDIES ABROAD

1995	The Other Thing
	with Bud Wood
1996	1st Year Core
1997	Towards a Conditional Architecture
	with Chris Macdonald
	Clearings
	with George Wagner
	Studies Abroad - Japan
	with George Yu
1998	The Urban Savage
	with Stephanie Robb
1999	1st Year Core
	Studies Abroad - Japan
2000	The Loved One
	Studies Abroad - Cairo and Athens
	with Ron Walkey
2001	Heavy
	Squatique
2002	Orphan Sites
	Urban Studio Concorde
	Tokyo Studio
	with George Wagner
2003	Heavier
2004	Terrains
	The Cemetery Studio
2005	Much Heavier
2006	Parallel Universe
2007	Culture of Making
	Giant City
2008	Culture of Making
	EcoDensity, Really?
2009	Sustainable Pleasures
	Culture of Making
2010	Culture of Making
	Even Heavier
	Studies Abroad - Brazil
	with Mari Fujita
2011	Culture of Making
	Comprehensive Studio
2012	Envelop(e) 2012
2013	Now and Forever
	It's a Material Culture
2014	Waste Space
	with Blair Satterfield
	Studiolo
2015	ThirdSpace
	T-House
2016	Material Facts and Fictions
	Comprehensive Studio - Life and Death
2017	Elements of Architectural Design
	Retail Therapy
	Studies Abroad – The Netherlands
	with Colette Parras
2018	SNACKITECTURE
	The Sensing Body
2019	Elements of Architectural Design
	Envelopes 2019
2020	Elements of Architectural Design
	The Sensing Body redux
2021	Elements of Architectural Design
	BL.Ending Space
2022	Elements of Architectural Design
	GoAway Green
2023	The Planes Between
	The Big in Small
	Studies Abroad - Japanese Noodles
	with Lőrinc Vass
2024	InsideOutside
	10 Versions Studio
	Studies Abroad - More Noodles Please
	with Lőrinc Vass
2025	InsideOutside redux

Watering Garden

BEACON HILL PARK, VICTORIA, BC • 2007

By the time *Watering Garden* opened in 2007, at Douglas Street and Circle Drive, Beacon Hill Park had long been embraced as more than a tranquil, picturesque landscape of meandering paths, lily ponds, well-manicured ornamental plants and free-ranging peacocks. Designed by John Blair, winner of an 1889 competition, the park was to be a heavily programmed public space with something for everyone. "... a good baseball diamond, a good cricket pitch, a good lacrosse ground and a good stretch of turf for exercising horses laid out in the Park and carefully protected for those who wish to play these games and to ride. [Organize] the resources of the Park... to get the greatest advantage to the greatest number out of it. ... And let no one imagine that the dull level of vacant monotony... is what the people as a whole enjoy." (*Colonist*, May 4, 1902)

Watering Garden was awarded to Pechet and Robb through a public bid/tender process. The team beat out their competitors, all splash park companies, by successfully making the case that while waterparks are forlorn in the winter months, a giant watering can would be intriguing even in cool, misty weather. Harkening back to his own childhood, when Bill was taken to tourist spots like "The Land of the Little People," "Anne Hathaway's Cottage," and "Fable Cottage," the scale jump trades on Victoria's traditional projection of itself as a place of enchantment. Encountering a giant watering can instantly shrink us to Lilliputian tiny. Additionally, as a symbol of the city's love of gardening in a play space for children, the project posits that "we are nurturing our little ones, like flowers being watered." BP *Watering Garden* is now on the official route of tour buses, where they point it out as a ginormous eccentricity.

The seventeen foot, stainless steel, gigantic watering can does not behave itself as one might expect, that is, pouring water exclusively from its spout. No, this is a naughty watering can which is all the more fun. On the north side of the plaza, four large buttons in primary colours scream out to the children: push me, push me! Of course, kids quite reasonably imagine that pushing one button, say the yellow one, would achieve an effect different than pushing another, so they race from button to button assuming they are producing the wild water effects. What they don't know is that the first push of any button starts one of ten randomly selected sequences, each sequence having ten to twelve water events—cheeky squirts and mists and downpours, jets, soft rain, the "rooster tail"—emanating from different nozzles: straight, spiral, mister, horizontal sprayer. Until that program has run its course, no pushing of buttons, however emphatically, does a darn thing except give the children a sense of agency, which is almost always good.

City worker Pete Baldini described the clever ploy well on the Friends of Beacon Hill Park website: "There is a computer inside the watering can that allows random spray patterns to evolve, which in turn increases the play value of the spray park for the users by keeping them guessing where the next blast of water will come from!" Small, low buttons on the side of the can produce better behaved, that is, more predictable squirts.

The city of Victoria's first Poet Laureate, Carla Funk, was commissioned to write a poem for the site. The words of "Invitation" are sandblasted onto a large sheet of granite at the northern edge of the *Watering Garden*, where the water drains off the gently sloping plaza. The water then empties in Fountain Lake, and from there, Goodacre Lake. On hot days, as a great deal of water is evaporating, the kids are unknowingly doing a good deed as they play, generating water to replenish the lakes. Win-win all around.

Pechet and Robb Art and Architecture

CLIENT: City of Victoria • TEAM: Bill Pechet with Andrew McLean, Heidi Nesbitt / PWL Partnership Landscape Architects / Carla Funk (poet) • FABRICATION: Accent Stainless Steel Manufacturing • CARTOON: John Bryant • PHOTOS: Michael Perlmutter (p. 209, 210 bottom, p. 211), Bill Pechet (p. 210 top left, right) • SKETCH: Bill Pechet • DRAWING: Lőrinc Vass • CARTOON: John Bryant • STATUS: Built

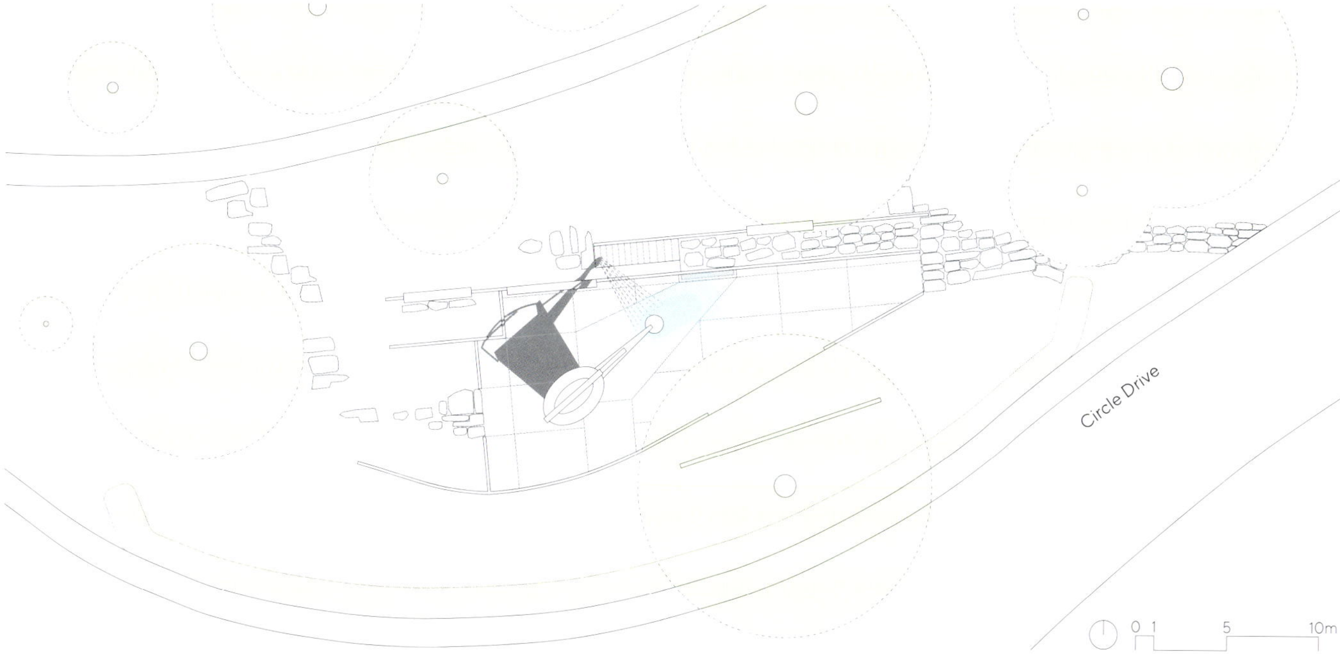
Circle Drive
0 1 5 10m

Invitation

Come step inside this story again,
inside this maze of leaf
and light and bloom.
Let your bare feet cool
in the hush of the grass.

Let yesterday be yesterday,
a bridge of stone, a swinging gate.
Follow peacock call, swallowtail,
Great Blue Heron, and the long-eyed snail
on his winding silver way.

At the shining pool, bend down
to see the water stir and ripple
Who are you? Where are you going?
And the clouds above you
sail and change

from whale to kite,
from smoke to swan,
from dark to light, like you
inside this jeweled garden
with the sun upon your face.

—Carla Funk

waving

GEORGE R. BROWN CONVENTION CENTER, HOUSTON, TX • 2015

"Everything is bigger in Texas," says everyone in Texas.

At five city blocks long and 100 feet high, the supersized, red, white and blue George R. Brown Convention Center in Houston is Texan through and through. In 2015, representatives of the surrounding entertainment district, Avenida Houston, wanted to "expand culture" by bringing art to the Convention Center and the neighbouring Houston Partnership Tower.

A specific site and requirements for this public art competition were given: the new work would occupy the space in and/or around an existing rectangular fountain and incorporate water and light features. Thanks to the highly successful public artwork, *emptyful*, PECHET-Studio was invited to submit a proposal.

waving harkens back to *hi-bye*, the 2011 competition entry for the 7th Avenue Transit Mall in Calgary, bringing its 900 rotating arms to Houston in a new configuration and radically different context. The arms—this time suspended from seven poles with stainless steel hoop-forms positioned in and around the fountain—would, like their predecessor, rotate when activated by a breeze, the hands waving a friendly welcome.

By day, the arms would sparkle in the sunlight as they catch a breeze and throw light beams across the water and plaza. By night, lights from below would cycle through multiple sequences creating a variety of effects. The changing patterns in the water and the lights would ensure the dynamism of the artwork. The programming of the lights could easily be altered to respond to special holidays, festivals, sports events. Imagine the Super Bowl under-way and the lights projecting the colours of the two competing teams. Or, on second thought, maybe just the colours of the home team if the Houston Oilers make it to the Bowl.

PECHETStudio

CLIENT: George R. Brown Convention Center • **TEAM:** Bill Pechet with Gabe Daly, Sam McFaul / Eos Lightmedia • **RENDERINGS:** Sam McFaul • **STATUS:** Competition finalist

West End Decorative Lighting

WEST END, VANCOUVER, BC • 2013

One of the first things a newcomer notices about Vancouver is how inky black the nights are. It is no wonder that Vancouver has a long history of debates about city lights. It is a century-long story of push and pull, between advocates for more illumination and those fighting light "pollution." Public opinion swings back and forth, but now it is light time again!

The West End Business Improvement Association approached Bill for his help in advocating for the integration of lighting into the city's masterplanning process. To that end, he was commissioned to design decorative lighting schemes for Davie, Denman and lower Robson. In collaboration with Eos Lightmedia, two proposals were developed and prototyped for review by the city, local businesses and residents.

In the first scheme, perforated aluminum "banner lights" were proposed to be attached to existing infrastructure to enhance the general illumination of the commercial streets and establish an identity for the WEBIA, much as the lights on Granville Street had unified a visually chaotic environment two years earlier. Large circles cut out of each side of the banners aligned only from specific viewpoints, "animating without moving parts." BP

While this proposal was not implemented, a second concept was realized, at least partially, and still functions today along the eastern end of Davie, just off Burrard. Readymade, off-the-shelf strings of coloured lights are draped along both sides of the street, inviting the neighbourhood to come out and party. The programmable lights change colour and "twinkle, travel or just gently pulse" according to the occasion. They even produce shimmering rainbow effects to celebrate the historic epicentre of Vancouver's gay neighbourhood.

PECHETStudio

CLIENT: West End Business Improvement Association • **TEAM:** Bill Pechet, Gabe Daly / Eos Lightmedia • **FABRICATION:** Main Sheet Metal Works (prototypes) / Eos Lightmedia • **PHOTOS:** Jose Gonzales (top, bottom left), Bill Pechet (bottom right) **SKETCH:** Bill Pechet • **STATUS:** Off and on

Whiskers on Mittens

OTTAWA ART GALLERY, OTTAWA, ON
FEBRUARY 6 – APRIL 13, 1997

In the PECHETStudio, the shelves are crammed with Bill's well-worn sketchbooks. Representing decades, they are organized chronologically: one book a year, sometimes two. In his early years, the books varied in size and colour, some spiral bound, others glued and stitched. Later, he settled on the most common of black sketchbooks, full-sized because a year is a long time. The books have experienced various degrees of abuse; many have lost their spines, some are held together with tape. Bill's sketchbooks are filled, not with personal confessions, but with sketches and meeting notes, collaged fragments, observations, reminders for doctors' appointments or meetings with friends. In short, the sketchbooks are a record of what is of interest to Bill. They are his calendar, Rolodex, scrapbook, tracing paper, all in one.

When curator Bruce Hugh Russell invited Bill to participate in a group exhibition, "Pentimenti: Process in Contemporary Canadian Architecture," at the Ottawa Art Gallery in 1997, Bill proposed *Whiskers on Mittens*. His installation would feature ten open sketchbooks, one from each of the past ten years, bolted onto ten wooden, wall-mounted shelves, each with a small wind-up music box attached. Visitors who wound the music boxes were serenaded as they perused the sketchbooks. In her review in *The Ottawa Citizen* (March 11, 1997), Nancy Baele described the sound accompanying his installation: "When several are going, there's not an unpleasant mix of Christmas carols, popular songs, a Brahms lullaby." Bill would describe the gentle cacophony of saccharine pop and classical tone accompaniment as "John Cage meets Ikea."

The title *Whiskers on Mittens* is a retelling (*mitate*) of "Whiskers on Kittens" from the *Sound of Music's* "My Favorite Things." The sound boxes have funny little steel rods that look like innocent whiskers, but the dark side of the title suggests something weirder. "Why are there whiskers on mittens? What man lurks in the forests of winter, ready to pounce? The ravine across from my childhood home was filled with menacing witches and goblins." BP

In a second review of the group exhibition in *Parachute* (1997), Brent Wagler singles out *Whiskers on Mittens*. "According to a handwritten comment in one sketchbook, the creative imagination should not be underestimated: 'Alchemical sachets... will promote fertility if placed in your underwear drawers.'"

CLIENT: Ottawa Art Gallery • **FABRICATION:** Granville Island Woodworks • **PHOTOS:** Michael Perlmutter (top right) / Bill Pechet

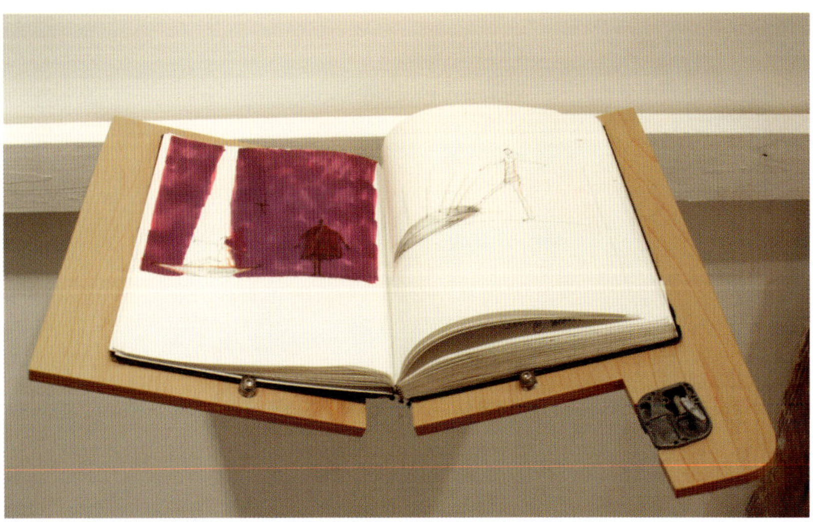

Who's there

VANCOUVER, BC AND XIAMEN, CHINA • 2007, 2012, 2022

It all started innocently enough with a painting of a bunny first exhibited in Bill's 2007 solo exhibition, *Finding Sudoku*, at the Helen Pitt Gallery in Vancouver. On an impulse five years later, Bill contacted several factories in China to inquire about creating 500 copies of the painting. As someone interested in the effects of multiples and familiar with Walter Benjamin's "The Work of Art in the Age of Mechanical Reproduction" (1936), Bill was curious about how non-mechanical reproductions might affect the original's aura.

The 500 copies were shipped from a factory in Xiamen to Vancouver, tucked away in plastic containers and stored in Bill's studio bathtub for a full decade. Unsure what his experiment meant, Bill wrestled with the discomfort of being a privileged westerner who commissioned low-wage workers in China to make copies of his work.

But in 2022, Bill was invited to exhibit the full array of paintings at Bothkinds Project Space in Vancouver's Gastown. When the 500 blue-green bunnies were lined up, the variation inevitable in non-mechanical reproductions created a kind of nervous visual jiggle. The so-called reproductions each exuded the aura of an original. Collectively, all those labouring hands, transformed a cute bunny painting into something almost sinister.

In an excellent review in *The Tyee* (November 16, 2022), Dorothy Woodened summed up the exhibition well: "*Who's There* ropes in many Pechet-ian interests: quirky characters, serendipity, a sense of play, and an openness to the randomness of the universe. All of these are embodied in the different qualities that make up the collected bunnymen. There is also a strange aura of mystery and uncertainty that clings to the project—or whatever you'd like to term the uncanny valley between impulse and execution. Maybe this is why the emotional quality keeps shifting like the surface of the sea. It's an experience that Pechet is well aware of. One moment, the bunnymen seem chipper and upbeat. In the next, they're all menacing."

PAINTINGS: Bill Pechet (top left original painting), Jingyi (Xiamen) Works of Art Co. Ltd. (copies) • **PHOTOS:** Lőrinc Vass (paintings), Michael Perlmutter (bottom left), Jingyi XWOAC (bottom right) • **STATUS:** Back in the tubs in the tub

X-ray Vanity

BILL PECHET'S BATHROOM, VANCOUVER, BC

A syntactical inversion of two meanings of "vanity," this installation transforms quotidian bathroom objects—toothbrush, floss container, comb, pharmaceutical container—into an evershifting playground of silhouetted objects. Backlit, these ubiquitous objects are reseen as beautiful and strange. "The glowing cabinet transforms the bathroom into a mermaid's lair during bathtime." BP

FABRICATION: Two & Two Design Innovations • **PHOTOS:** Bill Pechet

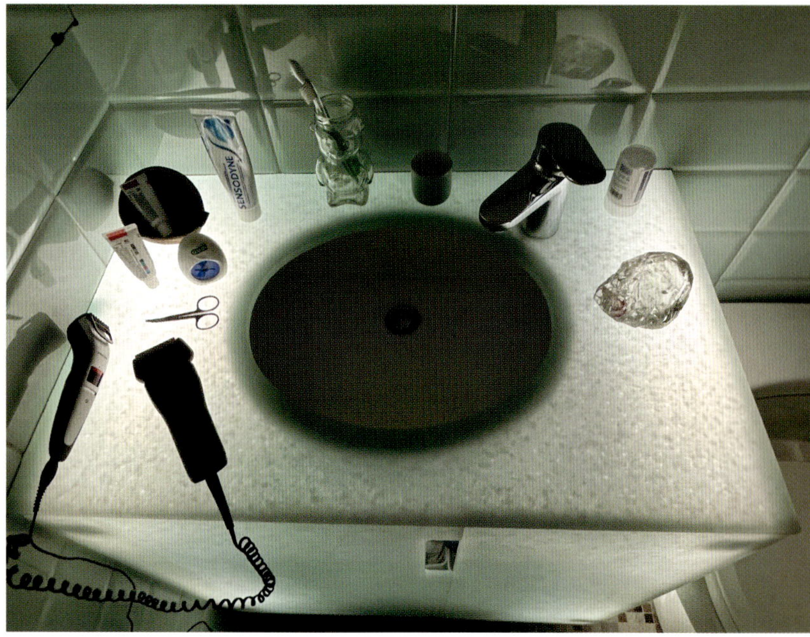

Ze'ev

Bill Richardson

SKETCH: Bill Pechet

On February 9, 1957—a slow news day—the *Edmonton Journal* reported that a letter sent by Mrs. M. Pechet, of 13836-106A Avenue, and addressed to Mrs. I. Kettner, 13618-102 Avenue, had reached its intended destination—a distance of a few city blocks—two months after being mailed. Mrs. Pechet and Mrs. Kettner, both active members of the city's Jewish community, might have shared a knowing chuckle when they learned the reason for the letter's attenuated journey; the *Journal* disclosed that it went astray "after apparently becoming entangled in a Christmas card envelope destined for England."

Here was one more demonstration—as if another were required—of the Yiddish proverb,"*Der mentsh trakht un got lakht*;" that is, "Man plans, and God laughs." Oh, well. No lasting harm was done. The prodigal post was restored. There was cause for celebration. Nine months (and change) later, William Joel Pechet, known as Bill, Hebrew name Ze'ev, was delivered, unentangled, and on time. He is to this day reliably punctual.

Bill Pechet's birth, as births go—this was according to his mother, Judy, aka Mrs. M. Pechet, who routinely told grownup Bill the story of his advent during her birthday phone calls—was straightforward, efficiently accomplished with a minimum of fuss. Benign and cooperative from the get-go, he evolved into a compliant child, conciliatory and self-reliant, requiring only the most usual tugs from the parental reins. It is true that at the age of five, or thereabouts, he risked being identified as an insurrectionist when, along with his cousin, Arna Panar, he appeared on *Romper Room*. It was Christmastime and Miss Sue, the local superintendent of the televised preschool, was met with stony stares from the two junior Jews when she inveigled them to take part in some seasonal sing-song or crafts project. Their two mothers cracked up watching it. There were, inevitably, the occasional brushes with danger that enliven and imperil most childhoods: a near drowning in a swimming pool, a visit to the hospital emergency department after experimentally swilling gasoline, a skating episode that resulted in a broken leg; momentary crises that proved surmountable. On balance, however, he was a placid, private presence come to roost among big personalities whose opinions were passionately held, freely aired, and among whom feelings ran high.

Virginia Woolf, in a letter to Vita Sackville-West, asked, "My God, how does one write a biography?" Implicit in the question is an acknowledgment of the near impossibility of the exercise; of finding an angle, a slant of light that will frame and compress but not obscure or obliterate the telling and necessary details. The subject and his work are the feast, the reason we gather at the table, but it was laid and prepared by those who went before. The ancestors, *sine qua non*, created the milieu, thickly marbled with old country traces, that nurtured the artist. They must be honoured, their voices conjured.

Bill Pechet's parents were first generation Jewish Canadians, the children of Romanian immigrants on his father Mitch's side, and Russian newcomers on Judy's. Both diasporic families were equally, if differently, remarkable. To his mother, Bill Pechet was particularly close. Between them was a deep and lasting bond, her affection for her third child and second son undiminished by his tendency as a preschooler to criticise her choice of lipstick shade.

Shapiro was Judy's maiden name. She was born in Calgary in 1924 and raised there. Her father, Morris, was a partner in a company that evolved to become United News, a successful wholesaler of books and magazines throughout Western Canada. Her mother, Bessie, was a Shumiatcher, still a well-known family, prominent in business, cultural, and philanthropic circles. Some branches of the Shumiatcher clan, Bessie's among them, upon arrival in Halifax or Montreal or Staten Island, anglicized the name to Smith. Some drifted, from one year to the next, depending on the prevailing winds of assimilation, from Smith to Shumiatcher and back again.

Bessie Shapiro was musical, an outstanding pianist. In her Calgary home, at 213 Superior Avenue, a concert grand that would have dominated any room was accorded exaggerated prominence by its elevated placement on a dais built for that purpose. Over the years, the stage in Bessie's living room was the site of many given-for-company performances by her children, then her grandchildren. (Bill Pechet was one of those recitalists, although the nun who had been his piano teacher was never able to persuade him to learn to read music. His sense of pitch was excellent, if not perfect, and he was able—is still—to play easily by ear.)

Both Bessie's daughters—Bill's mother Judy, and her younger sister, his aunt, Sylvia—inherited her musical gift. (It was their little brother, Larry, in whom the business drive was predominant.) Sylvia—she died in Victoria in 2024 at the age of 96—was an opera singer, a soprano who also sang lyric mezzo roles. As Sylvia Grant—her entry in *The Canadian Encyclopedia* notes that her "performances were marked by dramatic force and a voice of brilliant timbre"—she had a busy career in Toronto with the Canadian Opera Company. She was also a frequent guest of the New York City Opera before she retired in 1968 in favour of raising a family. Judy was an accomplished pianist and a frequent laureate at local music competitions and festivals. She was, what's more, a powerhouse tennis player. Even as a schoolgirl, her athletic and artistic triumphs were routinely touted in the Calgary press; she was a steady presence in the local papers from 1933 through 1944. That was the year when, at nineteen—she was by then a first-year commerce student at the University of Alberta, in Edmonton—Judith Shapiro was named a recipient of a scholarship funded by the Associated Board, Royal Schools of Music. It would have allowed her, postwar, to pursue her keyboard studies in London. But 1944 was also the year she met and married a hockey star and Flight Sergeant named Mitchell Pechet.

The Shapiros and Shumiatchers, arriving on the Canadian plains, gravitated to established population centres: Regina, Edmonton, Calgary. The Pechets, after coming from Romania, circa 1902 chose to initially settle in and around such Saskatchewan country towns as Lipton and Cupar. These were among the several sites of Jewish colonies established in Saskatchewan. Cupar was where Mitch Pechet (b. 1918) spent his formative years. He was the third of five brothers (and one half-brother) born to his mother, Sophie (nee Tessler, 1889–1947) and his father, William.

William Pechet (1884–1957) was the grandfather for whom Bill Pechet was named. (William was an anglicized version of "Wolf;" Bill Pechet's Hebrew name, Ze'ev, "Wolf," is another nominal link to this forebear who died a few months before he was born.) As new Canadians, the Pechets tried their hands at farming and business. In Cupar, they ran a general store; it burned, along with most of the commercial block in which it stood, in 1911. Another more ambitious enterprise, more along the lines of a department store, was established in 1918. Sophie and her children had a close call escaping from their upstairs apartment when that building, too, burned to the ground a few days before Christmas in 1921. These were Prohibition years, and there are family stories about William's adventures as a rum runner for another small-town Saskatchewan family, the Bronfmans, whose eventual Seagram empire began with prairie moonshine. Cross-border liquor smuggling was a sideline, lucrative but dangerous, to which Sophie called a halt—as the tale is told—after a near brush with the law where guns were drawn and bullets flew. William got into the hospitality game—like the Bronfmans—and ran hotels in Carberry, Manitoba and Fort Frances, Ontario. Eventually, he and Sophie settled in Winnipeg.

By then—those were the early years of World War II—Mitch Pechet's name and fame as a hockey star were well-established. After playing a couple of seasons with the Brandon Wheat Kings—he was a high-scoring forward—Mitch was drafted by the New York Rangers, then went to the Philadelphia Ramblers. Sidelined from active military service as a pilot—bad eyes—he played with the Armed Forces team. It was at a party, after a 1944 exhibition game in Calgary, that Mitch met Judy. No stranger to the hockey liability of puck-in-mouth, he was already wearing dentures. A jokester, his false teeth became part of his schtick. He'd goof around with them, extract them, use them as a comic prop. Judy was charmed. She thought he was hilarious, also attractive. Her parents were likewise impressed. He was engaging, successful, and a rarity, a Jew in the NHL; he remains one of the few to have played in the league. They were two good-looking, athletic, desirous young people. The tug between them must have been tidal. It was wartime. Everyone had lost the habit of banking on the future. The lag between meeting and marriage was often short. It was for Mitch and Judy. On their autumn mountain honeymoon they had a big row. Someone got locked out of the cabin, then was readmitted. So it went, for sixty-five years, less a day. They married on October 1; Mitch died on September 30, 2009.

Mitch Pechet left professional sports in 1949 after playing four seasons in St. Paul, Minnesota. By then, he was a family man, but still restless, alert, and responsive to opportunity's every knock. He followed his father's example, buying first a dairy bar, then a number of hotels and restaurants in Calgary and Edmonton. Judy was a homemaker, busy with the requirements of her four children. Sydney, the firstborn, now Sydney Kalef, was ten years older than Bill and took an active hand in raising him; he adored her—they remain close—and in his capacity as kid brother he was her willing minion and batman. He was dragooned into being her tanning assistant, remembers combing lemon juice through her hair as she sun-bathed in the backyard, remembers being deputized to hold a piece of cardboard (sometimes an LP jacket) covered in tinfoil at just the right angle to ensure even bronzing. Sydney, who was the associate choreographer for the opening ceremonies of Calgary's 1988 Winter Olympics, studied dance, as well as music. She honed her skills as a teenager by producing and directing musical revues for the Jewish Community Centre. Bill was now and then recruited as a cast member.

He was part of the chorus in an exciting rendition of "My Beautiful Balloon"—he has held onto the hand gestures and, if pressed, can demonstrate them—and particularly remembers a solo turn, singing "Standing on the Corner (Watching All the Girls Go By"). Sam, the firstborn son, the most mercurial of the children, a chance-taking adventurer who died in Copenhagen at forty-four, was born in 1950. Like Sydney, he recognized and encouraged the emergent artistic gifts in his kid brother; Bill Pechet names Sam as one of his first champions and true believers. A third son, Casey, the baby of the family, came along in 1959. Also musically adept, he was an accomplished flutist, a composer, and a programmer. Born into a family of joke-tellers and kibitzers, these two last born sons still slip readily into the easy, teasing banter of brothers who grew up sharing a room, albeit one they sometimes divided with a line down the middle. (When the Pechets migrated south for a few years, to Calgary, the boys had separate quarters. Bill was given free rein with his room's decoration, settling on a combination of smoky orange paint and rattan wall paper, hung with the posters that were then so *de rigueur*: one of a contented, smiling pig, and one he remembers as being *2001: A Space Odyssey* inspired, a medley of radiating light beams.)

It was in Edmonton, though, that Bill Pechet's nascent aesthetic sensibilities were fostered. He'd attended a parochial school, Talmud Torah, where the focus was less on art than on religion and core academic subjects. (He did, however, design the backdrops for a fourth-grade film version of the book of *Exodus*: dunes, pyramids, massive walls of water and so on. Tragically, no sketches or footage from the finished product remain.) Abstracted from the family passion for team sports—nor had an early attempt to interest him in things equestrian gone well—his interest in, and gift for, the visual arts was noted and encouraged.

He attended classes at the Edmonton Art Gallery. That was where—in an act of daringly deconstructive abstraction probably not seen in that city since the avant-garde kingpin Brion Gysin had been a boy there—he cut the pompom from his tuque and incorporated it into a collage. He remembers the feeling of adventure and freedom and discovery that came along with doing something creative in an environment that was not the familiar and domestic: a feeling of the world opening before him, Red Sea-like, the Promised Land in view. He remembers being a child in a room filled with much older students, everyone painting a still life from a vase full of mountain ash boughs, the branches replete with orange berries; remembers how he looked at it as might an ant, then made the choice to hugely exaggerate the size of the fruit.

Judy Pechet, aware that her son was uncommonly gifted and thirsty for stimulation, sought out private teachers. It was Jean Richards, a well-known local artist, who got him started drawing and painting ookpiks. About this undertaking he was enthusiastic and prolific; also giving. Pechet ookpiks were widely disbursed. They must have been memorable: in 2023, a school friend recipient of one of those early works contacted him to commission something similar for her grandchild. The ookpik legs and feet figured in his work long after he and Jean Richards parted ways; they still occur. Similarly influential was another tutor, Lino Tonnen, via whom Bill Pechet became fascinated by Picasso. He started producing work in a Cubist style, perfecting a technique for representing noses that he still uses today. He remembers the feeling of excited validation when his work was praised by his family, when it was displayed in their home, and sent off to, and acknowledged by, impressed and far-flung relatives in Los Angeles, New York, and Palm Springs.

Just as it had been his mother who arranged all these extracurricular classes, and chauffeured him there and back, it was surely Judy who did the legwork to make possible Bill Pechet's brief but glamorous career as a child model. Both he and Casey appeared in newspaper ads for GWG jeans; a family friend was in charge of the campaign. In one particularly memorable spread—from 1971, just before the family left Calgary, not that anything like cause and effect should be imputed to that coincidence—Bill was photographed, alongside his GWG family—as nuclear and heteronormative a cluster as ever you've seen—seated on the ground, chewing, rustically, on straw.

Nor was Mitch Pechet, the family provider, absent from Bill's aesthetic evolution. There was a postwar building boom underway in their Edmonton neighbourhood, and it was with Mitch that he, Bill, would go for walks to look at the mid-century modernist homes being built in such profusion. Mitch fostered in his son a lingering fondness for construction sites; Bill still recalls how excited his father was to follow the progress of Edmonton's CN Tower which, when completed in 1966, was for a few years the tallest building in Western Canada.

Height matters. At night, as a child, Bill Pechet would often dream of flying, and sometimes had the eerie experience of feeling himself detach from his carnal casing. Bobbing above, he looked down on his own sleeping body, looked down on the sleeping city, too. Astral projection? Possibly. You have time for that sort of possibility or you don't. He remains, well into his seventh decade, someone whose dream life—flying still figures and Barbra Streisand is often his co-pilot—is extravagantly inventive, and who—this seems related—is sensitive to the possibility of unseen presences, catching fleeting, peripheral glimpses of them in rooms, hallways, even in elevators. These episodes, infrequent, are never treated as extraordinary, and only occasion the most offhand and passing of remarks. (He's similarly *laissez-faire* about the time he met Farrah Fawcett in a frozen yogurt store on Robson Street and advised her on which flavour to choose.) Maybe it was this childhood habit of oneiric elevation that inspired his hankering, still active, for flight, and his passion for understanding the plans and inner workings of cities. Sometimes his father, and sometimes his sister, would drive Bill and Casey to an airfield to look at the little Cessnas: he remains an occasional plane spotter and images of aircraft, or their long shadows, recur in his doodles, sketchbooks, and children's books. He remembers a visit to Edmonton's Klondike Days festival where a sidewalk artist drew "what do you want to be when you grow up" portraits of Bill and Casey. Casey was portrayed as a fireman, and Bill as a pilot. These quick sketches—they were rendered with oversized heads—were hung on the walls of their bedroom. Bill Pechet added just a touch of colour to his lips.

These are a few of the many memories that have survived the sculpting ebb and flow of more than a half-century's passing. It's true that family stories, anecdotes, are soft, malleable. Subject to alteration, prone to slippage, they don't recommend themselves as foundation material. Nonetheless, they count for something. Seen through a glass, opaquely, there's something prognosticatory about them. Floating above, looking down, you can see the artist (the designer, the architect) still a boy, not quite a young man, already practicing his signature. He's experimenting with materials. He's thinking about structures. He's acquiring taste, discernment. He's steeped in the tragic riches of *shtetl* storytelling, is developing the humour, the art of deflection, that will become so much a part of his eventual brand. In his professional life, he would become adept at prosecuting a personal vision through intense, prolonged, sometimes uneasy, but most often productive collaborations with colleagues: landscape designers, engineers, fabricators, contractors, craftsmen, tradespeople, city bureaucrats, university administrators, boyfriends. He was coming into his own in a family that was loving and combative; was determining how to find his place as someone whose impulse was to pacify, who was conflict-averse, amongst siblings and parents who were argumentative, competitive, sporty. He was learning that success could derive from strategy, negotiation. From patience.

In 1971, after three years in Calgary, the family—save Sydney, now married—moved to Victoria. The early years on Vancouver Island were unsettled, domestically. Mitch intended to acquire a hotel but instead, as one does, bought a hockey team, Junior A, the Victoria Cougars. He kept his business interests in Alberta and, for the next several years, was a weekend visitor at home. The marriage hit a patch rocky enough to require a separation, then a reconciliation. The family kept moving from rental house to rental house, four in as many years, before one suitable for purchase was located in the Uplands neighbourhood of Oak Bay. Bill Pechet remembers 3110 Midland Road as his mother's "essay in wallpaper," many different patterns having been chosen for the various rooms. His room was in the basement, and he was allowed both to choose the wallpaper for his bathroom—a kind of large plaid in black, white, and yellow—and to paint a supergraphic on the stairway wall, pillars of light with a cloud and a lightning bolt.

Soon after the family arrived in Victoria, another powerful woman brought her influence to bear on young Bill Pechet. Asenath Petrie (1914–2001), a psychologist and poet, was born in London into an influential Jewish family: her father was Rabbi Avigdor Schonfeld. A Zionist much concerned with the cause of Jewish-Arab reconciliation, she worked after the war in refugee resettlement and then, as a psychologist, began a study of pain management. This led to an appointment at Harvard, and resulted in the book by which she's best remembered, *Individuality in Pain and Suffering* (1968). Bill Pechet can't recall the exact circumstances that led to her landing in Victoria; he thinks it was connected to her own pain, a serious back injury that resulted from a fall. For reasons that are murky, she chose Victoria as the site of her convalescence and somehow, via a cousin or friend or some other point of contact in the Jewish network, met and befriended Judy Pechet. They became close. These were the years of marital discord, and both women were, in their own ways, in pain. Bill Pechet remembers that his mother would go out of her way to offer the newcomer assistance—quite a lot was required—and that, for a few years, Asenath was very much a part of their family life. She took him under her wing, would talk with him about the life of the spirit and art. Together they would look at paintings, and she encouraged him to think, in every way, about light, its source. He remembers one particular Saturday afternoon when they discussed Rembrandt's *Jacob Blessing the Sons of Joseph* (1656) for what felt like hours, analyzing the image: its assembly, and how light and shadow informed the literal and allegorical story. It was an immersion both practical and soulful. Mitch, Bill remembers, found Asenath puzzling, and was probably not upset when she decamped and moved to Jerusalem in 1973.

In addition to owning the Victoria Cougars, Mitch Pechet became their coach. Hershey's was a team sponsor, donating massive chocolate bars, ten-pounders, that were awarded as prizes at games, raffle-style, to attendees whose tickets bore the winning number. Unclaimed bars, more than a few, were diverted to the garage where they were stored near an ice pick. The latter was deployed by Bill and by Casey to chip away at the former, covertly, not that anyone was fooled. To this day, Bill Pechet has a love-hate, binge-repent relationship with all things sweet. (Back in Edmonton, the garage had been the repository for a great many cases of an Israeli depilatory agent—Delilah, it was called—in which Mitch believed enough to invest but which never panned out.)

At Oak Bay High School, where he was the co-editor and principal photographer for the yearbook, Bill Pechet spent a lot of time hanging around the art room. Now and again, his exertions attracted wider notice, though he has no recollection of being named the laureate in a contest sponsored by United Way to paint murals on a construction hoarding at the corner of Fort and Douglas. Confronted with the evidence (see the *Times Colonist*, October 24, 1977), he wonders out loud if anyone thought to notify him of this triumph, so long absent from his CV. Who knows what doors might have opened, had only it been there?

By then, a month shy of turning twenty, he was a student at the University of Victoria. Although architecture had by this time insinuated itself into his vision of a possible future, he was still in a wide-ranging, experimental mode. He'd chosen his favourite high school subject, Geography, as a major, with a minor in Asian Studies, and then stayed on to complete the requirements for a Fine Arts degree.

At least as foundational to his emerging future as anything that was revealed in a classroom was the stuff of young life, happening. He took a job with an agency that assisted Japanese students with housing and settling. He moved away from 3110 Midland Road, with its clamour of wallpapers, and into the first of a series of communal households, first on Fairfield and then on Dallas roads. Here, among a rotating cast of roommates, many of them young artists, writers, designers, he forged friendships and began conversations that have lasted for forty years, and led to many collaborations, to say nothing of dinner parties, impromptu garden installations, and house redecorating jamborees. Importantly, he also began to travel, to Europe and to Asia.

Japan became a regular destination. He made his first long sojourn there in 1981, was exhilarated to discover how different the society he found was from the one he'd imagined, based largely on what he'd discerned from dining with his family at the one or two Japanese restaurants in Victoria. Economically, culturally, socially, the country was then in a state of febrile boom. These were palmy days for native English speakers who were much in demand as teachers. He got work, eye-opening, tutoring wealthy housewives who would never complain about their husbands in their native tongue, but opened up in a second language. He taught school children and classes of hipsters who were his contemporaries and in whose lives he became enmeshed. Many dinners. Many parties. Many day trips. He lived in a 10′ by 10′ room in Tokyo, and produced artwork that he took around to various galleries, trying to get shows. He remembers one dealer—very sophisticated, very serious—giving his work very sophisticated and very serious attention while she slowly, deliberately extracted errant hairs from his collages.

By this time, many of the denizens from the shared accommodations in Victoria had gravitated to Vancouver, either to study or work. A large house in the Dunbar neighbourhood, not far from the University of British Columbia campus, became their gathering ground, and that was where Bill Pechet lived when he came back to Canada to begin his architectural studies in 1982. Again, the cross-pollinating energy generated by the meeting and mingling of diverse but like-minded young artists, of emerging costume designers (like Nancy Bryant) and filmmakers (like Ann Marie Fleming), was certainly as vital to his consolidating sense of self as anything learned in the classroom.

Similarly formative was a second long Asian excursion that began as a semester abroad in Hong Kong, after which he took a leave from the UBC program to travel to Tokyo and a job with a Japanese firm. They did a lot of work in the Philippines, and he was sent as part of a team hired to draft a masterplan for central Manila, and to design mode interchange terminals for the nascent rapid transit system. He lived for nine months in that complex and chaotic city, deeply immersed in projects that allowed him to spend time both in the field and in the studio. Different ways of thinking, of building, of circulating; different environmental situations, materials, protocols, and priorities; it was a kind of apprenticeship that would serve him well when he returned to UBC, better able to animate theory with practical experience. It was during this time that Bill Pechet began to claim his gay identity and embarked on his first long-term relationship with another man.

Returning to Vancouver, and to the house in Dunbar, Bill Pechet picked up his studies where he had left off, distinguishing himself in seminars and also with his graduating presentation, the Tokyo-sited *Museum of Sand.* That was, arguably, the beginning of the work examined in this book, the early days of his affinity—by now one of longstanding—with concrete, with its casting.

The typical path for a newly-graduated architecture student would have been to find work with a good firm and begin the process of registration. Bill Pechet was hired right out of school by Gerald Kennedy Architects, but soon had to come to grips with the certainty that the "typical path" might not suit him. For one thing, he was, as he says, "a shitty employee." After Kennedy, he worked for a couple of years with Henriquez, and then part-time for several other estimable Vancouver firms: the Patkaus, Bing Thom, and landscape architect Judith Reeves, but found the assignments sometimes constraining or too much at variance with his own tastes and interests. More absorbing was the time he spent doing his own work with other young artists—sculptors, painters, set and costume designers, landscape architects—at a number of rented studios around the city.

It will astonish anyone who's more recently arrived in Vancouver to learn that there was a time, well within living memory, when such spaces—large, and able to accommodate a variety of semi-industrial uses—were available on such downtown streets as West Georgia and Richards. It was in these dawning days of his professional life, largely through word of mouth, that Bill Pechet came by some of his earliest important assignments. A major focus of his work has long been cemetery planning and design, and the first of these, the extraordinarily beautiful *Woods* columbarium, grew out of a chance meeting at a conference with a West Vancouver city administrator. Similarly, the ambitious and innovative *Southlands House* on Blenheim Street—house design is a relatively small part of the portfolio—came his way through a friend of a friend's recommendation made to the clients. (At this time of writing, mid-August 2024, that property, still in the hands of those original owners, has been listed for sale in the twelve million range. It is an extraordinary work, the more so given how young and untried was the architect.)

It was at this same time, when the city was more in the mood than is now the case to support the work of small dance companies, that he began to produce set designs for such choreographers and companies as Dancecorps, Holy Body Tattoo, Chick Snipper, Jennifer Mascall, and John Alleyne. Sometimes, as was the case with Alleyne, he would collaborate with his former housemate, costume designer Nancy Bryant. (Their story of the project that took them to Monte-Carlo, and all that that entailed, is, sadly, too long and involved to reproduce here. Which is a pity—it's a good one, antic, in all the best ways.)

The studio on West Georgia gave way to the studio on Richards which then became the studio on West Georgia again and then became the studio on Cypress and West Broadway. This last studio was spacious, occupying half of the main floor of a building shared with a Japanese massage parlour staffed mostly by young Korean women who would probably have preferred a different line of work. That proximity was its own study in managing traffic flow, as the rub and tug clients, unclear about who was where, often hammered on the studio door, and were surprised, when it opened, at the vast assembly of architectural models, blueprints, and draughting tables. It was here, in the main, in the Cypress studio, that the work of Pechet and Robb took place.

Stephanie Robb had been a UBC classmate; they first bonded over creating decorations for a student Hallowe'en party, and in the mid-Nineties —by which time Bill Pechet had returned to UBC to teach as a Lecturer in Practice—they began their long professional collaboration. Their first forays involved the interiors of restaurants and stores, most notably the downtown outpost of *Le Château* with its gingerbread people cutouts, their eyes illuminated, suspended above the exterior canopy at a crazy "run, run as fast you can" angle, and then expanded to residential renovations and house extensions. *Exeter House*, in Oak Bay, much published in design magazines and books, dates from the Pechet / Robb years. This is the stunning private residence on an extraordinary half-acre lot that Bill Pechet designed for his sister and brother-in-law, Sydney and Robert Kalef. In the last few years, the well-to-do Uplands precinct of Oak Bay has seen a great deal of construction and its citizens, once largely committed to Tudor style half-timbered piles, are less disturbed by heterogeneity of design than was the case at the beginning of the millennium when the drawings for *Exeter House* were submitted to the city for approval. It was granted, as Sydney remembers, with a wry, if wary, grin from the planning department, whose officer knew that feathers were primed for ruffling. "Look out, Uplands," was what he said. So began the concerted campaign against modernism from the woman across the street, one of the few people who proved resistant to the steady, patient, persistent charm of Bill Pechet.

She soon moved. Her bungalow was demolished. Something quite striking stands there now.

Ongoing work involving cemetery design came their way, as did opportunities for the installation—more quixotic than lucrative—of public art. They collaborated on such projects as the cheerful high-fiving hand of the "Stacks" at the False Creek Energy Centre, and the helmet-inspired lights at Victory Square, and, most notably, ambitiously, and possibly goofily, the vast polar fleece construction called *SweaterLodge* that represented Canada at the 2006 Venice Biennale.

When that partnership had run its course and was amicably dissolved, Bill Pechet moved his studio to its present location, a "live-work" building in the creative hub of East Vancouver's Mount Pleasant neighbourhood. It's a high-ceilinged, concrete space with the nerve centre / war room located atop a spiral staircase in the second-storey loft. A kind of curated chaos evolves around the floor-to-ceiling bookcases and the big drawing table on the main floor. Some of the many, small, glow-in-the-dark paintings that are often gifted to friends are adjacent to remnants of projects that evolved just a step or two beyond the drawing board stage, which are cheek by jowl with numerous examples of the honey bears he's been casting for years, from concrete, from resin, though not yet from the gold he's often said he intends to use for this purpose, liquidating his every asset to acquire the ore and fabricate a last honey bear hurrah: a King Tut treasure. Hanging somewhere is the lab coat and Groucho Marx glasses he wore for the pandemic Zoom launch of an illustrated children's book. The bathtub is, and has been for some years, a storage site for the white plastic totes containing the 500 paintings of bunny-men—bunnies are a recurrent, almost totemic subject—that were duplicated from an original cartoon, sent to a painting factory in Xiamen, China and duplicated in a dizzying array of multiples by the workers there. (They were exhibited, as a group, at the Bothkinds Project Space, in Vancouver, in 2022.)

His living quarters for more than twenty years have been in an equity co-op apartment building in Vancouver's West End, a few steps from Stanley Park. From the sixth floor, he has a winning view of Lost Lagoon. Here, too, are signs of what might be read as evidence of eccentricity, or something like it. The first thing anyone would notice on entering the apartment are the cacti and succulents that are there in extraordinary variety and abundance. Some of these he has nurtured since childhood. Now and again, they bloom. One produces a flower that smells like rotten meat, an extrusion meant to appeal to carrion-loving pollinators. There's the plastic bag in the kitchen that contains the thousands of stickers he's peeled from fruits and vegetables over the years. There's a large glass container, corked, beaker-shaped—it puts one in mind of *emptyful*, the water-spilling, steam-spouting, colour-emitting installation that's become one of the favourite landmarks in the city of Winnipeg—which was once brimming with rainbow coloured miniature marshmallows. They're there, still, but have gone dun-coloured in the sun and atrophied over the years into something resembling nothing found in nature. (Unlike, say, coloured miniature marshmallows.) Somewhere, in the nether reaches of a closet, is his collection of the hair he combed from Tuesday, an elderly and needy white cat he rescued one cold night (it was a Tuesday) from the alley, and with whom he fell in love. During a brief flirtation with felting, he used that hair, some part of it, to patch the moth holes in a cashmere sweater. It is a conversation starter, for sure. There's an enormous sea shell, weighing perhaps sixty pounds, once home to a clam of memorable dimension, through which various objects rotate, and there are two chrome-sided, horseshoe-shaped swivel chairs, in one of which wasps nested a few years ago. There's a statuette of Colonel Sanders, to whom Bill Pechet bears a passing resemblance, and there's a still-in-the-box Barbra Streisand doll, standing at a microphone, dressed in her *Funny Girl* sailor suit. There is no toaster. In all his adult life, Bill Pechet has never owned a toaster. There's a photo of his parents, Mitch and Judy, taken when they came to visit him in Japan. There are his mother's red driving gloves: a kind of shrine to her memory, may it be a blessing. She and Mitch are buried in the Jewish cemetery in Victoria, alongside their son, Sam. There's a fourth space in the family plot where Bill Pechet will lie, according to plan, though almost certainly not for many years yet. Longevity is a family trait.

Mitch Pechet was a legend at the Victoria YMCA, where he was a daily presence, usually the first to arrive, every morning. After he died, in 2009, a dedicatory plaque was installed on his locker. Bill, who inherited his father's barrel of a chest—that made-in-the-fields sturdiness (also insulating furriness) that often so distinguishes men of Eastern European and Ashkenazy heritage—is also devoted to physical culture, and takes excellent care of his body. He needs to be fit—he is very fit—to keep up his accustomed pace. His familiar, usually daily path, takes him from home to studio to gym to UBC where he's taught for more than thirty years. Many, many graduates of what is now the School of Architecture and Landscape Architecture (SALA) have participated in the studios and seminars and voyages abroad (most often to Japan) he's led in his role as Lecturer in Practice. Some of them, like Lőrinc Vass, another contributor to this book, have become colleagues and studiomates. Bill Pechet's interview with Thena Jean-hee Tak illuminates his ideas about life in the academy, and his thoughts on pedagogy.

It was perhaps an error for an undisciplined layperson who happens also to have a close personal connection to the subject to try to summarize, in a few pages, this remarkable, and very much still active, life and career. Someone disinterested in how the child becomes the father of the man would have spent less time with the formative years, would have been more analytical and descriptive about the work through which Bill Pechet is known and will be remembered. Someone more rigorous, more serious, would have been hard-headed about investigating how the career might have been differently complexioned had his interests been less far-flung and varied: the dreaded dilettante syndrome.

The best way to understand Bill Pechet is surely to spend time considering the record of his projects. They are the most persuasive teller of his story, bearing, as they do, such eloquent witness to his inspiration, creativity, persistence, patience, and collaborative gifts. They say more about him than can a compendium of cherry-picked particulars. It is astonishing to think that so much has come from him. So much that began as a concept, and that might have remained in the realm of the imagined, was turned into the built, the monumental, the lasting. So much that began in the folds of his brain was committed to paper, was modelled, was haggled over and negotiated in committee rooms and at meetings, was approved, was passed into the hands of fabricators, was made dimensional, was installed in the public realm. Someone who hasn't spoken to him every day for twenty-two years, either face to face or on the phone, would have had a more insightful, impartial, and intelligent take on all of this.

Just now he hung up after a conversation that recalled how, for a few years, he fed several generations of raucous seagulls from his balcony. They came every day, expecting the sardines he would feed them from his earthquake readiness kit. It was a hullabaloo, and also—noise, poop—a mistake. They stopped visiting during one of his occasional longer-term absences, probably one of the many Japan trips. He missed them, but he also saw that it was a relationship that had run its course. It was best to call it quits. But on the day of this writing, he happened to have some leftover scone (homemade, oatmeal-based, he bakes them every morning) and a crow, a juvenile, new from nest, happened to be on the balcony railing, looking in, looking hungry, looking like he might benefit from what was on hand. Bill Pechet did what Bill Pechet would do. He made a new friend, confident that something interesting will happen next. Something interesting always does.

Also, he does Sudoku.

PHOTO: Bill Pechet

We gratefully acknowledge the generous support of the Canada Council for the Arts and The Yosef Wosk Publication Fund at Vancouver Heritage Foundation.

Conseil des arts du Canada Canada Council for the Arts

VANCOUVER HERITAGE FOUNDATION | YOSEF WOSK PUBLICATION FUND

ORO Editions
Publishers of Architecture, Art, and Design
Gordon Goff: Publisher

www.oroeditions.com
info@oroeditions.com

Published by ORO Editions

Author: Leslie Van Duzer
Book Designer: Pablo Mandel
Project Manager: Jake Anderson

10 9 8 7 6 5 4 3 2 1 First Edition

ISBN: 978-1-961856-53-0

Prepress and Print work by ORO Editions Inc.
Printed in China

ORO Editions makes a continuous effort to minimize the overall carbon footprint of its publications. As part of this goal, ORO, in association with Global ReLeaf, arranges to plant trees to replace those used in the manufacturing of the paper produced for its books. Global ReLeaf is an international campaign run by American Forests, one of the world's oldest nonprofit conservation organizations. Global ReLeaf is American Forests' education and action program that helps individuals, organizations, agencies, and corporations improve the local and global environment by planting and caring for trees.